Roy Williams

Plays: 3

Fallout, Slow Time, Days of Si———'² Absolute i

Fallout: 'You stagger out of Roy Williams
shattered. Exhilarated because this dram
dramatist spectacularly achieves his full
though shot through with humour, is as b
youth culture in Britain today as you are e

Slow Time: 'The play is set in the bleak coni ⸺... ₃ msutution in
the hour before dawn [where] three boys – one white, one black and one Asian –
struggle to comprehend the brutality of their surroundings, and reveal the bullying, crime and peer group pressure that have brought them there' *Evening Standard*

Days of Significance: 'A play of passion and political anger . . . He uses the plot of *Much
Ado About Nothing* as a springboard to examine the naïve, adolescent and often racist
values that many of our young British soldiers have exported to Iraq . . . It makes
for a tough, pugnacious evening that shows Williams, who has impressively
charted the intricacies of Anglo-Saxon racism, widening his horizons to tackle the
poisoned state of society' *Guardian*

Absolute Beginners, a stage adaptation of Colin MacInnes's seminal novel of adoles-
cence set in London in 1958: 'Bags of energy and highly watchable' *Daily Mail*
'Williams in adapting . . . [has] seized on the stylised quality of the prose and
created something that, right from the off, looks, sounds and moves in a completely
distinctive way' *Observer*

Roy Williams worked as an actor before turning to writing full-time in 1990. He
graduated from Rose Bruford in 1995 with a first class BA Hons degree in Writing
and participated in the 1997 Carlton Television screenwriter's course. *The No Boys
Cricket Club* (Theatre Royal, Stratford East, 1996) won him nominations for the
TAPS Writer of the Year Award 1996 and for New Writer of the Year Award 1996
by the Writers' Guild of Great Britain. He was the first recipient of the Alfred
Fagon Award 1997 for *Starstruck* (Tricycle Theatre, London, 1998), which also won
the 31st John Whiting Award and the EMMA Award 1999. *Lift Off* (Royal Court
Theatre Upstairs, 1999) was the joint winner of the George Devine Award 2000.
His other plays include: *Night and Day* (Theatre Venture, 1996); *Josie's Boys* (Red
Ladder Theatre Co., 1996); *Souls* (Theatre Centre, 1999); *Local Boy* (Hampstead
Theatre, 2000); *The Gift* (Birmingham Rep/Tricycle Theatre, 2000); *Clubland*
(Royal Court, 2001), winner of the *Evening Standard* Charles Wintour Award for the
Most Promising Playwright; *Fallout* (Royal Court Theatre, 2003) which was made
for television by Company Pictures/Channel 4; *Sing Yer Heart Out for the Lads*
(National Theatre, 2002, 2004), *Little Sweet Thing* (New Wolsey, Ipswich/
Nottingham Playhouse/Birmingham Rep, 2005), *Slow Time* (National Theatre
Education Department tour, 2005), *Days of Significance* (Swan Theatre, Stratford-
upon-Avon, 2007), *Absolute Beginners* (Lyric Theatre, Hammersmith, 2007), *Joe Guy*

(Tiata Fahodzi/Soho Theatre, 2007), *Baby Girl* (National Theatre, 2007), *Out of the Fog* (Almeida Theatre, 2007), *There's Only One Wayne Matthews* (Polka Theatre, 2007), and he contributed to *A Chain Play* (Almeida Theatre, 2007). His screenplays include *Offside*, winner of a BAFTA for Best Schools Drama 2002. His radio plays include *Tell Tale, Homeboys, Westway*, which was broadcast as part of Radio 4 First Bite Young Writers' Festival, and *To Sir with Love*. He also wrote *Babyfather* for BBC TV.

by the same author

Clubland

Days of Significance

Fallout

The Gift

Joe Guy

Little Sweet Thing

Sing Yer Heart Out for the Lads

Starstruck/The No Boys Cricket Club

Williams Plays: 1

(The No Boys Cricket Club, Starstruck, Lift Off)

Williams Plays: 2

(The Gift, Clubland, Sing Yer Heart Out for the Lads)

ROY WILLIAMS

Plays: 3

Fallout
Slow Time
Days of Significance
Absolute Beginners

with an introduction by the author

Methuen Drama

METHUEN DRAMA CONTEMPORARY DRAMATISTS

3 5 7 9 10 8 6 4 2

First published by Methuen Drama in 2008

Methuen Drama
A & C Black Publishers Limited
36 Soho Square
London W1D 3QY
www.methuendrama.com

Fallout first published in 2003 by Methuen Drama
Copyright © 2003 by Roy Williams
Slow Time first published in 2008 by Methuen Drama
Copyright © 2008 by Roy Williams
Days of Significance first published in 2007 by Methuen Drama
Copyright © 2007 by Roy Williams
Absolute Beginners first published in 2008 by Methuen Drama
Copyright © 2008 by Roy Williams. Adapted from the novel by Colin MacInnes, published
in 1959 by MacGibbon & Kee
Copyright © 1959 Colin MacInnes

This collection copyright © 2008 by Roy Williams
Introduction copyright © 2008 by Roy Williams

Roy Williams has asserted his rights under the Copyright, Designs and Patents Act, 1988, to
be identified as the author of this work

ISBN: 978 1 408 10109 4

A CIP catalogue record for this book is available from the British Library

Typeset by SX Composing DTP, Rayleigh, Essex
Printed and bound in Great Britain by Good News Digital Books, Ongar

Caution

Contents

Roy Williams:
Select Chronology

1996   *Night and Day* (Theatre Venture tour)
       The No Boys Cricket Club (Theatre Royal, Stratford
       East). Nominated for the TAPS Writer of the Year
       Award 1996 and Writers' Guild Best New Writer
       Award 1996.
       Josie's Boys (Red Ladder Theatre Co.)
       Homeboys. Broadcast as part of the BBC Radio 4
       First Bite Young Writers' Festival

1998   *Starstruck* (Tricycle Theatre, London). Received the
       first Alfred Fagon Award, the 31st John Whiting
       Award and the EMMA Award 1999.

1999   *Lift Off* (Royal Court at the Ambassadors). Joint win-
       ner of the George Devine Award 2000.

2000   *Souls* (Theatre Centre tour)
       Local Boy (Hampstead Theatre)
       The Gift (Birmingham Repertory Theatre, transferred
       to Tricycle Theatre)

2001   *Clubland* (Royal Court Theatre Upstairs). Won the
       Evening Standard Charles Wintour Award for Most
       Promising Playwright.

2002   *Sing Yer Heart Out for the Lads* (National Theatre,
       Lyttelton Loft)
       Writer in Residence, Royal Court Theatre
       Offside (BBC Television). Winner of the BAFTA
       Award for Best Schools Drama.
       Babyfather (BBC Television)
       Tell Tale (BBC Radio 4)

2003   *Fallout* (Royal Court Theatre, Downstairs). Received
       the South Bank Show Arts Council Decibel Award.

2004   Revival of *Sing Yer Heart Out for the Lads* at the
        Cottesloe space, National Theatre.

2005   *Little Sweet Thing* (New Wolsey, Ipswich/Nottingham
        Playhouse/Birmingham Rep)
        Slow Time (National Theatre Education Department
        tour)

2006/7 Revival of *Sing Yer Heart Out for the Lads* by Pilot
        Theatre and national tour

2007   *Days of Significance* (Swan Theatre, Stratford-upon-
        Avon)
        Absolute Beginners (Lyric Theatre, Hammersmith)
        Baby Girl (National Theatre)
        Out of the Fog (Almeida Theatre)
        There's Only One Wayne Matthews (Polka Theatre)
        Joe Guy (New Wolsey Theatre, Ipswich, and Soho
        Theatre, London)

Introduction

Everyone was horrified When ten-year-old Damilola Taylor was murdered on that Peckham estate in 2000. As I watched the investigation slowly progress, my horror turned to fury. I was angry at the boys who killed him, angry with whoever let these boys down and angry with the police for failing to get justice for another black youth when the case fell apart. By the time the girl code-named Bromley gave evidence at the trial, I knew I had to write about this. Here was this girl who was at least as frightened as she was tough. I was interested in trying to get into the mindset of these youths, to explore what kind of Britain they are growing up in. As a teenager in the eighties, I was reading and hearing about riots in Brixton, Broadwater Farm, etc. The youths back then were angrier than the ones we have now. They were angry at being treated like second-class citizens in their own country. Today, for these young people , like the ones in *Fallout*, it's not about having too little, it's about having too much. It is about stepping over someone else to get what they want. If they want a new mobile phone, and they see some one else has it, they will just take it.

Much has been debated about why this is happening, poor education, family breakdown, a lack of positive male role models, especially among young black men. All true, I suppose, but for me the strongest issue is that we are exploiting our teenagers by making them obsessed with material wealth and their passage into adulthood is being lost along the way.

Another reason for writing *Fallout* was that I wanted to explore the world of the Metropolitan Police, especially in the light of the McPherson report, which accused the force of being institutionally racist after their poor handling of the Stephen Lawrence case. Some of this I looked at through the character of Joe, a black copper working in an organisation more politically correct and tolerant than it has ever been before. Yet he feels more isolated and alone than he ever would have in the eighties when racism was rife in the force. Some argue it was better then, because at least black people knew where they stood.

*

As well as the riots I lived through in London, I remember often being told about what took place in 1958 on the streets in Notting Hill where I lived. If you take a wander around the area now you will find it hard to believe there was any trouble between blacks and whites, because Notting Hill today is one of the most multiracial parts of London. I loved *Absolute Beginners* when I first read it. The energy of Colin MacInnes's writing is just spectacular, it is poetry and had a huge impact on me. MacInnes was so ahead of his time, in terms of what he was saying about the exploitation of those young people living in the fifties, who first coined the term 'teenagers', and about Britain emerging from the post-war years to a more colourful and, for the first time multicultural, nation. Those concerns don't seem to have gone away.

When David Farr asked me to adapt the book for the stage, I jumped at the chance, almost biting off his hand in the process. It was a new way of working for me and a surprise to learn that adapting is no easier than writing a play from scratch.

Slowtime was a story stolen from the headlines, about an Asian boy who was brutally murdered by his racist cell mate in a young offenders institution. As part of my research I visited a young offenders prison in Aylesbury. I met several of the inmates there. I was shocked to see how young they were, fourteen- to eighteen-year-olds, how innocent they all looked. I had difficulty believing any one of them could commit a serious crime. I wrote *Slowtime* for the National Theatre's Education Department and my aim was to scare the shit out of those young men who are one step away from a life of crime. I didn't want to bash them over the head with this issue, but I wanted them to see, or least try to understand, that Feltham and Aylesbury and other young offenders institutions are not cool places to establish a 'rep' . They are dangerous, frightening, lonely places that will destroy their souls.

In spite of its subject matter, *Days of Significance* is the play I've had the most fun writing. The RSC commissioned me in 2004 to come up with something inspired by a Shakespeare text, for the company's Complete Works Festival. I was persuaded by my 'sister' Indhu Rubasingham not to go for the obvious, like *Othello*, So I chose *Much Ado About Nothing*. Its returning soldiers, battle of the sexes, girls and boys in packs resonated with me. They seemed just like the young people going out boozing in city centres across the country. I wanted to write something about the war in Iraq, but I wasn't interested in exploring how it affects the people in power. I wanted to show the people who are not in power or rather those who feel powerless. When the Gulf War broke out in the early nineties, for the first time ever I found myself arguing with a friend, not over girls, but over whether that war was just or not. He thought it was, I did not. He then said he voted for the Tories in the last election (and he still does). We were beginning to see the world as a much bigger place.

For *Days of Significance*, I wanted to recapture that feeling. In the character of Hannah, I wanted to show a girl who goes from being a careless young binge drinker allowing herself to be defined as a sexual object into a more confident young adult. Although her mates are soldiers, she shuts out all talk of the war; as she says, she does not want it to matter to her. But when her cousin's fiancé is killed and her own boyfriend is in the dock for torturing Iraqi prisoners, she learns that it does indeed matter. On one side *Days of Significance* is about a society that allows its young to drink themselves into oblivion at weekends, then expects them to defend its moral values in a war thousands of miles away. On the other it is a plea to those young people to know that, no matter who they are or where they come from, they must value themselves.

A huge thanks goes to my directors Ian Rickson, Liam Steel, Maria Aberg and Matt Wilde. I have loved every minute I've spent working with you on these plays.

It has also been a privilege to have such great lovely actors speaking my words in these plays, giving them life.

You are all geniuses.

Roy Williams
December 2007

Fallout

For Dona Daley

Fallout was first performed at the Royal Court Jerwood Theatre Downstairs, London, on 12 June 2003. The cast was as follows:

Clinton	Jason Frederick
Dwayne	Michael Obiora
Emile	Marcel McCalla
Perry	O-T Fagbenle
Joe	Lennie James
Matt	Daniel Ryan
Shanice	Ony Uhiara
Ronnie	Petra Letang
Manny	Clive Wedderburn
Miss Douglas/Inspector	Lorraine Brunning

Director Ian Rickson
Designer Ultz
Lighting Designer Nigel J. Edwards
Sound Designer Ian Dickinson
Music Stephen Warbeck

Characters

Shanice, *late teens, black*
Emile, *late teens, black*
Dwayne, *late teens, black*
Joe, *mid-thirties, black*
Matt, *mid-thirties, white*
Perry, *late teens, mixed race*
Ronnie, *late teens, black*
Clinton, *late teens, black*
Miss Douglas, *early forties, white*
Inspector, *early forties, white*
Manny, *late thirties, black*

The roles of Miss Douglas and the Inspector should be
played by the same actor.

Time
Present

Setting
Various

Enter **Clinton**, **Dwayne**, **Emile** *and* **Perry**.

Clinton   Kick him in the head, kick him!

Dwayne   Yes!

Perry   My bwoi.

Clinton   Kick him.

Dwayne   Tek off him glasses and chuck dem.

Clinton   Chuck dem now, man.

Emile   Pass me de phone, yu fucker!

Clinton   Pass him de phone, yu fuck!

Emile   Pass it now.

Perry   Do it now.

Dwayne   My bwoi!

Emile   Trainers too.

Clinton   Gwan, Emile!

Perry   Walk barefoot, yu rass.

Clinton   Like yu do in Africa.

Emile   Trainers!

Clinton   Tell him, Emile.

Perry   Tell the fucker.

Dwayne   Bus his head.

Clinton   Bus him up.

Emile   Trainers!

Dwayne   Fuck dem over to us.

Clinton   Before yu dead.

Emile   Trainers!

Dwayne   Punch him.

Clinton   Kick him.

Perry   Bus him up.

Emile   Yu see yu! (*Kicks continuously.*)

Exit **Clinton**, **Dwayne**, **Perry** *and* **Emile**.

Enter **Shanice** *and* **Ronnie**, **Joe** *and* **Matt**.

Ronnie   Yer gonna love me, Shanice.

Shanice   I love yer awready, yu fool.

Ronnie   Well, yer gonna love me more, dread. See?
(*Shows a blouse.*)

Shanice   Nice.

Ronnie   Honestly?

Shanice   Honestly.

Ronnie   Yes.

Shanice   Bit small fer yu.

Ronnie   Got it fer yu.

Shanice   Ronnie!

Ronnie   It'll go nice wid yer black skirt, yer gonna look
the business, girl, no guy can refuse yu.

Shanice   Ronnie, wat am I doin right now?

Ronnie   Nuttin.

Shanice   I'm workin.

Ronnie   Shut up.

Shanice   Later.

Ronnie   Yeah, but I want see how well it fit.

Shanice   Why yu aways gettin me things, man?

Ronnie   It don't look right on me.

Shanice   So why buy it?

Ronnie   I didn't buy it.

Shanice   Ronnie, yu didn't?

Ronnie   I saw it in the shop.

Shanice   Oh man.

Ronnie   As soon as I lay my eye upon it, I thought of yu.

Shanice   Is it?

Ronnie   It was callin to me, Shanice.

Shanice   Shush.

Ronnie   I had to have it . . .

Shanice   Hold it down.

Ronnie   Why?

Shanice (*aside*)   Police.

Ronnie   Ware?

Shanice   Deh.

Ronnie   Wat, dem?

Shanice   Yes.

Ronnie   Yo!

Shanice   Ronnie!

Ronnie   Yo!

Matt   Yes?

Ronnie   Yu lot still here?

Matt   Can we help you?

Ronnie   Yu best go home. Ain't no criminals in here.

Matt   Is it written all over our foreheads or something?

Joe   How did you know?

Shanice   It's written all over yer foreheads.

Ronnie   Believe.

Shanice   Kwame?

Matt   That's right.

Ronnie   Don't yu lot get tired? Bin interviewin everyone, man. Over and over. How come yu Feds never come see me? Especially dat cute young one, wathimname. Oh man, yu should see him, Shanice. Not like these two. Bring him round, let him talk to me.

Joe   Who?

Matt   PC Adams, he has been getting this all month.

Ronnie   So yu like it den?

Shanice   It's awright.

Ronnie   Ca if yu don't like it . . .

Shanice   Wat, yu'll tek it back?

Ronnie   I'll get yu summin else.

Shanice   Yu stay ware yu are. Yeah, wat yu havin?

Joe   Two teas and a smile.

Shanice *feigns a smile.*

Joe   How big are dem chicken wings?

Shanice   I dunno, they're chicken wings.

Joe   Lemme have four.

Shanice   Comin wid yer tea.

Ronnie   No, try it on first.

Shanice   Shut up.

Ronnie   Come on.

Shanice   Awright! Love to go on. Keep an eye out.

Exit **Shanice**.

Ronnie   So, when are yu gonna send dat nice copper round to see me den?

Joe   What are you gonna tell him?

Ronnie   Watever he wants. Yu get me? (*Laughs.*)

Her phone rings.

(*Answers.*) Tracey! Wass up, girl? Hold up. (*To* **Joe** *and* **Matt**.) Keep an eye out.

Exit **Ronnie**.

Matt   Who let that out?

Joe   I like the other one.

Matt   Bit young for you.

Joe   Look me in the eye and tell me you wouldn't tap that.

Matt   I have a sister her age.

Joe   You've got a dick your age.

Matt   And a wife. What?

Joe   Something I heard.

Matt   Well, don't keep me hanging, Joe, let's have it.

Joe   A story I heard.

Matt   Yes?

Joe   When you were at Kilburn. PC Holmes was her name. Tits this big.

Matt   Nothing happened.

Joe   Oh yes?

Matt   We were friends.

Joe   No such thing.

Matt   I wasn't even married then.

Joe   You were engaged.

Matt   Are you always like this?

Joe   You must have heard what they said about me.

Matt   And they were right.

Joe   You don't have to like me, Matt.

Matt   Well, I do. Did you read the file?

Joe   I flipped through it. All this must be kicking your arse by now.

Matt   That's one way.

Joe   Funeral's tomorrow.

Matt   I know.

Joe   You going?

Matt   The super is.

Joe   Royalty.

Matt   You saw the Jubilee celebrations. We're all trying to be modern now. Shall we start?

Joe   You're the boss.

Matt   Kwame left the station at five forty-five. CCTV clocked him walking past the church towards the high street. Another one picked him up coming off the high, walking towards the swimming baths. He was inside for an hour. He went there, every Thursday. CCTV again, clocked him leaving the baths at 6.50 p.m. He bought a burger and chips from here at seven, left this place at seven ten. He was last seen walking towards the station, passing the church again. We assume he was going home. Seven fifteen. He was found at the bottom of the road.

Joe   Seven twenty-five.

Matt   It was like his head was used for a football. He died, two days later. There was another CCTV, but it wasn't

working properly that evening. Typical. It kept getting
jammed. All it got was a lamp post shining in its lens. We're
bringing in a specialist, see if he can do anything, just like
what we did for that missing girl. One witness says he saw a
young man matching Kwame's description arguing with a
group of boys earlier that evening. He also saw a silver
BMW several times driving around the area playing really
loud rap music. It was like the driver was lost or something.
Whoever that driver was, he or she may have seen
something, but so far, no one has come forward. Feel up to
speed?

Enter **Ronnie**.

Joe   I wonder what the fight was about.

Matt   There was no fight.

Joe   Drugs. Phones.

Matt   That doesn't compute.

Joe   Why?

Matt   He was a straight-A student. On his way to
university. He wasn't into gangs at all. We asked everyone,
they all said the same thing, his nose was in the books.

Joe   He must have been fighting about something with
them.

Matt   It wasn't a fight our witness saw, it was an
argument.

Joe   So what was the argument about?

Matt   I don't know.

Enter **Clinton**, **Emile**, **Dwayne** *and* **Perry**.

Emile   Troll? Ware's Shanice?

Ronnie   Kiss my arse.

Dwayne   Shut up, troll, and tell him.

Ronnie   How am I supposed to do dat with my mouth shut? And I ain't no troll.

Dwayne   Sorry, Shrek.

Laughter.

Perry   My stomach is empty.

Emile   Troll. Food.

Ronnie   Yu'll have to wait.

Perry   Tower burger, large fries.

Clinton   Is dat wat yer gonna have?

Perry   Yes, Clinton, dass wat I'm gonna have, dass why I ordered it.

Clinton   Yu had a kebab an hour ago.

Perry   I'm still hungry.

Clinton   Don't see how.

Emile   Oh man, not again.

Dwayne   Shut up, Clinton.

Clinton   Tower cheeseburger is a lot to eat by yerself.

Perry   Clinton? Yu want me to order fer yu?

Clinton   I didn't say dat.

Perry   Dis bwoi drive me mad, yu know.

Clinton   But did I say dat?

Perry   Do yu want me to order fer yu? Why yu love to go round the block wid dis?

Clinton   Wid wat?

Perry   Now he's tekin the piss. Yer broke, yeah? Yu ain't got enuff dollars to buy a meal. Why yu can't ask?

Clinton   Don't get vex, P.

Perry   I don't know why yu can't say wat yu wanna say?

Clinton   Which is wat?

Perry   Does dis bwoi wanna die?

Clinton   If yu can't eat all dat by yerself, P, I'll help yu out.

Dwayne (*laughs*)   Bredren!

Emile   Oh juss help the college bwoi out, P. Can't you see, he's wastin away?

Perry   It's aways me he does dis to.

Emile   He's yer cousin.

Perry   Dat ain't my fault.

Clinton *stares.*

Perry   Wat?

Clinton   Nuttin.

Perry   Yu want sum?

Clinton   Yu don't have to.

Perry   I go ask yu again. Yu gimme more than yes or no, I go bus yer head. Yu want sum food?

Clinton   Yeah.

Perry   Gw'y.

Laughter.

Dwayne   Cold!

Clinton   I knew yu'd do dat.

Perry   Troll, give the bwoi sum food.

Clinton   Nice, cous.

Perry   Get a job, man.

Dwayne   Gimme a number-one meal.

Emile   Number two.

Perry   Wat yu want?

Clinton   Only if yer sure.

Perry   Pick a number before I kill yu.

Clinton   Two.

Perry   And a one fer me.

Ronnie   Yu lot mus be deaf.

Emile   Yu wan' die?

Matt (*gets up*)   Hey.

Emile   Yu want tek yer hand off my jacket please?

Matt   Take it easy, son.

Emile   Who dis fool?

Ronnie   Five 0.

Emile   Oh! So dass wat de smell was.

Enter **Shanice**.

Shanice   Yeah, I like dis one. Fits nice. Awright, Emile?

Emile   Ware yu bin?

Shanice   Out back.

Dwayne   Like yer top, Shanice.

Shanice   Go away, Dwayne.

Dwayne   But it look good.

Emile   I didn't get yu dat.

Shanice   Yu don't have to get me everythin, Emile, I bought it myself.

Ronnie   No yu didn't, I got it.

Emile   Tell it to shut up.

Ronnie   Shut up yerself.

Shanice   Ronnie! Yu like it?

Dwayne   Love it.

Clinton   Believe.

Shanice   Emile?

Emile   It's awright.

Dwayne   Dass it, awright? Yer gal look fine.

Shanice   He don't like it.

Ronnie   Shanice, don't, man, it look good.

Shanice   I'm changin.

Exit **Shanice**.

Dwayne (*mocks*)   It's awright!

Perry   Emile man, yer lucky yer my bredren. Ca if yu weren't, I woulda dived on yer gal from time.

Clinton   Not before me.

Perry   Yu go down on it, Emile?

Dwayne   Cold.

Perry   She give good shine?

Emile   Shut up.

Perry   Ease up, blood.

Emile   I'm tellin yer.

Clinton   Soff.

Perry   Go sit over deh, if yu go cry.

Ronnie   See, ain't juss me who tinks yer a pussy.

Emile   Yu don't shut yer mout, troll.

Ronnie   Wat?

Enter **Shanice**.

Shanice   Oh man, will yu two stop? Every time.

Dwayne   Put the other top back on.

Shanice   So yu can watch me all night?

Perry   Believe.

Emile   Rah, he's still starin.

Clinton   Who?

Emile   Mr White Man over deh. Yu like my friend, Mr White Man? Yu want ask him out, get his number?

Joe *sucks his teeth.*

Emile   Sorry, brudda, we didn't quite catch dat. Wat, yu can't speak till him tell yu to?

Joe   Bwoi.

Emile   Yer the bwoi.

Dwayne   So wat yu doin here, Mr Policeman?

Matt   Having a tea.

Clinton   They're here fer Kwame, innit?

Dwayne   Nuh, Clinton, really?

Emile   Wastin yer time, man, yu ain't gonna catch dem.

Joe   Them?

Emile   Wat?

Joe   You said them.

Emile   I know wat I said.

Joe   Them, as in more than one?

Clinton   Guy cussin yu, Emile.

Perry   He thinks yer stupid.

Emile   Yu tink I'm stupid?

Joe   What makes you think we're looking for more than one person?

Emile   I don't.

Joe   So why say it?

Emile   I say wat I like.

Joe   True, but why say that?

Emile   Ca I felt like it.

Dwayne   Easy, dread.

Joe   Choose your words carefully.

Emile   Yu my dad now?

Joe   Maybe, wass yer mudda's name?

Clinton   Oh shame.

Matt   Joe?

Emile   Wass he say?

Clinton   He's cussin yer mum.

Shanice   Sit down, Emile.

Joe   Yes, Emile, sit down.

Emile   Go chat wid yer gal deh.

Perry   I hate to break dis to yer, Dwayne. Yer dad's comin, dis way.

Dwayne   Oh man, wass he want? He bin stalkin me all day. Don't let him in.

Manny, **Dwayne**'s *dad, enters.*

Manny   Hey, son! Son? Ware yu going? Come here, son?

Dwayne   Wat yu want?

Manny   Lemme have one pound. Beg yu fer one pound.

Dwayne   Come outta my face, yeah.

Manny   Hey, bwoi.

Dwayne   Come outta my face!

Manny   Yer too rude, yer nuh.

Exit **Manny**.

Dwayne   Jesus, man, he's an itch I can't scratch, a pain in the arse.

Perry, *by the door, laughs.*

Dwayne   Wat yu laughin at now, yu baboon?

Perry   Jamal mek me laugh, man.

Dwayne   Jamal still in Feltham.

Perry   No, he come out lass month.

Dwayne   So wat yu laughin about?

Perry   Ca he's over deh, breakin into sumone's car. Have a look. The man love to steal cars, he muss have a hard-on fer it.

Dwayne   But he always get catch.

Perry   Exactly! The guy can't even drive properly. I was in a car wid him one time, half the time we were on the pavement. But deh's no tellin him. Guy tinks he's Formula One.

Clinton   Yo, policeman, I hope dat ain't yer car outside.

Matt   What car?

Clinton   Light blue Escort.

Matt   Oh what! (*Jumps up.*)

Dwayne   Oh yes, run, run!

Perry   Why yu tell him?

Clinton   I want see dis.

Dwayne   Come.

Exit **Matt** *and* **Joe**.

Dwayne   Yes, bwoi, run.

Perry   Bredren stole a police car! Deh gonna throw his arse in prison again and keep it deh. Fer trut.

Dwayne   He run fast.

Clinton   Too late, yu fool.

Dwayne   Come, let's go, I want see dis. Emile?

Emile   I catch up.

Dwayne   Yeah, go sex yer woman.

Exit **Dwayne**, **Clinton** *and* **Perry**.

Emile (*to* **Ronnie**)   Out.

Ronnie *sucks her teeth*.

Shanice   Ronnie.

Exit **Ronnie**.

Shanice *and* **Emile** *kiss*.

Shanice   Missed yu.

Emile   Missed yu too. I love yer hands. Did I ever tell yu dat? Yu got lovely hands.

Shanice *laughs*.

Emile   Wat? Yu think dat was funny?

Shanice   No.

Emile   So why laugh?

Shanice   Ca yu mek me smile.

Emile   Shut up, man.

Shanice   Yu do.

Emile   Yer tekin the piss.

Shanice   If yu don't like it, don't say it.

Emile   I won't.

Shanice   But I want yu to.

Emile   Look, don't wear dat top again.

Shanice   Oh man.

Emile   Juss don't.

Shanice   I knew yu didn't like it.

Emile   So why wear it?

Shanice   Ronnie got me it, yu know wat she's like.

Emile   Why yu still wid her?

Shanice   She's harmless, man. She ain't got nobody.

Emile   So?

Shanice   Can we not fight please?

Emile   Sorry, yeah.

Shanice   Yu will be.

Emile   Shut up, man.

Shanice *and* **Emile** *kiss again.*

Shanice   Yu ordered yet?

Emile   Yeah, number two.

Shanice   Number two?

Emile   I'm hungry.

Shanice   Yu fat bloater.

Emile   Shut up, I ain't fat.

Shanice   Hate to break it to yer, Emile, but yer gettin a little bit wide in the gut department. Anyhow, yu turn into one a dem big fat men who can hardly walk, I'll step.

Emile   Yu won't leave me.

Shanice   Yu wan bet?

Emile   Yu love me.

Shanice   I know I love yer, juss as long as yu don't turn fat on me. Oderwise, I juss have to go and check one a yer brers dem.

Emile   Yu ain't jokin.

Shanice   Course I'm jokin.

Emile   Yu really tink I'm gettin fat?

Shanice   Yu are so easy to tease.

Emile   Do yer?

Shanice   No.

Emile   Yu shouldn't say dat.

Shanice   It was a joke, I'm sorry.

Emile   Wat if one a dem had heard yer?

Shanice   I don't care.

Emile   They'd dive on yu like dat, if they had the chance.

Shanice   Let dem try.

Emile   Dwayne man, he wants yer.

Shanice   Well, I don't want him, I got wat I want.

Emile (*slaps her hand away*)   Move!

Shanice   Emile! Yer wrong anyway. I ain't Dwayne's type.

Emile   Oh shut up, yeah.

Shanice   Yu shut up.

Emile   Yer everybody's type. Yer so fit.

Shanice   Awright.

Emile   Yer are.

Shanice   Yes! I'm fit. (*Beat.*) Wass botherin yu?

Emile   Saw Kwame's mum yesterday. Stuck up, man, always was. Lookin down on me like I'm shit. Come like her bwoi, well, he find out, innit.

Shanice   Don't.

Emile   See her face in the paper, appealin fer help. Den deh got de blasted funeral tomorrow, why can't she juss let it go, man? She don't even live round here no more.

Shanice   Her son's dead, she can't let it go.

Emile   I thought yu were on my side.

Shanice   I am.

Emile   Well, show it den.

Shanice   Wat do yu think I'm doin?

Emile   I keep seein him.

Shanice   Shush.

Emile   His face, man.

Shanice   He'll go soon. He'll go.

Beat.

Emile   Put the oder top back on.

Shanice   Yu hate it.

Emile (*smirks*)   It look good.

Exit **Shanice** *and* **Emile**.

Enter **Matt** *and* **Joe**.

Joe   So what did they say?

Matt   They dumped the car about a mile away. They shat all over the back seats. I mean, there's no need for that.

Joe   They don't make teenagers like they used to. They ought to burn that fucker down.

Matt   I'm sorry?

Joe   The estate.

Matt   It's not the estate, it's the people.

Joe   Them as well. Young ones anyway.

Matt   Are you trying to provoke me, Joe?

Joe   Provoke?

Matt   How am I supposed to react to that?

Joe   We're all friends here, you act how you feel.

Matt   And then what?

Joe   You're losing me.

Matt   Am I supposed to agree with you?

Joe   Do you?

Matt   No.

Joe   That's exactly why they took your car. They can see right through you. Take it easy! Do you think it was them who attacked Kwame?

Matt   Well, they fit the description.

Joe   I'm surprised you can tell. You can't tell them apart in the day now, let alone night-time.

Matt   Excuse me?

Joe   Joke.

Matt   I don't find that funny.

Joe   Sorry.

Matt   Our witness named one of them.

Joe   Which one?

Matt   The leader. Dwayne Edwards.

Joe   I thought it might have been the one who goes out wid the girl. What's a nice-looking gal doing with a little bwoi like that?

Matt   I couldn't say.

Joe   I'm going to get a headache tonight, just thinking about it.

Matt   Shall we go?

Joe (*smiles*)   You're very polite.

Matt   Thank you.

Exit **Joe** *and* **Matt**.

Enter **Ronnie** *and* **Shanice**.

Shanice   Twenty grand!

Ronnie   Tellin yu.

Shanice   Fer Kwame?

Ronnie   Yes! Yu know wat I'll do if I had dat money?

Shanice   Tell me.

Ronnie   Buy car.

Shanice   Yu can't even drive.

Ronnie   I'd buy it fer yu. Get sum clothes. Yu can tell me wat to buy, dress me up.

Shanice   I don't think the world is ready fer yu in a dress.

Ronnie   We go ravin every night. Hunt fer sum bwois. But only if deh buff.

Shanice   Of course. So wat about Dwayne?

Ronnie   Mek him jealous, innit? Emile as well. Can't wait, man. If yu weren't goin out wid him, we could claim dat money right now.

Shanice   Yu shouldn't say things like dat.

Ronnie   True though.

Shanice   I don't care if it's true, don't say it.

Ronnie   Yeah, but it's true.

Shanice   Shut up.

Ronnie   Yu sound like Emile.

Shanice   Sorry.

Ronnie   Call me troll while yer at it.

Shanice   Are yu deaf, wat did I juss say? I've never called yu dat, not even behind yer back. Ronnie, have yu told anyone wat yu saw?

Ronnie   No.

Shanice   Promise me.

Ronnie   I haven't.

Shanice   It's important.

Ronnie   I know.

Shanice   Ca we ain't at school no more, I can't aways be deh fer yu.

Ronnie   I know.

Shanice   Gotta think fer yerself.

Ronnie   I said I know.

Shanice   Be careful wid wat yu say.

Ronnie   Wat yu gettin wound up fer? Yu didn't do it.

Shanice   I feel as though I have.

Ronnie   Behave, man.

Shanice   I had him cryin his eyes out to me.

Ronnie   Wat, again?

Shanice   Goin on about seein Kwame's face.

Ronnie   Ejut.

Shanice   He ain't the only one, dread. I'm seein Kwame too, every day. Him standin right here. Him leavin, wavin to me. I'm the lass person who saw him alive, Ronnie.

Ronnie   No yu ain't.

Shanice   Yu know wat I mean. He had his lass food in here, double cheeseburger, large fries and a Coke. Dat was the lass food he ever had, double cheeseburger.

Ronnie   I don't know why yu gettin stressed.

Shanice   It's runnin thru my head, every day. Shit won't go.

Ronnie   I know it won't, ca yu love to chat about it.

Shanice   Why did Emile have to do it?

Ronnie   Ask him.

Shanice   Juss ignore me, yeah.

Ronnie   I know wat yu need.

Shanice   Tell me.

Ronnie   Barbados.

Shanice (*laughs*)   Is it?

Ronnie   Definitely. Go stay wid yer gran. I'll come wid yu, yeah.

Shanice   We go chase, man?

Ronnie   Trust.

Shanice Awright.

Ronnie We go swimmin.

Shanice Bacardi Breezer.

Ronnie Tropical Lime.

Shanice Ruby Grapefruit.

Ronnie Lie on beach.

Shanice Sun in my face.

Ronnie Yu see?

Shanice Oh Ronnie man! If only.

Ronnie We can, yu know.

Shanice No, we can't. Come on, enuff daydreamin. Clean up.

Ronnie Yer gonna love me, Shanice.

Shanice I love yu awready.

Ronnie Well, yer gonna love me even more.

Shanice Wat yu tief now?

Ronnie Nuttin. Guess who I saw? Guess?

Shanice I don't want to guess, juss tell me.

Ronnie Miss Douglas.

Shanice Is it?

Ronnie The slag herself.

Shanice She see yu?

Ronnie Yeah, she saw me.

Shanice So wat she have to say fer herself?

Ronnie Nuttin. She was comin outta Tesco's when I clocked her. She couldn't get across dat road fast enuff. She was clutchin her bag, like they do, well desperate to get away from me. She nearly walk right into the side of dis car, nearly get run over. Man scream out from his window, cussin her, I goes, yes, blood, tell her. I kept followin her though.

Shanice   She didn't see yu?

Ronnie   No, I was careful. Yu wanna know ware she lives now? Ashwood Gardens.

Shanice   Ain't much help without a number.

Ronnie   Twenty-nine C. Yu gonna get her, Shanice? I'm comin wid yu, yeah, I have to come wid yu.

Shanice   Calm yerself.

Ronnie   I'm juss sayin, I'm comin wid yu. Let's get her back, man, let's do her good, fer kickin us out. Please, Shanice?

Shanice   Awright!

Ronnie   Yes!

Joe *enters.*

Ronnie   Wass my man doin here?

Shanice   Yu here again?

Joe   No, it's what can I get you? You won't get many customers talking like that.

Ronnie   Chat is dry.

Joe   Ginger beer please.

Ronnie   Buff dough.

Shanice   I don't think so.

Ronnie   Oi oi buff bwoi!

Shanice   Yu mad?

Ronnie   Yu tellin me yu wouldn't?

Shanice   He's Five 0.

Ronnie   So yu would, if he wasn't? How old are yu?

Shanice   Ronnie!

Ronnie   How old?

Joe   Old enough.

Ronnie   Thirty-five or summin. Has to be. Yu look good though, fer an old man.

Shanice   Thirty-five ain't dat old.

Ronnie   She thinks yer buff.

Shanice   Will yu stop shamin me?

Ronnie   So ware's the oder one?

Joe   My partner?

Ronnie   No! Guy's a minger. The oder one. Fit one who wears uniform. Looks like Duncan from Blue. Yu should see dis guy, Shanice.

Shanice   Yu told me.

Ronnie   Oh man!

Shanice   Yu mind? Don't go creamin yer knickers in here.

Ronnie   So ware is he?

Joe   You mean PC Adams?

Ronnie   Yeah, him, ware is he?

Joe   I have no idea. I don't know him.

Ronnie   Well, yu can find out fer me.

Shanice   Yu love to drool. Yu don't feel slack?

Ronnie   Yu should see him dough.

Shanice Since when yu go fer white bwois? Yu muss be well moist.

Ronnie Juss tell him I gonna come lookin fer him. It's gonna be me and him soon, tellin yu. 'Me so horny . . .

Shanice '. . . me so sexy . . .

Ronnie/Shanice '. . . me love yu long time!'

Laughter from the girls.

Ronnie Wanna share him, Shanice?

Shanice I don't do white men.

Ronnie But if yu had to, who would yu go fer?

Shanice None.

Ronnie Shut up.

Shanice None, right.

Ronnie If I put a gun to yer face, yu still wouldn't choose?

Shanice No.

Ronnie Lie bad.

Shanice White bwois too soff.

Ronnie Blah, blah, bloody blah, who would yu choose?

Shanice David Rees.

Ronnie David Rees!

Shanice Yu have to shout?

Ronnie Oh shame.

Shanice Only if I had to.

Ronnie Oh yes?

Shanice Yu open yer mout to anyone, and yu die.

Ronnie I can see dat, yu and him.

Shanice   Ain't gonna happen.

Ronnie   Oh but he's nice, really sweet and dat.

Shanice   Oh don't chat like a white girl, please.

Ronnie   I reckon he looks like Will Young.

Shanice   No!

Ronnie   Only ca him gay.

Shanice   He don't look like Will Young!

Ronnie   Ask him out.

Shanice   Move.

Ronnie   I know his brudda.

Shanice   Don't involve me in yer stupidness.

Ronnie   Yu might be missin out.

Shanice   On wat?

Ronnie   He might have a PHD, yu get me?

Shanice   A white bwoi?

Ronnie   Why not? Ain't juss bruddas who have dem. I know sum bruddas who don't have dem. Yu have one?

Joe   What?

Ronnie   PHD?

Shanice (*laughing*)   Shut up, Ronnie man.

Ronnie   Bet he don't.

Shanice   Yu don't feel no shame.

Ronnie   Watch my man's face turn red now.

Shanice   Oi, go and get sum change fer me.

Ronnie   Oh I see.

Shanice   No yu don't see.

Ronnie Want sumtime alone wid yer man here. I'm tellin Emile. How yu know he ain't here to chirps me?

Shanice He ain't chirpsin neither of us.

Ronnie All the shops are shut.

Shanice Costcutter's ain't.

Ronnie Dass miles.

Shanice Pound coins and twenties.

Ronnie Awright, I'm gone. Comin back dough. She go eat yu alive, dread.

Exit **Ronnie**.

Shanice She's mad.

Joe No need to apologise.

Shanice I ain't, I'm juss sayin she's mad. So ware is he?

Joe Who, Adams? I don't know him.

Shanice Yer partner.

Joe Conducting interviews or something. I don't know. I gave him the slip.

Shanice Naughty.

Joe When you hear him ask the same questions 'bout twenty times, it gets a bit boring, you know.

Shanice Is it?

Joe You're a bit young to be running this place on your own.

Shanice Is it?

Joe Should be at school.

Shanice Is it?

Joe Oh, I see, you don't want chat to no policeman.

Shanice   Is –

Joe   – Is it? Beat you.

Shanice   Gimme summin worth chattin about.

Joe   Did you go to his funeral today?

Shanice   His parents wouldn't want me deh.

Joe   Why's that?

Shanice   They don't want none of the kids from round here deh.

Joe   Can't say I blame them. I wouldn't want a whole heap of kids comin to my boy's funeral when I know it's one of them that killed him, or know who did.

Shanice   I don't know who kill him.

Joe   I never said you did. Did yu know him?

Shanice   Course I knew him.

Joe   How well did you know him?

Shanice   I answered dis awready.

Joe   Yeah, but do it fer me. I'm new. Please.

Shanice   We were at school togeder.

Joe   He was attacked after leaving here.

Shanice   Yes!

Joe   How did he seem?

Shanice   Awright, he was fine.

Joe   He was here for ten minutes.

Shanice   He had to wait fer his food.

Joe   Wat did you talk about?

Shanice   Stuff, his college and that.

Joe   College?

Shanice   He had to leave home, he was scared about going away.

Joe   That's quite a conversation to have in ten minutes.

Shanice   Is it?

Joe   Was he a regular, Shanice?

Shanice   He aways used to pop in here after he went swimmin. He would sit down deh, read one of his books. Kept tellin him.

Joe   Telling him what?

Shanice   About his books. Guy loved to study, man.

Joe   And what is so wrong wid that?

Shanice   He was aways gettin teased.

Joe   By who?

Shanice   Bwois.

Joe   What boys? The same ones who were in here the other day?

Shanice   And others. Dass the way it was at school. Yu strut round wid books in yer hands, yer askin to get beat up.

Joe   Or killed.

Shanice   Ain't wat I said.

Joe   I know.

Shanice   He loved to carry on, like he was better.

Joe   What's wrong wid that?

Shanice   Sum people don't like dat.

Joe   What people?

Shanice   I'm juss sayin.

Joe   Like yer boyfriend?

Shanice   He couldn't tek a joke.

Joe   How so?

Shanice   One time we had dis new teacher in, yeah. So we all decided to play a joke on him. No one was gonna speak fer the whole lesson, not do any work, juss stare out, see wat happens, wat he does. Everyone was up fer it right, except Kwame. Deh he was, sittin deh, doin his work. He ruined the joke.

Joe   He wanted to work.

Shanice   It was juss a joke.

Joe   It was his choice, he didn't have to, if he didn't want to.

Shanice   Den he was a fool. I could tell yu oder tings 'bout him.

Joe   So tell me.

Shanice   Yu don't wanna know, yu juss want catch the guy who did it.

Joe   So, I'm lookin for a guy?

Shanice   No. I don't know.

Joe   Tell me.

Shanice   First day he come to our school, teacher put him next to me, so I had to look after him. I ask him, why me?

Joe   Because you have a nice face?

Shanice   Yeah.

Joe   You have.

Shanice   Yu come like my gran.

Joe   How so?

Shanice   Ca she aways sayin, sum people have it in their nature to be nice. No matter wat they do to hide it, it's aways deh. They can't help it. Well, I could help it, I didn't want no smelly-head African next to me, followin me. I told him to move, nuff times, but he wouldn't go. I felt sorry fer him after a while, especially when other kids would start on him.

Joe   You looked after him.

Joe   I bet Emile loved that.

Shanice   He weren't my boyfriend den.

Joe   And now?

Shanice   Kwame loved to show how smart he was, like deh is two kinds of black, and he come from the better one, he was havin a laugh. People weren't gonna tek dat.

Joe   Including Emile?

Shanice   Why yu love to chat about Emile, yu love him?

Joe   It's just a question.

Shanice   Yu ask too many questions.

Joe   It's my job.

Shanice   So's listenin.

Joe   Ain't I listening to you now?

Shanice   All dat shit in the paper, chattin like they knew him. He weren't special, he was juss anoder kid, he was nuttin.

Joe   So, he had it coming?

Shanice   I didn't say that.

Joe   So wat was he doing chatting to you about college?

Shanice   I dunno, he juss talked. I can't stop him from chattin.

Joe   But why you, Shanice?

Shanice   I dunno.

Joe   Maybe cos he thought the same way as your gran.

Shanice   Yer wastin yer time.   *just go now.*

Joe   Why?

Shanice   Go back to ware yu come from.   *you don't underst*

Joe   This is where I come from.

Enter **Dwayne**, **Emile**, **Clinton** *and* **Perry**.

Dwayne   Tyson's soff.

Clinton   Awright, watch.

Dwayne   Wass he got, after my man Lennox give him a slappin?

Clinton   He's still a force.

Dwayne   He's a joke. He ain't never bin the same since he come outta prison after wat dat gal said about him. He grind her, and wat happen, get banged up. Dat ain't right.

Perry   My dad says, women are here to fuck up the black man.

Clinton   Yu don't even know yer dad.

Perry   Yer mama don't know yer dad.

Clinton   Dry!

Dwayne   Like her pussy.

Joe *laughs*.

Dwayne   Awright, awright, who call the Feds?

Emile   Was it yu, P?

Perry   Yeah, I want dem to catch the bastard dat cut up Clinton's hair?

Clinton   Ha, yer so funny.

Dwayne   So wass my man doin here?

Shanice   We're juss chattin, so leave him, yeah.

Dwayne   Yu sexin him?

Shanice   Oh man, juss step.

Dwayne   Emile, have a word, man.

Shanice   Excuse me, I'm right here.

Emile   So ware's yer massa?

Shanice   Emile?

Emile   Ware him deh?

Clinton   Cold.

Perry   Gwan.

Emile   Him let yu off the ball and chain fer the night? Him lose his tongue or wat?

Joe   Toothpaste.

Emile   Wass he say?

Clinton   He said toothpaste.

Emile   Yeah, I know wat he said.

Joe   Well, you might want invest, ca yer breath stink, bredren.

Laughter.

Perry   Oh shame!

Dwayne   It's awright, Emile.

Emile   Get off.

Dwayne   Wat, yu go cryin to yer mummy now, ca the brudda here lick yu down wid sum lyrics?

Emile   He didn't lick me down.

Dwayne   And it was a dry one too.

Clinton   Toothpaste.

Emile   He ain't no brudda.

Dwayne   Look like one to me.

Perry   Yu want invest in sum specs as well, Emile.

Clinton   As well as toothpaste.

Emile   Look at the fool.

Dwayne   Yeah?

Emile   Don't even know he's bin used.

Joe   Why don't you enlighten me?

Emile   We ain't tellin yu shit.

Joe   So, you do know something?

Emile   No.

Joe   But you just told me you ain't telling us shit.

Emile   See, awready I know wat yer doin.

Joe   I'm only repeating wat you said.

Emile   Yu go try twist my words, watch him now.

Joe   You're twisting your own words.

Shanice   Emile?

Emile   Is who ask yu fer anythin?

Joe   You said you ain't telling us shit.

Emile   Yes.

Joe   Which implies, that you know something, but you refuse to share it with us.

Emile   No.

Joe   No, you refuse to share, or no, it isn't true?

Emile   See wat I mean about him?

Joe   You better watch yourself, Emile, that's a bad habit you picked up there.

Emile   Why don't yu juss go?

Dwayne   Shut up, yu fool.

Joe   Thank yu, Dwayne, control yer bwoi.

Clinton   Comin out wid dry lyrics himself now.

Joe   You had better keep a leash on this one, Dwayne. He may fold under questioning.

Dwayne   Sit down.

Joe   Bwoi.

Shanice   Why yu stressin him fer?

Perry   Rah, woman tougher than yu, Emile.

Shanice   Why don't yu juss go home?

Joe   I am home.

Dwayne   Wass dis?

Shanice   He say he comes from here.

Dwayne   Is it? Ware?

Joe   Dickens.

Dwayne   Knew it! Dat estate is soff!

Joe   Let me guess, Cleveland?

Perry   Believe.

Joe   Yu ain't all dat.

Dwayne   Shut up, man.

Clinton   Wid yer dry chat.

Perry   Yu definitely ain't bin back from time.

Joe   You Cleveland bwois are wurtless and you know it.

Dwayne Talk to the hand.

Joe Yu know it.

Dwayne Dat was back in the day. Tings change.

Clinton Believe.

Perry Yeah.

Dwayne Wat matters is now.

Joe Awright, I'm down with that.

Dwayne No yer not. Yu ain't from round here no more, dread. So don't carry on like yu tink yu know.

Clinton Chump.

Perry If yer so bad, why yu leave fer?

Joe I wanted a change. Cleaner air.

Emile Well, gwan den, if dass how yu feel.

Joe Yeah, but there's a little matter of a murder, Emile, remember?

Emile Yu ain't gonna find him here.

Joe Maybe, maybe not.

Emile Dis guy drive me mad.

Dwayne Chill.

Emile Juss say wat yu feel, yeah.

Joe Your boy is losing it again, Dwayne, have a word.

Emile Yu tink it's one of us, innit?

Joe You'll find out soon enough what I think.

Emile Wass so special about dat bwoi anyhow? How many black bwois bin kill up round here?

Joe That ain't my business.

Emile   Course it ain't. But Kwame was different, right. Ca he loved to act like a white man.

Clinton   Believe.

Joe   Whatever.

Emile   Go run back to yer slave masters.

Joe   Slave masters?

Emile   How yu know it weren't a white guy dat beat him?

Joe   I don't.

Emile   So wat yu doin here? A little bit of trouble.

Joe   A little bit?

Emile   And the first ting deh do is reach fer us. Always.

Joe   Oh look, don't gimme the 'police pick on us ca we're black' line. Ca I'd juss laugh in yer face. Why should people care about you, when you don't care about yourselves?

Emile   Ooh, man get vex.

Clinton   Oh yes.

Joe   Bwoi, you'll know when I get vex.

Emile   Is it?

Joe   You juss can't keep yer tail quiet, the lot of yer.

Dwayne   Awright, awright, let's juss chill now please, yeah. Peace. He don't speak fer the rest of us. Catch the rass dat did dis. Innit, bwois?

Chorus of agreement.

Joe   I see.

Dwayne   Good. Dass good.

Joe   Don't go mistaking me for some other fool, yeah. Cos I ain't leaving here till I catch somebody, and I will catch, trust. I'm gone. Shanice, always a pleasure.

Exit **Joe**.

Dwayne   Fool.

Clinton   He say he go catch sumone.

Dwayne   Catch wat? We supposed to be scared of dat?

Clinton   Nuh, man.

Perry   Safe.

Dwayne   And yu, lettin him get to yer.

Emile   I weren't.

Dwayne   He come like yer dad.

Emile   He don't look nuttin like my dad.

Dwayne   I didn't say he looked like yer dad, I said he
come like yer dad, clean out yer ears. He's right, yu nuh, yer
too touchy. No wonder my man's ridin yer arse. Hold it
down, bwoi.

Emile   I was.

Dwayne   Yu want get catch?

Shanice   Leave him.

Dwayne   Gal, shut up, I'm juss tryin to stop my bwoi here
from goin to prison, yeah.

Shanice   And yerself.

Dwayne   Yu want control yer woman please?

Shanice   Yu gonna let him speak to me like dat, Emile?

Dwayne   Emile!

Emile   Leave me!

Shanice   Oh man.

Emile   Every time yu two start, it's me in the middle. Yu
want fight, gwan.

Exit **Emile**.

Dwayne   Bring dat fool back.

Shanice   Let him sulk.

Dwayne   Gwan.

Exit **Perry** *and* **Clinton**.

Shanice   Wat am I doin?

Dwayne   Yu gonna cook me sum food?

Shanice   No.

Dwayne   Rude!

Shanice   Wat yu want?

Dwayne   Number two.

Shanice   Wat yu starin at?

Dwayne   Nuttin.

Shanice   I'm up here, yu know. Perv man. 'Bout yu lookin down my top.

Dwayne   I weren't.

Shanice   I saw yu.

Dwayne   Yu look nicer in dat oder top. Put it on.

Shanice   I don't have it.

Dwayne   Get anoder one. I'll pay fer it.

Shanice   Dry.

Dwayne   I chat better than Emile. Wat yu doin wid him?

Shanice   Who, yer best friend? I love him.

Dwayne (*sucks his teeth*)   Yer juss lookin after him. Like yu look after troll.

Shanice   Don't call her dat.

Dwayne   Shut up.

Shanice   Yu know she fancies yer.

Dwayne   Who's lookin after yu? When yu go have sum fun?

Shanice   Yu think I want fun wid yu?

Dwayne   Don't yu get bored?

Shanice   I'm gettin bored right now.

Dwayne   Come on.

Shanice   Don't touch me.

Dwayne   Yer lucky dass all I'm doin. Nuff brers round here want ride yu, yu nuh.

Shanice   Yu on crack?

Dwayne   How yu gonna fight dem all off? Dass how bad it's gettin. Yu don't know wat yer doin, yu got no idea. The fact dat yer goin wid sum fool, mek dem want it even more. I keep tellin dem nuff times, no one touches yu, but I can't hold dem off for ever, Shanice.

Shanice   Yu couldn't hold yerself.

Dwayne   Yu wanted it dat night.

Shanice   I was drunk.

Dwayne   Yu were sexed up. Yu know if one a dem so much as looks at yu funny, I'd kill dem.

Shanice   How nice.

Dwayne   Yer so fit. Wat? Yu rather I chat rubbish to yu?

Shanice   Go on den, try.

Dwayne   Move.

Shanice   Deh's no one else here. Come on, I want to see dis. Try. Come on. Fer me.

Beat.

Dwayne   I love yer hands, yu got nice hands.

Shanice *laughs.*

Dwayne   Yu want die?

Shanice   Yu are so sad. Yu run Emile down day and night, den yu have nerve to steal his lines. Sad!

Dwayne   Move.

Shanice   But oder than dat, not bad, I'd have to think about it.

Dwayne   Yu know wat else I can't get over. Seein yu, yer first day at school, I thought, Rah! Dat can't be the same Shanice Roberts who I used to live next door to, went primary school wid. Wid yer pigtails, and her nappy head. Playin football wid me.

Shanice   I whopped yer arse at football. Remember dat five-a-side tournament?

Dwayne   Yu score a couple of goals and yu think yer it.

Shanice   Three.

Dwayne   Dat third one was not a goal.

Shanice   Deh yu go.

Dwayne   It weren't.

Shanice   Oh Dwayne man, it was seven years ago.

Dwayne   It weren't a goal.

Shanice   Give it up.

Dwayne   I can't stop thinkin about yu.

Shanice   Dwayne, please.

Dwayne   Yer hauntin me, yu know dat?

Shanice *laughs.*

Dwayne   Don't laugh at me.

Shanice   Yu want have yerself a cold shower, dread.

Dwayne   Yu carry on.

Shanice   I will.

Dwayne   Yer gonna get hurt, yer gonna get hurt bad! Wass dat fool Emile gonna do den?

Shanice   He wouldn't be if he stopped mixin wid yu.

Dwayne   Is it my fault he keeps reachin out to me?

Shanice   I'm the one dass holdin him when he has his nightmares.

Dwayne   Is it? Ware?

Shanice   Yer nasty.

Dwayne   Chill.

Shanice   'Kick him in the head, kick him.'

Dwayne   I didn't tell him.

Shanice   Yu made him.

Dwayne   No, Shanice, yu made him. Yu told him Kwame was sexin yu. Sorry, yeah.

Shanice   Don't touch me.

Dwayne   Shanice.

Shanice   Go brush yer teeth.

Dwayne   Yu go free it up soon, yu know it.

Shanice   Not fer yu.

Dwayne   I hope they rape yu up bad.

Enter **Ronnie**.

Ronnie   Got yer change. Yu know how far I had to go. Awright, Dwayne?

Dwayne Troll.

Exit **Dwayne**.

Shanice Gimme my change.

Ronnie *throws money to the ground.*

Shanice Oh Ronnie.

Exit **Ronnie**.

Shanice Yeah, gwan, run!

Exit **Shanice**.

Enter **Joe** *and* **Matt**.

Joe See that basketball court.

Matt You are changing the subject.

Joe That is where the old huts used to be, for the dustbins.

Matt Really?

Joe I lost my virginity in there.

Matt I beg your pardon?

Joe I was fifteen. Mandy Cook, oh man, she was fine. Huts were the only place we could go to. Mandy Cook. First white girl I had, you know. Tellin you, she was –

Matt Fit, thank you.

Joe Just trying to lighten the mood.

Matt Look, Joe, I know you haven't been with us for long.

Joe Uh-huh?

Matt So you might not be up to speed with how we do things here.

Joe Probably not.

Matt   I'd appreciate it if you did not go off on your own. We work together.

Joe   Of course.

Matt   We follow our lines of inquiry together.

Joe   Absolutely.

Matt   So we understand each other?

Joe   Of course, Matt.

Matt   Good.

Joe   The thing is though.

Matt   Yes?

Joe   The girl knows something.

Matt   Did you think you could charm it out of her?

Joe   Well, we don't have much else.

Matt   I'm aware of that.

Joe   Haven't you noticed, everything's scaling down?

Matt   I'm aware of that as well.

Joe   It's not news any more. Soon, he'll just be another dead black kid. Kids round here aren't made to feel important. They never have. They know a token gesture when they see it.

Matt   I was beginning to think you didn't care.

Joe   I don't. (*Beat.*) I want to know what he was doing in there.

Matt   Ordering food.

Joe   So she said. But he never came out wid any.

Matt   He was eating in.

Joe   For ten minutes? Counting the five or six it takes to cook. I was thinking, maybe he was buying drugs there.

Matt   Joe, can I ask you something?

Joe   Just tell me, don't ask.

Matt   Why are you so eager to demean him?

Joe   Oh man.

Matt   He was a bright young lad. Four weeks away from starting university, he had a future, he didn't deserve to die like that.

Joe   You trying to impress me, Matt?

Matt   With what?

Joe   What a cool liberal you are.

Matt   Meaning?

Joe   Meaning that. I mean, come on, it's really got to get to you, all this PC shit.

Matt   Not particularly.

Joe   Not even a little?

Matt   The Met needs to change. We can't keep making mistakes.

Joe   It's the uniforms I feel sorry for. Now they're thinking of asking them to provide written records for every stop and search. I mean, what kind of stupidness is that?

Matt *sighs.*

Joe   What? What is it?

Matt   I don't understand you.

Joe   Good.

Matt   Joe, if you have a problem working with me on this case . . .

Joe   What case? We both know why I'm here. It's bring out the poster boy. Make the Met look good. McPherson report. Well, that's fine, but you had better step back, boy, and let me do my job.

Matt   First off, I am not your boy. Second, I am the senior officer.

Joe   Yes! Go, Matt! Stand yer ground, don't take shit from anybody.

Matt   Please, don't patronise me.

Joe   Ditto.

Matt   I was not.

Joe   It's always going to be in our job, prejudice.

Matt   I am not prejudiced.

Joe   Easy, Matt, it's only a word, you don't have to shit yourself.

Matt   I'm not. Alright?

Joe   If you're walking down the street at night, you see a bunch of black lads walking towards you –

Matt   Oh, come on.

Joe   – you know you're gonna cross that road, as fast as your legs can tek you. You know! It's all preconceived. Maybe this Kwame was a good kid, I don't know.

Matt   He was.

Joe   But he's from that estate. We've got to find out if he's a bad boy. We have to ask those questions, and I don't care.

Matt   That doesn't make it right.

Joe   It's the way it is.

Exit **Joe** *and* **Matt**.

Enter **Shanice** *and* **Emile**.

Emile   Rape yer!

Shanice   Dass wat the bastard said.

Emile   Wat yu mean rape?

Shanice   Wat yu think I mean? The bwoi nasty, dass wat I keep tellin yu.

Emile   Like he meant it?

Shanice   Whether he meant it or not, it was a nasty ting to say, don't yu think? Emile?

Emile   I don't blasted know.

Shanice   Yu don't know?

Emile   Wat yu stressin me fer?

Shanice   It's not a hard thing to work out, Emile. Was he right or wrong to say it?

Emile   He was wrong.

Shanice   Don't strain yerself.

Emile   I said he was wrong, wat yu want?

Shanice   Deal wid it.

Emile   I'm aways dealin wid it.

Shanice   Talk to him.

Emile   Yu mad?

Shanice   Tell him I'm yer gal, tell him he can't treat me like dis.

Emile   Awright!

Shanice   Why yu so soff?

Emile   Yu gonna dog me out now?

Shanice   No.

Emile   Lie.

Shanice   I want things the way they were.

Emile   Go college like Clinton?

Shanice   Yes.

Emile   Gal, dat ain't fer us, Miss Douglas took care of dat.

Shanice   Don't worry yerself about her.

Emile   Maybe yu should.

Shanice   Should wat?

Emile   Fuck him. Fuck him, Shanice. One time, yeah.

Shanice   No, yu did not say dat.

Emile   Dwayne's right, yeah, yu don't know wat yer doin, wat yer givin out. I can't tek it, man. Whenever my back's turned, wonderin all the time if Dwayne or anyone else is sexin yu. It's drivin me mad, not knowin, so juss fuck him, yeah. Least I'll know, I'll have sum peace, I'll forgive yu, we'll move on.

Shanice *screams. Attacks* **Emile**.

Emile   I'm sorry, I'm sorry!

Shanice   Yu love doin dis to me or wat?

Emile   I don't know wat I'm doin, yeah.

Shanice   It's aways about yu.

Emile   I keep seein his –

Shanice   – his face, yeah!

Emile   I'll talk to Dwayne.

Shanice   Don't worry yerself.

Emile   I said I'll talk to him. Don't leave me.

Exit **Emile**.

Enter **Ronnie**.

Shanice   Yu sure dis is the right road?

Ronnie   Yes.

Shanice   Ashwood Gardens?

Ronnie   Yes.

Shanice   Not Ashwood Square?

Ronnie   No.

Shanice   Twenty-nine C?

Ronnie   Yes.

Shanice   Are yu gonna say more than word to me tonight?

Ronnie   No.

Shanice   Bet yu do.

Ronnie   Bet I don't.

Shanice (*laughs*)   See!

Ronnie   Oh, juss leave me.

Shanice   Yer soff, Ronnie. Ronnie?

Ronnie   Get off me, don't do dat, Shanice. Move!

Shanice   Oh, so yu want fight me now?

Ronnie   Kick yer arse. It's big enuff.

Shanice *grabs her, holds her playfully in a headlock.*

Ronnie   Get off.

Shanice   Say it.

Ronnie   Get off me.

Shanice   Say it!

Ronnie   Yer arse ain't big.

Shanice   Better.

Ronnie   It's Jurassic!

Shanice *grabs her again.*

Ronnie   Awright!

Shanice (*backs off*)   Well, gimme a smile den.

Ronnie   I don't feel like smilin.

Shanice   Oh Ronnie.

Ronnie   Don't Ronnie me.

Shanice   Come here and gimme a hug. Come here.

Ronnie   I don't hug hos.

Shanice   Excuse me?

Ronnie   Yer a ho.

Shanice   Listen, I'm gonna say dis one lass time, yeah, deh is nuttin goin on between –

Ronnie   – between me and Dwayne!

Shanice   So yu think yer funny now?

Ronnie   Yer a liar.

Shanice   I ain't lyin to yu, Ronnie.

Ronnie   Yu lied to me before, den I had to find out from Clinton, yu were grindin Dwayne.

Shanice   Once, I grind him once.

Ronnie   Yu still lied dough.

Shanice   Only cos I know how yu go all menstrual when it comes to Dwayne.

Ronnie   Yu love to do dis to me.

Shanice   Yu know wat, yu can fuck off, yeah.

Ronnie   Wat?

Shanice   Fuck off. Move. Now.

Ronnie   Wass up wid yu?

Shanice   Yu! Yer so jealous.

Ronnie   Yu got everythin.

Shanice   I got nuttin but grief.

Ronnie   Yu got Dwayne droolin.

Shanice   I don't know wat yu see in de fool, I really don't.

Ronnie   He likes yu.

Shanice   So?

Ronnie   Why can't I be yu?

Shanice   Yu not turnin lesbian on me?

Ronnie   Move.

Shanice   Dat I don't need.

Ronnie   I said no.

Shanice   Look at me. I said look. (*Beat.*) Don't chat fuck ries in my face again, yu understand?

Ronnie   Yes.

Shanice   Don't be me, Ronnie. It's overrated.

Ronnie   I won't den.

Shanice   We awright?

Ronnie   Yeah.

Shanice   Yu sure?

Ronnie   Yeah.

Shanice   Cool.

Ronnie   She's comin.

Shanice   Right.

Enter **Miss Douglas**.

Shanice   Awright?

Miss Douglas   Yes, thank you.

Shanice   Yu got a light?

Miss Douglas   I don't smoke.

Ronnie   She don't recognise us.

Miss Douglas   That's not true.

Shanice   See, yu get Ronnie all upset now.

Miss Douglas   Then I apologise.

Shanice   Ain't yu gonna say hello?

Miss Douglas   Hello, Shanice.

Shanice   Hello, Miss.

Ronnie   I love yer house, Miss. Nice.

Miss Douglas   Thank you.

Shanice   Ware yu goin?

Miss Douglas   I'd like to go home.

Shanice   Stay and chat.

Ronnie   Yeah, stay and chat.

Shanice   Yu bin shoppin, Miss?

Miss Douglas   Yes.

Shanice   Let me see.

Miss Douglas (*pleads*)   Please.

Shanice   Please wat?

Ronnie   Ain't even touched her yet, and she's sweatin awready.

Miss Douglas   What do you want?

Shanice   To chat.

Ronnie   Yu deaf?

Shanice   So how's it goin, Miss?

Miss Douglas   Fine.

Shanice   How's school?

Miss Douglas   Fine.

Shanice   Yu miss us?

Ronnie   Do yu miss us?

Shanice   Course she does, Ronnie, check her face.

Ronnie   She's sorry.

Shanice   Is dat true, Miss, yu sorry?

Miss Douglas   Yes, I am sorry.

Shanice   Yu lie bad.

Ronnie   She'd say yes to anythin, to get away.

Shanice   Believe.

Ronnie   Yu a prostitute, Miss? Say yes.

Miss Douglas   I don't know what it is you want.

Shanice   To chat.

Ronnie   Still deaf.

Miss Douglas   Please don't do this.

Shanice   Don't do wat, Miss?

Miss Douglas   You are only making things worse for yourself.

Shanice   Is it?

Miss Douglas   Let me pass.

Ronnie   Yu don't tell us wat to do no more.

Shanice   Nice watch. Take it off.

Miss Douglas (*removes watch*)   May I go now?

Ronnie   Yu know, I'd shut up if I were yu.

Miss Douglas   You haven't changed at all.

Shanice   Don't chat to her like dat. We're out here now.

Ronnie   Believe.

Shanice   Dis is our school.

Miss Douglas   Look, I will not be intimidated like this.

Shanice   Is it?

Ronnie   Can hear her heart pumpin from here.

Miss Douglas   I won't allow it.

Shanice   Yu won't allow it?

Ronnie   Gonna put us in detention? Miss tink she bad now.

Miss Douglas   You cannot keep doing this, blaming everyone else for your mistakes.

Shanice   Wat have I said about talkin like dat? 'Bout yu darkin us?

Miss Douglas   You stole Mr Ferns's wallet, girl.

Shanice   I was puttin it back.

Miss Douglas   Oh come on.

Shanice   I was.

Ronnie   Yu were puttin it back?

Shanice   Quiet.

Miss Douglas   We have been through this.

Shanice   We go thru it again.

Miss Douglas   I caught you red-handed.

Shanice   Yu caught me puttin it back.

Ronnie   Yu soff.

Shanice   Shut up.

Miss Douglas   You had his money in your pocket, explain that to me.

Shanice   I don't have to explain shit.

Miss Douglas   Oh Shanice.

Shanice   Step!

Ronnie   Wat yu tryin to touch her fer? Yu a dyke, Miss?

Miss Douglas   Listen to me.

Shanice   Couldn't wait, man, yu wanted me outta deh.

Miss Douglas   You know that isn't true.

Shanice   And den yu had to start on Emile.

Miss Douglas   He threw a chair at me.

Ronnie   Did yu like wat I did, Miss?

Miss Douglas   Oh yes, Veronica, you trashing my car was a nice touch.

Ronnie   Cool. Gimme yer money.

Miss Douglas   Shanice, please listen to me.

Ronnie   Gimme it.

Miss Douglas   Why are you still letting yourself get led around by her?

Ronnie   She is dead.

Shanice   Hold it down.

Ronnie   Nuh, man.

Shanice   Hold it down, Ronnie.

Ronnie   Shanice!

Shanice   Go stand over deh. Go. Yu betrayed me.

Miss Douglas   What is it you think you did to me?

Shanice   It's all yer fault.

Miss Douglas   All I ever did was try and help you. I had no choice.

Shanice   It was juss a wallet, man.

Miss Douglas   It was wrong.

Shanice   I was puttin it back, yu deaf?

Miss Douglas   It was too late. You came so far, you were doing so well.

Shanice   So why open yer mout den?

Miss Douglas   Why did you take it?

Shanice   I dunno, I juss did.

Miss Douglas   Was it her?

Shanice   Leave her.

Miss Douglas   Did she put you up to it?

Ronnie   Wass she say?

Miss Douglas   When are you going to learn, Shanice, people like her don't want to be helped? They don't want to listen.

Shanice   I am people like her.

Miss Douglas   No, you are not. You're just scared.

Shanice   Don't play me. I wasted nuff times listenin to yu, and I still got fling out.

Ronnie   I'm bored now, man, do her, den let's go.

Shanice   Hand over yer money.

Miss Douglas   No.

Shanice   Miss!

Miss Douglas   I will not. You won't hurt me.

Shanice   I will.

Miss Douglas   No, you won't.

Shanice   I will.

Ronnie   Juss do it.

Miss Douglas   Stay out of this, Veronica.

Ronnie   Stop callin me dat.

Miss Douglas   Still thinking a foul mouth is going to get you everything you want.

Ronnie   Let's juss tek her money and go, Shanice man.

Shanice   I want her to gimme it.

Miss Douglas   You are going to have to take it.

Shanice   Gimme it.

Miss Douglas   No.

Ronnie   Shanice!

Shanice   Leave me!

Miss Douglas   Why couldn't you leave her alone?

Ronnie   She renk!

Miss Douglas   You are nothing, Veronica Davis, you always were.

Ronnie   Yu gonna let her chat like dat?

Miss Douglas   Please, Shanice.

Ronnie   Yu think yu be sellin burgers if yu didn't get fling out?

Miss Douglas   Listen to me.

Ronnie   Wid yer shit money every month, hair smellin of onion.

Miss Douglas   Shanice?

Ronnie   Every night, dread.

Miss Douglas (*pleads*)   Please.

Ronnie   Do her!

Shanice *strikes her.*

Ronnie   Oh! Shame! I felt dat from here. Tek her money and let's go.

Shanice   Yu happy now?

Ronnie   Shanice!

Shanice   Yu happy?

Ronnie   Wat yu goin on wid?

Shanice   Are yu?

Ronnie   Come on!

Exit **Shanice**.

Ronnie   Ware yu goin? (*To* **Miss Douglas**.) Ware yu goin? Money.

Miss Douglas   I knew you'd end up like this.

Ronnie   Is my name Shanice? I don't business wat yu think of me, yeah. I know yer scared. Believe.

Exit **Ronnie** *and* **Miss Douglas**.

Enter **Dwayne**.

Dwayne   I'm here. Come on!

Enter **Emile**.

Dwayne (*laughs*)   Wat?

Emile   Bastard, man.

Dwayne   Shut yer noise.

Emile   Yer a bastard, Dwayne. Leavin me like dat.

Dwayne   Is it my fault yu can't run?

Emile   I know how to run, I can run faster than yu.

Dwayne   So wat happened? Yu go cry?

Emile   Shoulda told me yu weren't payin him.

Dwayne   We done it before.

Emile   Still shoulda said. Coulda bin prepared.

Dwayne   Bwoi love to moan.

Emile   Guy nearly caught me.

Dwayne   I bet he's still lookin.

Emile   I bet he calls the police.

Dwayne   Hey, it's me who should be callin. 'Bout he charge us ten squid from town. Tief! Hear how the controller said it would be seven or summin. But my man deh try and shake us fer ten. Hear how he spoke. 'Ware yu goin, boss, ten pound, boss.' Stupid Arab. Should tell him about him claart! Go back to Iraq! See how long his beard was? Bin Laden's brudda. Yu know how many bruddas dat man's got? Untold! His mama's hole muss be dat big.

Emile   Ain't his mum. His dad have a whole heap of women.

Dwayne   Must be a bro. Gimme a draw. Bloody cheer up, man, wass up wid yu?

Emile   Juss don't leave me like dat again.

Dwayne   Yeah, wass yer wurtless rass gonna do?

Emile   I ain't no rass.

Dwayne   Rass.

Emile   Don't call me dat.

Dwayne   Rass! Yu still comin out wid nish, Emile, wat yu gonna do?

Emile   Yu'll find out.

Dwayne   Chill. Before I slap yu.

Emile   Juss tell me wat yer doin.

Dwayne   I'm tellin yu to chill. Hey, don't step up, unless yu gonna jump.

Emile   Yer mad.

Dwayne   Is it?

Emile   Outta control, dread.

Dwayne   Me?

Emile   Yu didn't have to hit the guy.

Dwayne   He ask fer it.

Emile   Six times? Have a heart, blood.

Dwayne   Like yu had fer Kwame?

Emile   He deserved it.

Dwayne   So yu tink yer bad now?

Emile   I want respect.

Dwayne   Wat yu goin on wid?

Emile   Shanice said –

Dwayne   Shanice? Don't come to me wid shit from yer gal, 'bout Shanice!

Emile   Yu still don't respect me, do yer?

Dwayne   Yer chattin like a spas.

Emile   I did wat yu all wanted.

Dwayne   Yu don't want to start dis wid me.

Emile   I want respect, I want it now, bredren.

Dwayne   Well, yu ain't gonna get it.

Emile   Yu love to put me down.

Dwayne   Yer too soff.

Emile   I've had enuff.

Dwayne   Is it?

Emile   Wat more I have to do?

Dwayne   Yer soff!

Emile   And stop tryin to sex Shanice, she's my woman.

Dwayne   I'll sex who I like, bwoi!

Emile   Yu ain't.

Dwayne   Yu really are stupid, innit? Dat policeman know it too.

Emile   Leave her alone, Dwayne.

Dwayne   Watch me stroke her leg, every time yer deh. Watch me run my train up her arse, watch me. Yu might learn summin. I'm gonna run it good, man, gonna run it. And yu ain't gonna do nuttin, ca yer soff.

Emile *pulls out his blade, aims it at* **Dwayne***'s face.*

Dwayne   Yeah? Wat? Wat?

Emile   Yu see it?

Dwayne   Yu tink I'm blind?

Emile   I buy dis fer yu.

Dwayne   Yu pull it, yu best use it.

Emile   I will.

Dwayne   Wat she see in yu?

Emile   She my woman. And I want respect!

Dwayne (*laughs*)   Yu.

Emile   Idiot? Fool? Arsehole? Who's soff now? Who's soff now?

Dwayne   Me?

Emile   Who have the blade?

Dwayne   Yu.

Emile   Yu know who yu look like, Dwayne? Like one a dem white cunts who clutch their bags warever we see dem.

Sound of police sirens.

Dwayne   Yu hear dat?

Emile   Yu a white cunt, Dwayne?

Dwayne   Dass the cab driver tellin dem about us, we gotta go.

Emile   Are yu a white cunt?

Dwayne   Yeah.

Emile   Believe.

Exit **Dwayne**.

Enter **Joe**.

Joe   Bwoi, Emile! You know how to run fast, man! Look at me, I have no breath left. You alright? Take deep breaths, my man.

Emile   Move.

Joe   Alright.

Emile   Yer lucky I trip up.

Joe   Yeah.

Emile   No way could yu catch me.

Joe   I almost had you.

Emile   Yu want go again?

Joe   You mad?

Emile   Yer soff.

Joe   I bet you used to run for your school. Am I right?

Emile   Yeah.

Joe   Medals and shit?

Emile   Untold.

Joe   Me too.

Emile   Yu?

Joe   What, you don't believe?

Emile   Yer outta shape, blood.

Joe   That was then, this is now.

Emile   Believe.

Joe   So what happened to you, Emile? Didn't you want to be an athlete? Why aren't you running now?

Emile   Dunno.

Joe   Don't chat like you're an idiot.

Emile   Move.

Joe   What happened?

Emile   I dunno. Shit, shit 'appens.

Joe   Like what? What shit? Tell me what happened to you.

Emile   Yu tink I want tell yu?

Joe   Fine. Stay stupid.

Emile   So wat about yu?

Joe   Me?

Emile   Dickens, bwoi. Wat 'appen to yu? Didn't yu want to be a policeman?

Joe   Are you cussing me?

Emile   Yeah, I'm cussin yu.

Joe   Lose the tone, Emile. Have some respect.

Emile   Yer not my dad.

Joe (*laughs*)   Look, just tell me what you were running from just then?

Emile   Heard the sirens.

Joe   Yeah, so what you running for? What's your naughty little black arse been up to now, Emile? What you do?

Emile   Nuttin.

Joe   You're a bad liar.

Emile   Is it?

Joe   People who run have something to hide.

Emile   Is it?

Joe   Yes, it is.

Emile   People also run ca they don't like gettin stressed by all yer friends, innit? I ain't got time fer dat.

Joe   You? Where the hell you going, work? (*Laughs.*) I was lookin for yu, I want to chat to you.

Emile   I don't wanna chat to yu.

Joe   Now you're hurtin my feelins.

Emile   Is it?

Joe   I was hoping we could spend some quality time together.

Emile   Wat yu tink I am?

Joe   Come, stand up.

Emile   Ware we goin?

Joe   Take a guess.

Enter **Matt**.

Joe   So, Emile, the guy on your left is your boy Clinton, and over there, we have Perry, and that has got to be Dwayne, right here, see that boy there, you see him?

Emile   I ain't blind.

Joe   That's Kwame.

Emile   I know.

Matt   You know?

Emile   Yeah. I know. I went school wid him.

Joe   Well, that's good, because you're going to recognise this young fella right here. That's you.

Emile   That ain't me.

Joe   Hold up a second, I've got a better picture here. It really gets your face. You wouldn't believe the trouble we went through to get these pictures.

Emile   Is it?

Joe   Trust. Here we are. See it there?

Emile   Yeah. Ain't me.

Joe   That's not you?

Emile   Ain't me.

Joe   Well, that's a big relief.

Emile   Yeah?

Joe   Yes, cos then, if that was you, and your friends, at this particular place, at this particular time, with Kwame, approximately five minutes before he died, then you and your friends would have some serious explaining to do, me and my friend here wouldn't have to reach for a search warrant, knock on your mother's door, you still live at home, course you do, go through all her things, same thing with your friends, bring them all in here, one by one, see what they say, find out if they are a bigger jackass than you. But like you said, dat ain't you.

Emile Can I go now?

Joe Sit down.

Emile Yu can bring in who yu like. Deh won't say nuttin.

Joe Say what? What aren't they going to say?

Emile Nuttin.

Joe So, they do know something?

Emile Don't play me, yeah.

Joe Play you with what?

Emile Wid dem words.

Joe Are you stupid?

Matt Joe?

Emile Yeah, tell yer bwoi to chill.

Matt Why don't you stop wasting our time.

Emile I'm juss messin wid yu.

Matt Tell us about these.

Joe You're all laughing in this one, what's that about?

Emile Nuttin to say. We're juss laughin about, havin a laugh.

Joe Did you kill Kwame for a laugh?

Emile No.

Joe So why did you kill him?

Emile I didn't.

Joe You know who did?

Emile No.

Joe   This picture was taken five minutes before he was beaten up, Emile.

Emile   And yer point is?

Joe   You are probably the last ones to see him.

Emile   Yer point?

Joe   And you don't know anything?

Emile   Is wat I said.

Joe   Alright. So tell me something you do know. What was the conversation about. (*Holds up photo.*) Tell me. What were you laughing about?

Emile   Can't remember.

Joe   Try.

Emile   I was tellin a joke.

Joe   A joke?

Emile   Yeah.

Joe   Must have been a good joke.

Emile   It was.

Joe   Well, let's hear it then. The joke.

Emile   Yer soff.

Joe   And you're a liar.

Emile   Wat do yu call a lesbian dinosaur?

Joe   I give up.

Emile   A lickalottapus.

Joe   That's it?

Emile   Yes.

Joe   Weren't that funny.

Emile   Yeah, well, dass yu.

Joe   That was the same joke you told Kwame?

Emile   It's wat I said.

Joe   But it isn't funny. Ignorant, yeah, but not funny.

Emile   We laughed.

Joe   I don't see Kwame laughing.

Emile   Well, he was.

Joe   It looks he's crying.

Emile   He weren't cryin.

Joe   Like he's scared. What has he got to be scared about?

Emile   Yu tell me.

Joe   You threaten him?

Emile   No.

Joe   What did you do to him?

Emile   Nuttin. We pass him by the street, told the joke, and we left him.

Joe   You left him there to die.

Emile   No.

Joe   Yes.

Emile   We juss left him.

Joe   Did you like him?

Emile   He was awright.

Joe   Why?

Emile   Wass dis fool sayin now?

Joe   Why did you like him? He was nothing but a bookworm, a nerd, a little fool. What was he going do with his life? Go to university, get a nice job, forty grand a year, you think? He was heading out of the estate for good. Then, there's you. Dashed out of school at fifteen. What have you got in common with him? How could you be friends with him?

Emile   Did I say we were friends?

Joe   Alright, now we're heading somewhere.

Emile   I said I liked him.

Joe   Are you a battyman, Emile?

Matt   Joe!

Emile   Yer the battyman.

Joe   You liked him? That Zulu warrior, who's as black as coal? Who thought he was smarter than the lot of you?

Emile   Yer words, dread.

Joe   You liked him?

Emile   Yeah.

Joe   Does Dwayne know you're this soft?

Emile   I ain't soff.

Joe   He was a nice-looking boy though.

Emile   Yu are a battyman.

Joe   He must have had a lot of girls reaching for him.

Emile   Yeah?

Joe   Him and Shanice would've made a nice couple, don't you think, if she wasn't going out with you, that is.

Emile   She is goin out wid me.

Joe   I know. But if she weren't. Did he step to your woman, Emile, is that how it was? You ain't having that, some bwoi tryin to grind your woman. I wouldn't have that. Is that what occurred, Emile? Is that what occurred?

Emile   No.

Joe   You can talk to me.

Emile   I am talkin.

Joe   See, what I can't figure out, what I can't get my head round, is this. This picture. You and your friends, other end of the high street, laughing your heads off, look at the time, five minutes after Kwame was found in the street, with his head cracked open. You lot, laughing like it didn't mean a thing.

Emile   Ca we didn't know.

Joe   Tell me.

Emile   I am.

Joe   Tell me what happened. We all get a little upset.

Emile   I ain't upset.

Joe   Especially over a woman. I know how it goes, come on, Emile, bend my ear, bro to bro.

Emile   I ain't yer bro. I ain't yer nuttin. Yu love to tink yer down wid us.

Matt   Alright.

Emile   Yer nuttin to me.

Matt   Sit down, Emile.

Emile   So don't come it, yeah, don't play the big man.

Matt   Sit down please.

Emile   Well, tell yer bitch to chill den. Ca dass all yu are now, dis fool's bitch! And I ain't growin up to be no white man's bitch, yu get me?

Joe   You don't like bitches, do you, Emile?

Emile   No.

Joe   Was Kwame a bitch?

Emile   Yes.

Joe   Is that why you killed him?

Emile   No.

Joe   So why did you kill him?

Emile   I didn't.

Joe   You couldn't stand it.

Emile   I don't talk to yu.

Joe   He was a reminder.

Emile   I'd rather chat to him.

Joe   Of what a wurtless, useless rass you are.

Matt   Let's take a break.

Joe   Innit, Emile?

Matt   Interview suspended at 16.10 p.m.

Exit **Emile**.

Matt   I'm releasing him.

Joe   Are you mad?

Matt   We're going round in circles in there. We've got nothing to charge him with. You need to calm down.

Joe   For fuck's sake.

Matt   Will you please calm down?

Joe   Facety little nigger.

Matt   Joe?

Joe   You want to see yourself, eyes as big as saucers. Yes, Matt, I said nigger. Do you want say it, go on, give it a try, let it out. Cos if I'm thinking it, so are you. Nigger!

Matt   Stop it.

Joe   Little shit.

Matt   Are you done?

Joe   Boy wanna learn respect.

Matt   Calm down, please.

Joe   Oh, will you stop saying please, it drive me mad! He did it. I know he did it. You know he did it. Bwoi thinks he's bad, him and his crew. I'll show dem who's bad. Ain't nuttin but a low-life useless cold-blooded black bastard. He thinks he's summin, he ain't nuttin. I'm havin him.

Matt   With what exactly? You've got nothing.

Joe   Don't butt in like that again.

Matt   I'm sorry?

Joe   Mek me look bad.

Matt   You were losing it.

Joe   It was working.

Matt   He wanted to talk to me more than you.

Joe   Love to hold his hand.

Matt   Your way wasn't working.

Joe (*laughs*)   Fool don't even know he's bin insulted.

Matt   Don't push your luck.

Joe   You do nish for one black kid, too much for the other one.

Matt   Oh that's right, go there.

Joe   You all think you're doing them a favour by patronising them.

Matt   I wasn't patronising him. Look, I do not wish to fight you, Joe.

Joe   Why? What you so bloody 'fraid to say, man?

Matt   Hold it down.

Joe   I don't want to hold it down. I want to talk. I want us to talk. I want us to have the conversation. Yeah? So let's have it.

Matt   I'm releasing him.

Exit **Joe** *and* **Matt**.

Enter **Shanice**, **Ronnie**, **Perry**, **Emile**, **Clinton** *and* **Dwayne**.

Shanice   Perry, dat had better not be spliff yer smokin.

Perry   Nuh, man.

Shanice   Wat have I told yu? Not in here.

Perry   Shut up and gimme my fries.

Shanice   Who yu tellin to shut up? Yu mad?

Perry   Emile?

Emile   Chill.

Shanice   Dat had better be him yer sayin dat to.

Perry   Emile?

Shanice   Emile!

Emile   Yer shamin me, Shanice.

Perry   Thank yu.

Ronnie   Yu shame yerself.

Perry   Yu gonna take dat?

Emile   Shut yer mout.

Perry   Oh right, so bwoi tink he man now.

Emile   I don't think, I know.

Perry   Dwayne, put dis fool under manners again fer me please.

Emile   Why don't yu?

Perry   Awright den, come.

Dwayne   Sit down.

Perry   Yu fight like a gal anyhow.

Emile   Is it?

Perry   Believe.

Dwayne   Put out the spliff.

Perry   Dwayne man.

Dwayne   Yer fuckin up my sinuses wid dat, put it out.

Clinton   Are we all done now? Can we divvy up now please?

Clinton *produces a handbag, the boys rifle through it.*

Perry   See dat woman's face? See how scared? Feel my heart.

Clinton   Move.

Perry   Feel it, dread.

Clinton   Like a drum.

Perry   Better than weed.

Emile   Better than speed.

Clinton   Better than a line.

Perry   Yu tek line?

Clinton   Yes.

Perry   Since when?

Clinton   A boy at college had sum.

Perry   I thought I tell yu to stay away from dat?

Clinton   Step off, P.

Perry   I'm telling yer mum, yu get dis! (*Raises his hand.*)

Emile Yu got the rest of the money in yer pocket deh, Dwayne?

Dwayne Wat?

Emile Rest of the money, dread.

Dwayne Rest of the money here.

Emile Nuh, man. I saw yu open the purse, deh was more deh.

Dwayne Is it?

Emile Yer holdin out on us, bro. Come on, man, cough up the rest, ain't got all night.

Dwayne Deh is no more.

Emile Right now, on the table, if yu please.

Perry Emile, yu mad or wat?

Dwayne I'm tellin yu now, Emile, dis was all the money dat was in dat bag.

Emile Well, yu mus be high from Perry's weed den, ca I definitely saw more dough in dat purse. Now I know yu don't wanna skank us, so wa gwan? Yer dad still fleecin yu or wat?

Dwayne Don't do dis. Awright? Yu understand?

Emile Awright, blood, ease up.

Dwayne Yu ease up.

Emile I'm cool. Keep the money.

Dwayne Deh's no more money.

Emile Awright, man, watever, I made a mistake den.

Dwayne Yer damn right.

Exit **Dwayne**.

Emile Oh come on, Dwayne!

Clinton   Yu are well and truly mad, yu nuh.

Perry   Believe.

Emile   I thought he was skankin us.

Clinton   Sounded like yu knew, a minute ago.

Perry   Bwoi sweatin now.

Clinton   Must be.

Emile   About wat?

Perry   I know my man Dwayne longer than yu, Emile.

Emile   Yer point is?

Clinton   Leave him, cous, his time comin.

Perry   Yu know.

Emile   Speak English, yu fools.

Perry   Dwayne comin fer yu now, rude bwoi, when yu least expect it. Him comin fer yu. Yu challenged him.

Exit **Perry** *and* **Clinton**.

Ronnie   Oh man, yu fucked up!

Shanice   Shut up, Ronnie.

Ronnie   Tell me now, if dat ain't wat he did.

Emile   I don't business.

Shanice   Emile.

Emile   Let him come, I had him before.

Shanice   Listen to me.

Emile   I'll tek him again, let him come.

Ronnie   Yu sweatin big time, Emile.

Shanice   Clean up.

Ronnie   Yu know he's got a gun now.

Emile   Move.

Ronnie   I've seen it. Watch him put a hole in yer head.

Shanice   Enuff.

Emile   Dis is a test.

Shanice   Emile man.

Emile   I'm ready fer him. I ain't tekin any more of dis, I ain't tekin it from nobody.

Shanice   Yu best listen to me now.

Emile   Yu want me, Dwayne! Well, I'm ready now. Come fer me now!

Shanice   Yu gotta go.

Emile   Don't start.

Shanice   No. Leave.

Emile   Wat do I have to go fer? It's Dwayne dass gotta go. He's goin. And if Perry and Clinton don't like it, they can go too. He's the one who's soff, I tell him who's soff. Me. Emile. Say summin. I defended yu. Tell him yu my woman. No one sexes yu.

Shanice   Did you think he'd listen?

Emile   I did wat you wanted, man.

Shanice   He only backed off cos yu had a knife, wat happens if Ronnie's right, wat if he's got a gun now?

Ronnie   He has!

Emile   It'll be awright.

Shanice   No, it won't.

Emile   Why yu love to piss on everythin I do?

Shanice   Ca yu don't think.

Emile   I dealt wid him. Like I said.

Shanice   I meant talk.

Emile   Deh yu go again, wid dis talk business.

Shanice   Prove yer better dan him.

Emile   Yu mad or wat?

Shanice   Dan all a dem.

Ronnie   He's gonna kill him.

Shanice   Ronnie!

Ronnie   It's true and yu know it, man. Run and hide, Emile, cos Dwayne is gonna fuck yu up.

Shanice   I'll come wid yu.

Ronnie   Shanice man.

Shanice   Quiet! (*To* **Emile**.) We'll go anyware. We'll leave now, yeah. Right now, come. Emile?

Emile   Dis was supposed to be my time. It was me who had Kwame, not dem. Deh jealous.

Ronnie   Fool.

Shanice   Yu don't have time fer dis.

Emile   They love to put me down, love to mek joke. Do they wake up every night, seein his face?

Ronnie   I thought yu said the nightmares were gone. Ain't so big now.

Shanice   Do yu wanna die, Ronnie?

Ronnie   Oh bloody hell, Shanice.

Shanice   Do yu wanna die? Shut yer hole! Emile, ware yu goin?

Emile   It's my time.

Shanice   No.

Emile   I don't business no more!

Exit **Emile**.

Ronnie   Yu were gonna go?

Shanice   Ronnie man!

Ronnie   Without me?

Shanice   We ain't even blood, wass up wid yu?

Ronnie   Yu go, they'll know it was him.

Shanice   And if we stay, he's dead.

Ronnie   Juss don't leave without me, yeah? Shanice?

Shanice   Beg yu, girl, get a life.

Ronnie   I hate it when yu come like dis. Look yer nose down.

Shanice   Calm down.

Ronnie   Plannin on goin without tellin me.

Shanice   I was gonna tell yer.

Ronnie   Yu lie bad. Yu love to lie.

Shanice   Fine, if dass wat yu tink.

Ronnie   And yer still a ho.

Shanice   I dunno wat I am.

Ronnie   Yer a ho, Shanice. Love to have man fuss over yu. Yu get all moist cos of it.

Shanice   Ronnie?

Ronnie   Don't Ronnie me. Go run off wid dat fool, run! I tek care of myself, I don't need yu.

Shanice   Are yu done? Come here.

Ronnie   Fer wat?

Shanice   Come here.

Ronnie   Yu go slap me?

Shanice   I'll slap yu if yu don't come here.

Ronnie *approaches.* **Shanice** *kisses her on the forehead.*

Shanice   Don't ever chat fuck ries in my –

Ronnie   – in my face again, yeah, watever.

Shanice   I'd never set out to hurt yu.

Ronnie   Yu ain't goin.

Shanice   I have to.

Ronnie   Not without me.

Shanice   Deh's gonna come a day, when yu have to look after yerself, Ronnie.

Ronnie   I don't care.

Shanice   I don't have time fer dis.

Ronnie   I'll do it.

Shanice   Wat?

Ronnie   I'll tell dem wat I saw. I'll get the money, den we can both go.

Shanice   Ronnie!

Ronnie   If Emile's in prison, Dwayne can't hurt him. Right? Am I right? Well, deh yu go den, problem solved. I'll tell the police, Dwayne can't hurt Emile, den we can go. Yer up fer it? Shanice? Are yu up fer it?

Shanice   He wanted to be a designer.

Ronnie   Buildings and that. He was a smart-arse.

Shanice   So he had it comin, he deserved to get beat up?

Ronnie   Don't yell at me.

Shanice   It's not right. Wat 'appened to him weren't right, he didn't deserve to have us comin into his life, man, endin it fer him. It's not right, and no one's sayin it.

Ronnie   I'm sayin it.

Shanice   Yu want the money.

Ronnie   Was it yu who saw him gettin kicked in the head? Lyin on the ground bleedin, cryin fer his mum? I don't think so. Let me tell the police. Yu want Emile alive and in prison, or dead? It's a good plan, Shanice, it'll work. Please! Let me. Yeah? Yeah?

Shanice   Awright.

Ronnie   Awright wat?

Shanice   Yes, go on, do it.

Exit **Shanice** *and* **Ronnie**.

Enter **Dwayne**, **Perry** *and* **Clinton**.

Perry   Yu shoulda had his claart deh and den.

Clinton   Juss tell me ware and when yer gonna do it, Dwayne. Please. Ca I wanna see dat fool on his hands and knees, cryin like a gal in front of my laughin face, before yu kill him. Please, Dwayne, tell me, a favour to me, man.

Perry   He heard yu, Clinton.

Clinton   Well, tell him to speak up den, can't hear him.

Perry   Dwayne?

Dwayne   Yeah, man, watever.

Clinton   Thank yu. I dunno why yu let it get dis far.

Dwayne   Yu my mum?

Clinton   He pulled a knife on yu, dread, shoulda taken care of business deh and den.

Dwayne   He proved his worth, I thought he was due.

Clinton   Now he's tekin the piss.

Dwayne   Who yu barkin at?

Clinton   Awright, man, ease up.

Dwayne   Yu wanna come it as well, Clinton?

Clinton   All I said was –

Dwayne   Don't say anytin.

Perry   Clinton, leave us alone fer a minute, yeah.

Clinton   I didn't say nuttin –

Perry   Juss go stand over deh. (*To* **Dwayne**.) So, wat?

Dwayne   Guy gives me a headache wid his voice, man.

Perry   Try livin wid it. Yu go tek care of Emile, everytin sweet, yeah?

Dwayne   Yeah.

Perry   Cool. Crack a smile fer me nuh, man. I tell yu wat though. When dat fool's gone, Shanice.

Dwayne   Shanice?

Perry   It's me and her, man. Trust.

Dwayne   No.

Perry   Wat yu mean, no?

Dwayne   I mean, no. She's off limits, before and after, yu understand?

Perry   Don't tell me yer still sweet fer her? It is, innit?

Dwayne   None of yer business.

Clinton   Oh man.

Perry   Wat yu want?

Clinton   Yer dad, Dwayne.

Dwayne   Oh man.

Enter **Manny**.

Manny   Good evenin, gentlemen. Wat say yu?

Clinton   Bwoi! (*Waves the air.*)

Perry   Bredren!

Manny   Yu don't have a hug fer yer Uncle Manny?

Perry   I'm awright, Manny, juss stand over deh please.

Manny   Who loves yu more than me?

Clinton   Don't touch me, yeah.

Manny   Bwoi, yu can't say hello?

Dwayne   Hello.

Manny   My bwoi, yu nuh, my bwoi.

Dwayne   Yeah, they know.

Manny   Yu have a pound fer me? Juss a pound, bwoi, please.

Dwayne   Wat yu want it fer?

Manny   I have to go see my mudda, yer granmudda, I need bus fare.

Dwayne   Yeah.

Manny   Gimme a pound please.

Perry   Dwayne, we're not here now, catch yu later, yeah. Let's go up west, catch a bus.

Clinton   Yu get it, I'll walk.

Perry   Yu want walk all the way up west?

Clinton   I don't mind, it keep me fit. Seriously.

Manny   Son?

Perry   Why can't yu jus say it?

Clinton   Say wat?

Perry   We have to go through dis every time.

Clinton   Say wat?

Perry   Yer skint.

Clinton   I ain't skint.

Manny   Listen.

Perry   Yu want me to pay fer yer bus fare.

Clinton   If yu want to pay fer me, dass up to yu, innit.

Perry   Clinton! Juss say it.

Clinton   Awright. I'll come wid yu, if yu don't want to come on the bus by yerself.

Perry   Shut up, will yu, please, can yu do dat? Shut up. Hold up. Yu got money, from the purse.

Clinton   Yeah, I got money, but I ain't got change fer the bus.

Perry   Yu woulda walked all the way up west, even though yu have money?

Clinton   I don't have change.

Perry   Yu are gone, Clinton man, yu are so far gone.

Exit **Perry** *and* **Clinton**.

Manny   Hey, yu my bwoi, yu nuh.

Dwayne   Don't touch me.

Manny   Juss gimme two pound.

Dwayne   Yu said one pound.

Manny   Two pound fer me, please.

Dwayne   Do yu even know wat yer sayin, half the time?

Manny   Yu my bwoi.

Dwayne   Go brush yer teet, man.

Manny   Juss gimme sum change. Yes, yes. Hey, let me have sum more of dem silver ones yeah, please.

Dwayne   Take it all. Juss take it.

Manny   My bwoi.

Dwayne   Two words fer yu yeah, please. Soap and water.

Manny   Yu my bwoi.

Dwayne   Yeah, yeah.

Manny   Yu my bwoi. Good bwoi, Junior.

Dwayne   Wat?

Manny   Wat?

Dwayne   Wat did yu juss call me?

Manny   Yu my bwoi.

Dwayne   Yu juss called me Junior.

Manny   Nuh, man.

Dwayne   I ain't deaf, yu called me Junior.

Manny   Junior? Who dat?

Dwayne   Who is Junior? Did I hear yu right? Who is Junior?

Manny   Bwoi?

Dwayne   Junior is yer son, who live up by Shepherd's Bush, my half-brudda, dass who Junior is. Junior live wid his two little sistas, Tasha and Caroline, yer daughters, my half-sistas! Remember dem? Nuh, it muss be Anton yu remember, yer son who live up by Dagenham way. Or is it Stuart, my little brudda, who live two minutes away from my yard, who I never see. Nuh, nuh, it muss be the latest one, Kenisha. Wass my name?

Manny   Bwoi?

Dwayne   Move yer hand away from me. Wass my name? Yer so drunk, yu don't even know which yout of yours yer chattin to. Wass my name? Say my name before I buss yer claart all over dis street. Say it.

Manny Dwayne. It's Dwayne, yer name Dwayne.

Dwayne Yu musta bin beggin to God, to tell yu.

Manny Yu Dwayne.

Dwayne Get off me.

Manny The one in trouble.

Dwayne Who tell yu I was in trouble?

Manny It was yu who beat up dat bwoi, weren't it? Weren't it?

Dwayne It weren't me dat beat him, right.

Manny One a yer friends den.

Dwayne Who tell yu?

Manny Everyone know, 'bout who tell me? See, I do know yu. I know my own children right, I know! Don't tell me I don't know.

Dwayne So, wat yu gonna do?

Manny Why yu do it, son?

Dwayne Answer my question first. I didn't do it, I told yu. So, wat yu gonna do? Wat yu gonna do?

Manny Yu shame me.

Dwayne Yu want chat 'bout shame? Shame is seein yu, in the off-licence tryin to buy a can of beer wid only twenty pence in yer hand. Beggin dat Indian man to let yu have it.

Manny So wat, yu gonna mess up yer life?

Dwayne Wat are yu gonna do?

Manny Yu mad?

Dwayne Wat are yu gonna do?

Manny   Dwayne?

Dwayne   Wat are yu gonna do? Wat are yu gonna do? Wat are yu gonna do?

Exit **Dwayne** *and* **Manny**.

Enter **Joe**, **Matt** *and* **Ronnie**.

Ronnie   Is dat it?

Joe   Not quite.

Ronnie   So, when I get my money?

Joe   Hey.

Ronnie   Wat?

Matt   Why do they call you troll? Can't be nice.

Ronnie   Wat yu think?

Matt   Do they call you it? The boys?

Ronnie   Not just dem.

Matt   Is that why you're here?

Ronnie   Wat?

Matt   To get back at them.

Ronnie   No.

Matt   Get them into trouble.

Ronnie   No.

Matt   You had better tell us the truth now.

Ronnie (*to* **Joe**)   Him deaf?

Joe   Answer his question.

Ronnie   I just did.

Matt   This is a serious allegation you're making.

Ronnie   I know.

Matt   I want you to be sure now.

Ronnie   I am, I saw dem kill him. I thought they were jackin him at first. They were standin around him, in a circle, scarin him. They were shoutin and laughin, darin Emile to beat him, so he did.

Matt   Did what?

Ronnie   Kicked him. He was kickin him in the head.

Matt   Anything else?

Ronnie   One a dem, I think it was Perry, knocked off his glasses.

Matt   What else?

Ronnie   I saw dem run off. I ran too, in the opposite direction.

Matt   What else?

Ronnie   What else wat? I saw him beat him, Emile beat him up, they run off. Wat? Wat!

Joe   Tell me about the trainers.

Ronnie   Whose trainers? My trainers?

Joe   Kwame's trainers.

Ronnie   His?

Joe   Yes!

Ronnie   Oh, right!

Joe   Well?

Matt   Ronnie?

Ronnie   Wat?

Matt   We're waiting.

Ronnie   Cool. (*Nervous laughter.*)

Joe   Listen to me, Ronnie, yeah. You told us all about what you saw, Kwame gettin attacked, that's good, that's all good. But we still need you to help us clear up a few things. Such as the trainers, Kwame's trainers. You saw them take them off him, right, right?

Matt   Joe?

Ronnie   Right, yeah, I saw dat. They took the trainers off him.

Joe   Before or after he was attacked, Ronnie?

Ronnie   Before. It was before.

Joe   Good. That was all I wanted to know. When I turn on the tape, yeah –

Matt   I need to speak with you.

Joe   – that's what yer going to tell me. Right?

Ronnie   Cool.

Matt   Joe!

Exit **Ronnie**.

Matt   Tell me you didn't just do that.

Joe   Believe.

Matt   She had no idea what you were talking about.

Joe   That's not how I read it.

Matt   We held back that info about the trainers, for a reason.

Joe   Yeah yeah yeah.

Matt   She didn't see a thing.

Joe   She must have done.

Matt   Her story was all over the place.

Joe   So she couldn't string two sentences together, so
what? It's the way those kids talk. You're treating them like
they don't belong. That's how they feel, they're not stupid.

Matt   Do you have any idea what will happen if we screw
this? Do you?

Joe   She knew about the BMW.

Matt   That was in the local paper.

Joe   She saw it happen. We got him, what did I say? You
don't like it, you should have spoken up, Sarge!

Matt   You had no right leading a witness like that, without
consulting me.

Joe   I didn't think you'd be comfortable with it.

Matt   Do not patronise me!

Joe   You telling me you haven't bent a few rules in yer
time?

Matt   Of course I have. What kind of a wanker have you
got me down as?

Joe   So you'd fit up some white kid? Oh, but this is
different though, innit?

Matt   You know it is.

Joe   A black kid. You have to watch yourself. Got be Mr
Politically Correct Man of the Year.

Matt   You just won't give that up. You have done nothing
but push me and push me.

Joe   So push me back.

Matt   I have had enough.

Joe   It should only matter if it's true.

Matt   I won't have it.

Joe   You know he did it.

Matt   Course I know.

Joe   So, what?

Matt   So I need to think, is that alright with you?

Joe   There are two kinds of people.

Matt   Are you going to let me think?

Joe   Ones that break the law, ones that don't. I'm just dealing with the ones that do.

Matt   What do you think I'm trying to do?

Joe   Prove it.

Matt   Why do you hate them so much?

Joe   Prove it.

Matt   It's really got to hurt that you're not black enough for them.

Joe   Wass this fool going on with?

Matt   Joe, I'm warning you.

Joe   I'm gone.

Matt   Answer my question.

Joe   You think you can get to me like this?

Matt   I'm not trying to get to you, I want you to answer my question. They're your people, why do you hate them?

Joe   Listen, yeah, those boys are not my people. You think I care what they think?

Matt   Yes, I do think you care. You were Kwame. Weren't you? Look, I'm sorry, Joe.

Joe   Hey, don't you dare apologise to me. Don't turn soff now. Just keep your *Guardian*-reading shit to one side, yeah, or whatever it is you read . . .

Matt   I'm not like that!

Joe   You fucking people!

Matt   That is enough, Constable!

Joe   Wid your wishy-washy liberal crap. Are you so afraid to say what you really feel?

Matt   No.

Joe   Give me back the old school of police. Give them boys something to really cry about.

Matt   Not another word.

Joe   At least they'd know where they stand.

Matt   Don't push me.

Joe   To do what? To say what?

Matt   Leave it.

Joe   Come on, Matt, let them know where they stand. That's all they want.

Matt   Is that what you want, Joe?

Joe   This isn't about me.

Matt   You don't know where you stand?

Joe   All yer doin is cloudin the issue.

Matt   And you're running away. You're hiding. Alright, you want to hear about the time when I was in uniform, when I had to stop my first black person?

Joe   Yes.

Matt   He had a defective headlamp, I waved him down in the middle of the night, he comes out of his car screaming, I'm only picking on him cos he's black. He was doing forty. How the hell did I know what colour he was? All I saw was a defective headlamp.

Joe   Dumb nigger. Worst kind.

Matt   He was a prat. A stupid ignorant prat. That's what I thought, it's what I said. I got a reprimand.

Joe *claps slowly.*

Matt   There's no clouding of the issue for me, Joe. You'll never get me to say it. I don't want to say it. I'm not going to feel bad for what I believe in, and I do believe in it. The job, wishy-washy views, everything.

Joe   He's going to walk then.

Matt   You don't know that, that's not up to you.

Joe   Are you going to man up or what?

Matt   It's not our call. We'll let the DI decide if we have enough to charge him with, alright? And you're lucky, I'm not going to mention what you just did.

Joe   Well, thanks.

Matt   You can fuck off, I'm not doing it for you. Because, you see, Joe, I know where I stand. Now I'm going to tell you where you stand. Right here, beside me with your mouth shut.

Joe *goes to leave.*

Matt   You move one more inch, and you're finished. You speak when I say, you do as I say. Is that clear enough for you, Constable? This is what you wanted, to be like everyone else. Well, come on then, crack a smile, Joe. That's an order.

Exit **Joe** *and* **Matt**.

Shanice   Yu ain't gonna do nuttin.

Dwayne   Is who yu darin me?

Shanice   Yer soff.

Dwayne   Is who are yu?

Shanice   Can't yu see wat he's doin?

Dwayne   Playin big man.

Shanice   Like yu.

Dwayne   I'm better.

Shanice   Let me have him.

Dwayne   Ware yu gonna go?

Shanice   Sumware.

Dwayne   Yu ain't gonna go. Yu ain't.

Shanice   Gonna miss me, Dwayne?

Dwayne   See yu. Love to flirt.

Shanice   Yu can't say it.

Dwayne   I ain't backin down, Shanice, he dissed me.

Shanice   Yes yu can.

Dwayne   Don't chat rubbish to me. Why him? Wat is special 'bout him?

Shanice   He's the first one to ask me out.

Dwayne   I've asked yu out.

Shanice   He didn't juss yank my arm, and say, come!

Dwayne   I bet he can't even kiss.

Shanice   Him kiss better than yu. When we first went out, I knew he wanted to put his arm round me, I look at him, and goes, get on wid it. He was so shy.

Dwayne   Soff.

Shanice   He asked if he could kiss me.

Dwayne   Him a bwoi!

Shanice   He asked me, Dwayne.

Dwayne   Yu don't ask to kiss, yu juss kiss.

Shanice   I couldn't believe it.

Dwayne   Ca yer a slapper.

Shanice   Dass why I went wid yu. Ca I didn't want to believe it. Whenever anyone says I'm good, or nice, I don't wanna believe it.

Dwayne   I wanna kiss yu.

Shanice   Wat?

Dwayne   Is that awright?

Shanice   Yu mad?

Dwayne *kisses her.*

Shanice   Wanna grind me as well now, Dwayne?

Dwayne   No. (*Strokes her face.*)

Enter **Emile**.

Emile   So now wat, yu want me to beat him up now?

Dwayne   Come.

Shanice   Emile, no.

Emile   Why?

Shanice   Cos he'll kill yu.

Dwayne   No, let him come.

Emile   He was sexin yu, like Kwame, I have to.

Dwayne   So, come. (*Pulls out gun.*) My friend here waitin fer yu, come.

Shanice   Dwayne, back off, man, please.

Dwayne   Tell yer bwoi first.

Shanice   Put the gun down, wass wrong wid yu?

Emile   I can get a gun too, Dwayne.

Dwayne   Is it?

Emile   Believe.

Shanice   STOP! Dwayne man?

Dwayne   Yu love to think I won't do it.

Shanice   I know yu can do it, I know yu will do it. But I'm askin yu, I'm beggin yu, yeah, please don't do it. (*Beat.*) Emile, come on, man, yu don't want to do dis.

Emile   Well, stop makin me. It's yu dass makin me, it's yu dass makin me do dis.

Dwayne   Yer soff.

Emile   I might as well fling yu at him.

Dwayne   Yer givin me yer gal, Emile, cheers.

Emile   Yu love to have man chase yu.

Shanice   Awright, do it, fight him, go fight him, kill each oder ca I don't business no more, bloody fight him.

Dwayne   Come.

Shanice   He's waitin.

Dwayne   Yu comin or wat, Emile? I tell yu wat, I let yu mek a move first, yeah?

Shanice   Emile?

Dwayne   Come!

Shanice   He ain't.

Dwayne   Ca him soff.

Shanice   Dwayne, juss leave us, yeah.

Dwayne   Yu best start runnin.

Exit **Dwayne**.

Emile   Well, go on den.

Shanice   Wat?

Emile   Go follow him.

Shanice   Go follow him ware, Emile? I told yu not to hang round wid him. I told yu wat he was like.

Emile   First Kwame, now him.

Shanice   No. Kwame weren't tryin to sex me.

Emile   Shut up.

Shanice   He was juss bin nice. He didn't do anythin, he weren't after anythin.

Emile   Yu told me.

Shanice   I know wat I told yu.

Emile   So, why?

Shanice   Yu made me feel special, I weren't juss sum yattie to yu. Dwayne comes along, and yu stop noticin me. Yu were too busy impressin him. Yu made me lose faith, not juss in yu, but in me, man. So I goes, fuck yu, Emile, fuck yu. I thought Kwame fancied me, so I thought yes! I'll rush dat.

Emile   He did try and sex yu.

Shanice   Hello! I tried to sex him, he blew me off, Emile. Ca he was nice! Juss nice.

Emile   Yu?

Shanice   Ronnie's gone to the police. I told her to. Don't look at me like dat. Yu were supposed to juss give him a slap or summin. Why yu have to kill him?

Emile *grabs her.*

Shanice   It's dis place! Let's go, right now, come. I'll look after yu. Ronnie, she's so stupid, man, she thinks we're gonna run off togeder wid the reward money. Yer the one I want to run off wid. Yu were right all the time. I can't keep lookin after her, I don't want to. Yu ain't got a choice no more. Emile!

Exit **Shanice** *and* **Emile***.*

Enter **Ronnie**, **Matt** *and* **Joe**.

Ronnie   And I want a room wid cable.

Matt   Don't start.

Ronnie   It best have a telly wid cable.

Matt   You might have a video.

Ronnie   I want DVD.

Matt   What's the difference?

Ronnie   Obvious yu don't have one.

Matt   You will go where we put you.

Ronnie   Yu joke.

Matt   So be quiet.

Ronnie (*to* **Joe**)   Yu gonna let dis geezer chat to me like dat?

Matt   Take it or leave it.

Ronnie   I'll leave it den.

Matt   Where do you think you're going?

Ronnie   Home.

Matt   That is the last place you want to be, Veronica.

Ronnie   It's Ronnie, how hard is it to say dat, Ronnie!

Matt   Alright, Ronnie. I don't think you realise how serious this is.

Ronnie   I do.

Matt   You are, potentially, an important witness in a murder investigation.

Ronnie   Yeah, yeah. Love to go on.

Matt   What do you think your friends would do if you went home?

Ronnie   I don't know, go mad fer me, innit? (*Laughs.*) Call me troll, I don't care. Used to it. Don't care wat they think. Except Shanice, but she knows why I'm doing it, she knows.

Matt   This is as serious as it gets. Right, Constable?

Joe *nods his head.*

Matt   Right, Ronnie?

Ronnie   Yes! Awright. Bloody hell.

Matt   So we'll have no more talk about cable TV, MTV base, DV bloody Ds, PlayStation.

Ronnie   PlayStation 2, actually. Get it right. Joke!

Matt   Constable?

Joe   Hold it down, yeah.

Ronnie   Why don't yu kiss his arse while yer at it.

Joe   Just ease up, OK.

Ronnie   Yu white man's bitch.

Joe   This is it for you. Focus. Behave.

Ronnie   So I'm supposed to stay in sum room and do nish?

Matt   We can take you out.

Ronnie   When do I get my money?

Matt   You know when.

Ronnie   You can't even dash me a few dollars till den?

Matt   That is not up to me.

Ronnie   Can I use a phone?

Matt   Who do you want to call?

Ronnie   Shanice.

Joe   Why Shanice?

Ronnie   Tell her I'm awright.

Matt   I think your mind should be on other things.

Ronnie   I want call Shanice. I want a McDonald's Happy Meal.

Matt   Later.

Ronnie   I'm hungry, dread.

Matt   I said later. We're expecting company. Our inspector would like to speak with you.

Ronnie   Why yu lot love to ask borin questions?

Matt   Hey!

Ronnie   Awright.

Joe   Ronnie?

Ronnie   Wat?

Joe   Come on, just behave yourself, please.

Ronnie   I said awright.

Joe   This is important.

Ronnie   I know.

Joe   Right!

Ronnie   Yes, man!

Matt   This is hopeless.

Ronnie   Yu want calm down, dread. Can I have my McDonald's now?

Enter the **Inspector**.

Inspector   How far away were you?

Ronnie   A bit.

Inspector   A bit what? Give it to me in yards.

Ronnie   I dunno, juss a bit. I can't remember exactly.

Inspector   Well, you will have to remember.

Ronnie   Wat fer? I don't know.

Inspector   How could you forget that?

Ronnie   I didn't forget, I said I don't know.

Inspector   The point I am trying to make, Veronica –

Ronnie   Ronnie.

Inspector   – if you were there –

Ronnie   I was.

Inspector   – I do not think it is something you could forget.

Ronnie   Love to chat.

Inspector   Listen to me, you may find this amusing, Veronica –

Ronnie   Ronnie! Yu deaf?

Inspector   – I can assure you, those people in the courtroom will not.

Ronnie   Watever.

Inspector   You thought there was a robbery going on over the street, that they were 'jackin' somebody?

Ronnie   Yeah.

Inspector   You were standing behind the bus-stop shelter, across the road?

Ronnie   Yeah. Bloody hell.

Inspector   And you were hiding behind the bus-stop shelter because you did not want the boys to see you.

Ronnie   Dwayne don't like it when I'm followin him.

Inspector   Yes or no?

Ronnie   Yeah.

Inspector   Now, at that point in the evening –

Ronnie   Yer talkin too fast again.

Inspector   – At, that, point, in the evening, a silver BMW pulls up, by the bus stop, the window of the front-passenger side rolls down, a young white woman leans out, and you have a conversation with this woman.

Ronnie   Yeah.

Inspector   She asked if you lived in the area.

Ronnie   Yeah.

Inspector   She asked you for directions.

Ronnie   Yeah, yeah, yeah!

Inspector   Whilst Emile and his friends were attacking Kwame?

Ronnie   Yes. (*Aside.*) Slag.

Inspector   I beg your pardon?

Joe   Ronnie!

Ronnie   Nuttin.

Inspector   Furthermore, the music playing from the car radio is rather loud.

Ronnie   At first, but her man turned it down.

Inspector   But you could still hear the music?

Ronnie   Yeah, it was Jay Z.

Inspector   I'm sorry?

Ronnie   Jay Z the rapper. Dass who was playin on the radio. Are we done now?

Inspector   Not yet. Now help me out here. Despite the conversation, despite the 'Jay Z' music playing from the car radio, you were not distracted at all, from witnessing the attack?

Ronnie   No.

Inspector   And the boys do not notice that you are watching them?

Ronnie   No.

Inspector   You didn't hear about the BMW from the newspaper, did you?

Ronnie   No.

Inspector   But you knew we were looking for it, so did you decide to use it, to make your story more credible?

Ronnie   No.

Inspector   Did you really speak to that woman?

Ronnie   Why she carryin on?

Inspector   Did you see those boys?

Ronnie   Callin me a liar?

Inspector   I need you to be absolutely sure about this.

Ronnie   I thought yu wanted me to help?

Inspector   So you weren't following the events in the newspaper quite closely then?

Ronnie   No.

Inspector   You weren't desperate to grab the opportunity, to be the centre of attention?

Ronnie   Look, I might have glanced at summin in the paper, yeah.

Inspector   So, you do admit to lying?

Ronnie   Everyone was readin it. It had a picture of our estate and dat, it was cool.

Inspector   You didn't do more than read?

Ronnie   Why, why would I, wass so special about him?

Inspector   Twenty thousand pounds?

Ronnie   Oh man, I've had enough of dis. I'm done.

Joe   Come on, Ronnie!

Inspector (*to* **Joe**)   Yes, thank you, Constable. Sit down, Veronica.

Ronnie   Call me dat one more time.

Inspector   Sit down please. Just tell us the truth.

Ronnie   I am tellin yu the truth.

Inspector   I don't think you are.

Ronnie   I don't care.

Inspector   You were lying when you said you were on the street.

Ronnie   No.

Inspector   You were lying about seeing what happened, you know everyone is going to be watching you.

Ronnie   Yer point?

Inspector   You love it.

Ronnie   No I don't.

Inspector   You will love anything that will stop you from being reminded of what you really are, a sad, lonely little girl, with no friends.

Ronnie   I've got loads of friends. Shanice is my friend.

Inspector   What is your nickname? What do your friends call you?

Ronnie   I'm tellin the bloody truth, is dis wat happens when yu tell the truth? Well, fuck dat!

Inspector   Calm down please.

Ronnie   Try and help the police, say wat they want me to say, dis is the thanks I get.

Inspector   What was that? What was it that we told you to say? Ronnie?

Joe   Alright, look, I made a mistake, yeah.

Inspector   Quiet.

Joe   It's my fault.

Inspector   Sergeant?

Joe   But she saw him kill him.

Matt   Joe?

Joe   She saw the boy do it.

Matt   Don't.

Ronnie   Him goin mad or wat?

Joe   Tell her, Ronnie, tell her what it felt like seeing Kwame lying there on the ground, how it made you feel. That it made you care. Tell her.

Ronnie   Is who yu screamin at?

Inspector   Look at me, Ronnie. I said look at me.

Ronnie   This is fuck ries.

Inspector   What did they tell you to say?

Ronnie   Dat I saw dem tek the trainers.

Inspector   You said before you saw them do that.

Ronnie   I know. Musta happened when I was talkin to dat woman, innit?

Inspector   So, you were distracted.

Ronnie   No. Fer a second, yeah.

Joe   Shit.

Inspector   You have just lied to me. If we had put you in a courtroom, you would have committed perjury.

Ronnie   I'm not lyin. I saw dem do it, man. I saw dem kill him. Yu know wat they'll do to me if I go back home? How can I be lyin?

Inspector   I see.

Ronnie   Yu don't bloody see. Yu don't see us. None of yer. 'Bout yu see! I ain't lyin.

Inspector (*to* **Joe** *and* **Matt**)   What the hell are you two playing at?

Joe   Ma'am?

Inspector   Not another word. You've got nothing.

Ronnie   So we done now? Are we done?

Inspector   Get her out of here.

Ronnie (*pleads*)   Shanice!

Exit **Inspector**, **Ronnie** *and* **Matt**.

Enter **Emile**.

Joe   See, Emile, dis is gettin vex! I wanna tell you something, yeah? Cos, that's all I got time for now, thanks to that little friend of yours, that troll. One time, when I was in uniform, yeah, early in the afternoon, it was 'bout four or summin, got a call, two pissheads fighting outside a pub, one black, one white. One a dem spilled the other one's drink, I can't remember who, whatever. Anyhow, they were having a right go at each other. Pushing, and sum shoving. Both a them are as bad as each other, effing and blinding, tellin you! I didn't want to get involved. Shitting myself, if truth be told. But I stepped in, arrested them both, boom boom! (*Slaps* **Emile**.) The white guy, calmed himself down, straight off, he stood there, knew he was in the wrong, didn't even try to run off. Black guy, different story. He couldn't stop mouthing off to me. What do you think he said? Guess.

Emile   Dunno.

Joe   Cocksucker. Pig. Bastard. Traitor to my own, white man's bitch. The lot. Goin on about, how I was only nickin him cos he was black and I want to be white. By the time we got him back to the station, he was still carrying on. Still shoutin, mekin up all kinds of noise. It took five of us to throw him in a cell. (*Slaps* **Emile**.) You know what the white guy was doing during all this? Nothing, nish. From the time I showed up on the street, to when we got back to the station, he didn't say a word. And he was the one throwing out the most licks, when they were havin the fight. You see wat I mean, Emile? (*Slaps him.*) You see where I'm goin wid this? White man get caution, get sent home the very same day, black man spend the rest of the day and night in the cell, cos he couldn't keep his stupid wurtless mout shut, couldn't play the game! White man played the game, played it beautifully, I wanted to shake his hand and go, 'Yeah, nuff respect.' I tell you, Emile, when it comes to that, them white bwois are poles apart. Niggers, Emile, can't play the game. You can't play the game, Kwame played the game, Kwame had a life. He was a decent kid. But you, you! (*Slaps him repeatedly.*) You want a life, bwoi, get yer own. Why you have to tek his? You know what, it's fuckers like you, like that pisshead, is why I had to leave. Now it's fuckers like you that bring me back to where I started. You had to drag me down, innit? You had to drag Kwame down. You feel good about that? You love that? Is it? Do you? Do you? (*Slaps him.*) Do you?

Enter **Shanice**.

Joe   Yer wurtless!!

Shanice   (*stands between* **Joe** *and* **Emile**)   Leave him.

Joe   Shanice, move.

Shanice   Are yu mad?

Joe   Move.

Shanice   Leave him.

Joe   I'm letting him know where he stands.

Shanice   Yu think dis is gonna change him?

Joe   Bwoi drowning, girl.

Shanice   Wat else yu expect him to be?

Joe   You want drown too?

Shanice   Wat yu know about him? Wat yu know about me?

Emile   Get off.

Shanice   Emile?

Emile   Leave me!

Exit **Emile**.

Joe   Where you goin?

Shanice   Yu best step back.

Joe   Don't go after him, Shanice, remember your gran. He ain't even sorry for wat he did.

Shanice   Yu don't know him.

Joe   I know him.

Shanice   Yu don't know him.

Joe   Fine, go drown with the idiot.

Shanice   Wat about yu? Yu sorry? Yu sorry fer wat yu did, Joe? Say yer sorry, say it.

Joe   Sorry for what? You know what him and that friend of yours have done to me? You want drown yerself, go.

Shanice   Yu go. Carryin on like we should tek after yu, why should we be like yu?

Exit **Joe**.

Shanice (*aside*)   Yer fool.

Enter **Manny**.

Manny   Hey, pretty gal.

Shanice   Oh please.

Manny   Yu know yu love me.

Shanice   Is it?

Manny   Yu have a pound fer me? Beg yu fer a pound, please.

Shanice   Do yu even know how to wash yerself?

Manny   Beg yu.

Shanice   Yu stink.

Manny   Juss a pound.

Shanice   Step.

Enter **Dwayne**, *carrying a football*.

Manny   My bwoi, yu awright? Yu have a pound fer me? Beg yu fer a pound. Son? Bwoi?

Exit **Manny**.

Shanice   Yu see how black his teet is?

Dwayne   Yu hear from Emile?

Shanice   No.

Dwayne   Yu don't know ware he's gone?

Shanice   Stay wid his sista.

Dwayne   Wat about troll?

Shanice   Gone sumware wid her mum.

Dwayne   I dunno wat she's gonna do without yu.

Shanice   She's gonna have to learn, innit? They both are. I told her to do it.

Dwayne   I ain't here fer dat. Yu don't have to be scared, yeah.

Shanice   I ain't.

Dwayne   Yu are. Don't.

Shanice   Fine, I won't.

Dwayne   Did I tell ya? Clinton pass his BTEC.

Shanice *laughs.*

Dwayne (*feeling self-conscious*)   Wat?

Shanice   Nuttin. Dass good. Wat yu doin wid dat?

Dwayne   Wanna show yu summin.

Shanice   Wat?

Dwayne (*places football on ground*)   Gonna prove to yu dat third one was no a goal.

Shanice   Oh man, yu are sad.

Dwayne   Scared I'm right, Shanice?

Shanice   No.

Dwayne   So come.

Shanice   It was seven years ago, how am I supposed to remember ware I was, please?

Dwayne   I'm Neil, remember him?

Shanice   Yes.

Dwayne   I'm here.

Shanice   Yeah, and?

Dwayne   Yer outside the box, Perry's in goal, he's clocked yu makin yer move.

Shanice   I knew exactly ware I was gonna shoot.

Dwayne   Bottom right-hand corner.

Shanice   Right.

Dwayne   I'm givin yu chase, tryin to stop yer.

Shanice   But yu can't.

Dwayne   I nearly had yu.

Shanice   Right, den I scored.

Dwayne   No.

Shanice   Rest yer lip 'bout no.

Dwayne   Yu did strike, I'd give yu dat, but it bounced right off Clinton's knee.

Shanice   Deflection. Case rested.

Dwayne   If it hadn't, it woulda gone wide.

Shanice   No.

Dwayne   Tellin yu.

Shanice   Shut up.

Dwayne   Ask Clinton.

Shanice   Dwayne, put the ball down. Put the ball down. Wat are we doin?

Dwayne   Yu really think I woulda shot Emile?

Shanice   Yeah.

Dwayne   Believe. Yu know wat stopped me?

Shanice   Wat?

Dwayne   Yu, Shanice.

Shanice   So, wat now?

Dwayne   Go out and dat.

Shanice (*laughs*)   Go out and dat.

Dwayne   Yeah.

Shanice   Awright.

Dwayne   Wat?

Shanice   Yu deaf? I said awright.

Dwayne   Cool.

Shanice   But Dwayne?

Dwayne   Wat?

Shanice   Yu ain't grindin me.

Exit.

Slow Time

Slow Time was produced by the National Theatre's Education Department and toured to schools from January to April 2005. The cast was as follows:

Nabs	Dharmesh Patel
Delroy	Ashley Rolfe
Ashley	Aml Ameen

Director Matt Wilde
Designer Lisa Lillywhite
Sound Designer Mathew Smethurst-Evans

An education workpack on the play devised by the National Theatre can be downloaded from the National's website: http://www.nationaltheatre.org.uk/Past%20Workpacks%20+24838.twl

Characters
Nabs, *Asian, late teens*
Delroy, *white, late teens*
Ashley, *black, late teens*

Setting

A Young offenders institution. Three single-roomed prison cells.

Enter **Ashley**, **Delroy** *and* **Nabs.**

It is morning. Sound of boys shouting from other cells can be heard from the windows. The boys seen here have barely slept all night. **Ashley** *is first to be out of bed. He is sitting on the edge of the bed, staring out at his poster-covered wall. He looks pensive, almost agitated. He is building up the courage to do what he got up for. He stands up, walks towards the wall and slowly starts removing all of the posters he has pinned up. He folds each one and places them on his bedside table.* **Nabs** *is next to get up. He removes a folded photograph from his pocket. He sits up on his bed and stares at the photo lovingly. He gives it a kiss.*

Nabs   Morning, babes.

He puts the photo away.

Delroy *is walking around his cell like a little boy lost. He does not have a clue where to put himself. He is terrified. He looks out of his window, but sighs when there is little to see, apart from walls.*

Ashley *finishes putting away the posters. He sits on the edge of the bed again, staring.* **Ashley** *believes he is capable of doing this, but can't quite find the strength yet.*

Nabs   Hey! Hey! New boy. New boy! I know you can hear me, new boy. Walls are thin, dread. New boy? Are you going to talk to me or what?

Delroy   Yeah.

Nabs (*laughs*)   He speaks.

Delroy   What you want?

Nabs   It's me asking the questions, you understand?

Delroy   Yeah.

Nabs   Good. Enjoy your first night in, new boy?

Delroy   How you know?

Nabs   Boy, you deaf?

Delroy   No.

Nabs   So, you musta heard me say I ask the questions!

Delroy   Yeah.

Nabs   Just for that, I go ask you again. Did you enjoy your first night in? New boy?

Delroy   It was alright.

Nabs   Alright? You were crying like a baby, man, wid yer head down.

Delroy   I wasn't crying.

Nabs   Are you calling me a liar, new boy?

Delroy   No.

Nabs   That's what it sounds like.

Delroy   I wasn't crying.

Nabs   Wait until I catch you outside. One hour from now. Canteen, hallway, don't matter, gonna have words, you and I, new boy. 'Bout you chatting back to me.

Delroy   Alright then, I was crying.

Nabs   Nuh, nuh, too late now, new boy! Trying to be nice and everything, welcoming you to your new home and that, and do I get? Thank you? No, all I get for being nice is a mouthy little white boy trying to have beef with me, you think you're bad, new boy?

Delroy   No.

Nabs   Wanna be top boy?

Delroy   What?

Nabs   Top boy?

Delroy   What's that mean?

Nabs   What you think it means?

Delroy   Best boy at . . .

Nabs   Go on . . .

Delroy   Fighting?

Nabs   So now you know?

Delroy   That's not what I want.

Nabs   Suck yer mum!

Delroy   What?

Nabs   Suck yer mum.

Delroy   No. Don't say that.

Nabs   Or what? What can you do?

Delroy   I don't want no trouble.

Nabs   You got trouble.

Delroy   I just want to keep me head down.

Nabs   Who you bin talking to, new boy?

Delroy (*reciting*)   Just keep your head down, son. Keep your head down.

Nabs   One of them guards tell you that last night? On your way in here? Keep yer head down you'll be alright? Just do your time. First lesson, new boy, them guards, they don't know jack! You in hell now, rude boy, you best just learn to deal with it. You ain't nothing, you ain't even a name now. They give you a number when you come in?

Delroy   Yes.

Nabs   Let me hear it.

Delroy   FB963.

Nabs   That's your name now, new boy, best not forget it. Innit, Ash?

Ashley *cannot take any more of this noise. He begins ripping up his bed sheets.*

Nabs   Ash? What you doing in there, man?

Delroy   Are you gonna leave me now?

Nabs   This boy, man! One night in and he's barking orders at me.

Delroy   I weren't!

Nabs   Suck yer mum!

Delroy   Stop saying that.

Nabs   Sing me a nursery rhyme.

Delroy   Why?

Nabs   'Humpty-Dumpty'.

Delroy   I don't know it.

Nabs   You know you're lying. 'Humpty-Dumpty', sing it.

Delroy   Why you picking on me? Leave me alone.

Nabs   Telling me what to do again, you're asking for a beating! Ash? Ash! You still asleep?

Ashley   Well, I ain't now, am I?

Nabs   Tell this fool who the top boy is. New boy thinks he's bad.

Delroy   I don't think I'm bad.

Nabs   Won't sing me 'Humpty-Dumpty'. You know what that means, don't yer, Ash? Remember? Ashley? You left your tongue outside or what, Ash? Tell him, tell who's top boy?

Ashley   You!

Nabs   Believe.

Ashley   Alright, Nabs!

Nabs   Alright, Nabs, what?

Ashley   You made your point, leave the brother alone.

Nabs   You heard him, Ash, he said no. So you know what means, yeah?

Ashley   Sing 'Humpty-Dumpty' for him.

Delroy   Leave me alone.

Ashley   I'm trying to help you, yer fool.

Delroy   Why can't you leave me alone?

Ashley   Don't you get it? If you don't sing 'Humpty-Dumpty' for him, it means you're challenging him to a fight. You want to be top boy.

Delroy   But I don't want that.

Ashley   Come to your window and sing it for him. Sing it and he'll leave you alone, I promise.

Delroy (*mumbles*)
'Humpty-Dumpty, sat on a wall –'

Nabs   Nuh, nuh, nuh, louder.

Delroy
'Humpty dumpty, sat on a wall –'

Nabs   Louder.

Delroy
' – Humpty-Dumpty had a great fall –'

Nabs   What you doing? Go back to the beginning, and louder!

Ashley   Come on Nabs.

Nabs   You hear me talking to you, Ash? Louder, new boy, and I want it in rap.

Ashley   Come on, bro, just sing it. Sing it!

Delroy (*in rap*)
'. . . Humpty-Dumpty sat on wall,
Humpty-Dumpty had a great fall;

All the king's horses and all the king's men,
Couldn't put Humpty together again.'

Nabs *claps and cheers.*

Nabs   Gwan, new boy! Yes! It weren't so bad, now, was it? I knew you could do it. You're good new boy, you really are. Should be on *Pop Idol* or summin, what you think?

Delroy   I dunno.

Nabs   Well, I do. Trust.

Delroy   I'm not bad. I don't want to be top boy.

Nabs   Well, guess what? I believe you. So relax. What's your name, new boy?

Delroy   Delroy.

Nabs   You taking the piss, new boy?

Delroy   No.

Nabs   Just wait till I catch you in the hallway.

Delroy   What have I done now?

Nabs   As soon as they open our doors. You've got some proper beatings coming your way.

Delroy   You wanted to know my name. I told you my name.

Nabs   Your name is Delroy?

Ashley   It's what he said!

Nabs   But you're white.

Delroy   Yeah.

Nabs   You are white, innit?

Delroy   Yes.

Nabs   Proper white, not Ryan Giggs white?

Delroy   I don't get yer.

Nabs   Is your mum or dad black?

Delroy   No.

Nabs   So tell me something, how did a little white boy like you, wind up with a brother's name like that? Please, pray tell, I have to know.

Delroy   My mum used to live next door to this black family, the dad's name was Delroy, Mum liked the name, so thass what she named me.

Nabs   Oh, I see.

Ashley   Allow it, Nabs.

Nabs   This black guy, was he . . . you know . . . ?

Delroy   What?

Nabs   Giving your mum a service? (*Laughs.*)

Delroy   What?

Ashley   Was he sexing her?

Delroy   I know what he meant.

Ashley   Well, stop saying what then.

Delroy   I ain't said it much.

Ashley (*sighs*)   Ejut!

Nabs   Ah, excuse me, I'm talking to our friend here first.

Ashley   He ain't my friend.

Delroy   Good, cos you ain't mine!

Ashley   Good!

Delroy   I know it's good.

Ashley   Well, I know it's good as well.

Nabs   Excuse me! You both mind? Delroy! What kind of a name is that to give you? Your mum must hate you. How ugly were you when you were born? Stupid name.

Delroy (*snaps*)   No more stupid than Nabil.

Ashley *holds his head. He cannot believe* **Delroy** *could be that stupid.*

Nabs   First off, how did you know my name?

Delroy (*panicking*)   You said it.

Nabs   No I didn't.

Delroy   Then he did.

Nabs   No he didn't. Stop lying.

Delroy   I ain't lying.

Nabs   He's been calling me Nabs. He always calls me Nabs. You don't know who I am, you ain't got a clue. How did you know my name? You best tell me how you know, new boy, or in exactly fifty minutes, you're gonna get beat like you've never been beat before.

Delroy   One of the boys last night pointed you out.

Nabs   Which boy?

Delroy   A black boy. I don't know his name.

Nabs   Well, when you see him today, you point him out to me.

Delroy   I will.

Nabs   I know you will. Second, who are you to tell me my name is stupid?

Ashley (*whispers*)   Nobody.

Delroy (*repeats*)   Nobody.

Nabs   You're learning. You got your little bag there?

Delroy   Yes.

Delroy   Ain't opened it.

Nabs   So open it.

Delroy *opens the pack, empties the contents on his bag.*

Nabs   Come on, what you have?

Delroy   Bottle of squash.

Nabs   What flavour?

Delroy   Blackcurrant. Custard creams.

Nabs   No, you can have that.

Delroy   Sweets.

Nabs   Sweets? You have Liquorice Allsorts?

Delroy   No, Starbursts, Fruit Pastilles.

Nabs   Yeah, I'll take them off yer hands. Cheers, bro. Just bring them by me later. Yer supposed to say you're welcome, when someone says thank you. Didn't yer slut of a mum teach you manners? Or was she too busy getting serviced by man?! Is it?

Delroy *throws the bag against the wall and screams.*

Nabs   Delroy? Is that you getting vex now?

Delroy   I don't wanna be here.

Nabs   Yeah, I know. Yer so scared, you want to cry, yeah, I know. Ash knows it as well, innit, Ash? Come on, new boy, let it out, cry for me!

Delroy *begins to cry.*

Nabs   Yes, and the winner is – Nabs! I told you I'd make him cry, Ash, you backed the wrong horse, yer soff! How much is it you owe me? Tell me, please. (*Runs to door.*) Yo, bredrens, my horse came first, you all owe me, and you better believe, Nabs is coming to collect.

Delroy (*breaks down*)   Ashley!

Ashley   Oh man.

Nabs   What you calling him for?

Delroy   Ca I know him.

Nabs   You know this fool then, Ash? Ash?

Ashley   What?

Nabs   You know him?

Ashley   He lives on my estate.

Delroy   I knew you saw me last night. I knew it –

Ashley   Shut up, Delroy.

Delroy   Ash?

Ashley   Just shut yer mouth.

Nabs   Well, ain't this nice, couple of homies back together again. How you know each other? Where you find him, Ash?

Ashley *steps out of his cell.*

Ashley (*to audience*)   When I got sentenced here for two years, my dad was hollering and screaming at the judge. I've never seen my dad go on like that, not even at Mum's funeral. He was saying, 'He ain't no hardened criminal, he's like any other boy. Please, Your Honour, give him a chance.' My family all grew up on an estate in Acton, far from here, you get me? I used to be so naughty when I was little, putting salt in Dad's tea, knocking on people's doors and running off. Everyone said I was naughty. But not my mum, she really loved me, yeah, I really loved her. I reckon I was her favourite, I knew I was. When Mum was diagnosed with cancer, we all took a big family holiday to Barbados where she was born, we knew it was close to the end for her. She died three months later. I was fifteen. After that, that was it, started drinking, smoking, hanging wid dem bigger boys from the estate. I did anything I could not to remember her, to keep seeing my mum's face. I'd wake up in the morning, and have a can of lager. I started shoplifting. One night I was in this shop, and I get in a ruck with the shopkeeper, over a packet of Pringles, that was it, that's all it was, a packet of Pringles. Barbecue flavour. The guy try and have a beef with me. I tell him to move, but he wouldn't back off. What was I supposed to do? I slashed his face with my knife.

Delroy *steps out of his cell.*

Delroy (*to audience*)   As far back as I can remember, I always wanted to hang round with Ashley and his mates. To have them call me bredren. I knew I belonged with them, to be somebody, not a nobody like my mum and dad. Why should I be like them, work in a crappy factory like him, clean people's houses like her, watch some dry programme on TV like one of the soaps, or *Who Wants to Be a Millionaire?* – it's Alexander the Great, phone a friend, you watching tele with us, Delroy? No! We don't even have Sky Digital. Everyone I know has Sky Digital. And a plasma widescreen TV to go with it. Honestly, would you do what your mum and dad do? When you know you could earn twice as much on the street? Be honest. When Ashley asked me to go shop wid him, I was so proud, I felt like one of his brers. Any minute now, he's gonna call me bredren.

Ashley   Stuff these in your pockets.

Delroy   What, Pringles?

Ashley   You have to shout?

Delroy   Sorry.

Ashley   Stay behind me, we go walk out quietly, yeah?

Delroy   Don't you have money?

Ashley   Course I have money.

Delroy   So why we tiefing it?

Ashley   Why pay when can get it for free? Besides, all I got is a twenty, I don't want to break into that yet.

Delroy   I got change.

Ashley   Don't chat rubbish, Delroy.

Delroy   I ain't.

Ashley   If yer scared, say so.

Delroy   I'm not.

Ashley   So come.

Delroy   Oh no.

Ashley   What?

Delroy   Shopkeeper's seen us.

Ashley   Shit.

Delroy   He's coming.

Ashley   Chill. (*To shopkeeper.*) Yeah, what you want? Put what back?

Delroy   Ash, don't.

Ashley   Eh, mind who you're pushing Mr Shopkeeper, yeah. This jacket cost more than what you got on.

Delroy   Come on.

Ashley   I ain't going nowhere, this fool wants to have a beef with me.

Delroy   It ain't worth it.

Ashley   You love to act soff, Delroy.

Delroy   Ash man.

Ashley   You always did. Wait till I tell everybody how soft you are.

Delroy   He's gonna call the police.

Ashley   So what? (*To shopkeeper.*) So bring dem, bring dem come.

Delroy   I'm scared!

Ashley   I told the shopkeeper nuff times not to touch me. So what's he go and do? That was it. That was it for me.

(*Mimes slashing the shopkeeper's face.*) Two years for malicious wounding.

Delroy   Ashley was true to his word, telling everyone how soft I was, getting accused by everyone that I got scared, left him there in the shop. I had to do something, prove myself, that's why I took that woman's phone. It's how I get catch. I didn't mean to hurt her, but she shoulda given it up. What she fight me for?

Ashley *and* **Delroy** *step back into their cells.*

Nabs   Where you find him, Ash?

Ashley   He always used to follow me around the estate, even when we were little.

Nabs   You love him, new boy?

Delroy   Not like that.

Nabs   So you do love him, yes or no? Yes or no?

Delroy   Well . . . yeah.

Ashley (*embarrassed*)   Delroy, will you shut up?

Delroy   Sorry.

Ashley   You love that word or summin? Shut up, man.

Nabs   No, don't shut up, Delroy. Chat to me, if yer best mate can't be bothered.

Ashley   Delroy, you gotta ignore every word he says, yeah?

Nabs   Now yer hurting my feelings, Ashley.

Ashley   Find Andy, he's a guard here, he's alright.

Nabs   He's an ejut.

Ashley   Listen to Andy, he's alright, he is.

Nabs   He's a fool. And he's Irish.

Delroy   So?

Ashley   Exactly, so? So what? So what if he's Irish? It doesn't mean a thing. Keep thinking like that, Delroy, you'll be alright.

Nabs   Keep thinking like that, new boy, yer gonna get beat up, every day. By me!

Ashley   There's nothing stopping you from going to Andy, tell him Nabs is bullying you.

Nabs   He won't grass, he's too scared to. I can tell. Besides, you didn't.

Ashley   Didn't have to, not after I shoved that knife in yer face.

Nabs   Any time you want to try again boy, any time.

Ashley   Leave him alone, Nabs, you got me, he ain't nothing, you know he ain't.

Nabs   No.

Ashley   Why?

Nabs   Cos you asked. I'll have you both, don't bother me.

Delroy   I'm scared, Ashley.

Ashley   It's alright, man. He won't touch you.

Nabs   You think so? Forty minutes left, new boy.

Ashley   Go to Andy. He'll help you.

Nabs   He ain't going anywhere.

Ashley   He'll keep you away from Nabs.

Nabs   Yes, new boy, listen to every word he says, like some fool.

Ashley   He's gonna look after himself.

Nabs   He won't last a week.

Ashley   He will, I'll make sure of it.

Nabs   You'll fail. I still remember what you were like. Crying like a bitch. How long did it take for you to sing a nursery rhyme? 'Bout two seconds.

Ashley   Well, how long did it take you, motormouth?

Nabs   I never did.

Ashley   Lie!

Nabs   Ask Jermaine. He's been here longer than any of us. I ain't afraid of nuttin.

Ashley   Everyone is afraid of summin.

Nabs   Not me.

Ashley   Yes you are.

Nabs   You deaf?

Ashley   You're afraid of being afraid.

Nabs   What kind of dry chat is that?

Delroy   I'm afraid I'll never go home.

Ashley   Delroy, just remember what the guard said. Keep yer head down. Don't get involved.

Nabs   That's the first thing you do if you want to get noticed.

Ashley   He's my friend.

Nabs   Some friend!

Ashley   Just let me do this.

Nabs   There are only two kinds of people in this place, new boy, those who do it, those who take it. Yer the latter, I'm the former. You don't want to take it, you best learn to man up. Tell me right now, what I'm saying ain't true.

Delroy   Is it true, Ash? Ash?

Ashley   Yes, it is.

Delroy *sighs*.

Ashley   But don't keep it to yourself, talk to Andy, or Jenny.

Nabs   Oh yeah, Jenny, that girl is fine.

Delroy   Who's Jenny?

Nabs   English teacher – sweet! She comes round once a week. Looks like Jessica Alba.

Delroy   Ooh, I like Jessica Alba.

Nabs   Sure about that?

Delroy   Course.

Nabs   Are you sure you don't like Orlando Bloom?

Delroy   I ain't like that.

Nabs *laughs*.

Delroy   I ain't like that. I like girls! Jessica Alba is fit, I love Jessica Alba.

Nabs   Whatever.

Delroy   No whatever about it.

Ashley   It don't matter.

Delroy   It does matter.

Ashley   Will you shut up? I've got things to say.

Delroy   No.

Ashley   Don't get in a strop, I need to talk to you. Go straight to Andy or Jenny when you get bullied.

Delroy   When I get bullied?

Ashley   I ain't gonna lie to yer, it's going to be bad. It don't mean you have to suffer, don't mean you have to take it. Just go to Andy or Jenny, they'll know what to do.

Delroy   Why are you telling me all this?

Ashley   Cos you need to know.

Delroy   Yeah, but –

Ashley   There's no buts, Delroy. It's like what Nabs said, you gotta do it, or take it.

Delroy   I know that.

Ashley (*distraught*)   So what you asking for? Yer always asking!

Delroy   I'm sorry.

Ashley   Stop saying that.

Nabs   He ain't gonna last. Watch him, Ashley.

Delroy   You gonna let me talk?

Ashley   So talk.

Delroy   Yer always doing that, think you know me. Well, you don't.

Ashley   What you got to say, Delroy?

Delroy   I know all this, I'll do all this.

Nabs   No, you won't.

Delroy   You're saying this like you're going away or summin. I'll still have you?

Ashley   Yes, you will.

Delroy   What is it, Ash?

Ashley   Nothing. Nothing is wrong.

Nabs   He's just upset, cos he told Jenny he fancied her and she laughed. Said he was sweet, but just a boy.

Ashley   Don't you ever shut up, Nabs?

Nabs   No, funny enough.

Ashley   Try it.

Nabs   Or what?

Ashley   Yer lucky, cos I woulda had you.

Nabs   What you waiting for, big man? Doors open in half an hour, have me then, come!

Ashley   I won't be here in half an hour.

Delroy   Eh?

Nabs   What you chatting about?

Ashley   Forget it.

Nabs   Prick.

Ashley (*changing the subject*)   You love to think yer the bad bwoi.

Nabs   I don't think, I know.

Ashley   Oh, so that wasn't you crying like a baby when yer gal last came to see you?

Nabs   Don't go there, Ash.

Ashley   What's her name? Neela? So, how she doing? Still carry her photo.

Nabs   Yes, you keep talking, Ash.

Ashley   Shoulda seen him, Delroy, going mad whenever someone talks about her. Fighting anyone.

Nabs   Yes, that's right, I'll fight anyone. I don't cry like you two. I'm never gonna cry, no one is gonna see me cry in here, I'll die first, you get me? I'll fight anyone. Neela is my woman, yeah, and she's gonna be waiting for me when I come out.

Ashley   I was dying to see what this girl looked like, you know. See if she lived up to the hype. When was the last time she come to visit?

Nabs   I don't know.

Ashley   Yeah, you do. Don't lie.

Nabs   Six months, three days.

Ashley   I took one look, hmm, not bad, she looked like that Asian girl from *Bend It Like Beckham*. But not all that.

Delroy   She was gorgeous.

Ashley   Whatever.

Delroy   No whatever about it. She was fine.

Ashley   Yes, alright, Delroy.

Delroy   But we went to see it when it come out.

Ashley   Delroy?

Delroy   You were going into one about her, saying you were loved up.

Ashley   Shut up.

Nabs   She is all that. She's all that and more.

He steps out of his cell.

(*To audience.*) First time I ever saw Neela was when I was twelve years old. Her and her sister came into my dad's shop. They had just moved into the area. She was dressed in a little sari and she looked good, man. She was a couple of years older than me, she looked at me like I was dirt or summin, going, 'Who you looking at, you ugly little rat?!' My mum keeps telling me that when I first saw her, yeah, I asked Mum if Neela was an angel, ca she looked so beautiful. But nuh, that ain't me, I wouldn't say that. I do remember that I couldn't take my eyes off her. I had competition though, my best mate Tariq liked her as well. 'Neela is my woman, Nabs.' 'What you chatting about, Tariq? She's my woman.' 'She may be your woman, Nabs, but I showed her my thing the other day, and she loved it.' After that we had a fight. I beat him up of course. I could always beat up Tariq, he's soff. He was still my best mate though. It was silly, cos Neela wouldn't look twice at us, she

thought we were little boys. Well, little boys grow up. I was
fifteen, yeah, and Neela got her cousin Jasmine to pass a
note to me in school. She said, 'I'm waiting, Nabs, waiting
for you to ask me out, you fool! And you had better be
taking me to nice places, Nabs, cos I've got expensive tastes,
you get me?' 'Do you have any idea how sweet I felt? A
fifteen-year-old, going out with a seventeen-year-old, and a
fine one as well! But it was more than feeling sweet. It really
was. Whenever I'm with Neela, whenever I see her, think
about her, I can't breathe. I get this feeling in my stomach
that goes mad up. Like one of dem rides at Alton Towers. I
can't deny it, you get me? I'm loved up! She felt the same,
but whenever I did summin bad, she get vex fer trut.
'Watcha go and do that for? You a fool or what? What is
the matter wid you? Come here so I can clout you round the
head, come here! You ejut!' But she always looked after me.
She promised she'd always do that, she promised she'd love
me for ever. Like I love her. So much, that if any guy, any
guy mess wid her, I go mess wid his head, you get me?
That's how it is. It's like my heart is so big for her, the rest
of my body can't take it. And it's all full of love. She needs
to know, everyone needs to know how much I love her,
what I would do for her. I didn't ask for trouble. All I
wanted was to stand in the queue at McD's and get our Big
Mac and large fries. I didn't ask for that fool to sit in my seat
and insult my woman. Calling her a terrorist, stupid
Muslim, bin Laden's sister. What was I supposed to do? Let
him walk? Or smash his head against the wall nuff times?
What do you think I did? Neela wouldn't stop screaming. I
tried to explain to her, 'Don't you get it, Neela, I love you,'
but she's going on with, 'I know you do, Nabs, you keep
saying it, but it's too much, man, yer crowding me!'
'Alright,' I goes, 'alright.' Too much noise. 'Neela, don't
cry, I hate it when you cry. I'll be out soon, I will take
everything that place will throw at me and dash it back at
them. Then I'm coming back to you.'

Lights change.

She's waiting for me.

Ashley   Says who?

Nabs   My boy Tariq, he's looking after her, taking her out for me. Tells me how she's missing me.

Ashley   Tariq's taking her out? Looking after her?

Nabs   That's what I said. What you trying to say?

Ashley   Nuttin.

Nabs   Bollocks, I know exactly what you mean.

Ashley   Ca yer thinking it too. Why you think she ain't come back? Maybe she's having too much of a good time being 'looked after' by Tariq, innit, Delroy?

Nabs   Carry on.

Ashley   Hit a nerve, Nabs?

Nabs   I'll hit you.

Ashley   Remember this, Delroy, he soff.

Delroy   Leave him alone, Ashley.

Ashley   What you taking his side for?

Delroy   Shouldn't tease him.

Ashley   Well, he shouldn't dish it out if he can't take it.

Delroy   Don't make it right though.

Ashley   What is wrong with you? You really think he'll back you up?

Delroy   That's not why I'm saying it. Just because he's like that, doesn't mean I have to be.

Ashley   Go to sleep, I ain't chatting to you.

Nabs   You've upset him now, new boy. Thanks, yeah.

Delroy   You hear that, Ashley?

Ashley   I heard.

Delroy   He said thanks.

Ashley   Boy never listens!

Delroy   To me.

Ashley   He's still gonna pound yer arse in twenty-five minutes though.

Nabs   Believe.

Ashley   I can't stop him.

Delroy   Well, let him beat me up then, let him, cos I don't care any more.

Ashley   You will.

Delroy   He did it you, you're alright.

Ashley   Yes, Delroy, I'm alright.

Delroy   Well, so will I.

Ashley   Well, you won't be needing me.

Delroy   Cos you won't be here.

Ashley   Right.

Delroy   Why won't you be here?

Ashley   Eh?

Delroy   Why won't you be here?

Ashley   I'm out.

Nabs   Early release, says who?

Ashley   Says me.

Nabs   Since when?

Ashley   Since ages.

Nabs   I've never heard you say anything.

Ashley   What, I'm supposed to tell you everything now?

Nabs   You ain't got early release.

Ashley   And it's your business how, Nabs?

Nabs   Yer lying, man.

Ashley   Move.

Nabs   Yer chatting rubbish, yer arse ain't going anywhere.

Ashley   Oh yes it is.

Nabs   I know yer lying, mate.

Ashley   Don't call me mate.

Nabs   Only the governor can sign off on prisoners.

Ashley   So?

Nabs   So, he's away, ain't he? I heard yer mate Andy
talking about it.

Ashley   Yeah!

Nabs   Yeah, yeah what?

Ashley   The governor is coming back later today.

Nabs   No he ain't, he's only just left. It's like what I told
my new friend here, if you're going to tell a lie, make it a
good one. You of all people should know that.

Ashley   Oh, just leave me, will yer, both of yer. Yer
spoiling it.

Nabs   Spoiling what? What is going on in there? What are
you doing? Ejut?

Delroy   I don't get it, Ashley.

Ashley   Oh, what a surprise, Delroy doesn't get it.

Delroy   Why say you're leaving, when you're not? What's
going on, man? Tell me.

Nabs   Oh shame!

Delroy   What?

Nabs   I know what he's going to do.

Delroy   Do what? Ashley?

Nabs   Pussy.

Delroy   Someone tell me.

Nabs   Gonna do a bit of sheet-ripping, are you, Ashley?

Delroy   Wass that mean?

Nabs   Is it, Ash?

Delroy   What's sheet-ripping?

Nabs   Tell him, Ashley. Tell him what yer up to.

Delroy   Will somebody?

Nabs   You prefer if he heard it from me? Ashley? I'd give him all the gory details, yeah?

Delroy   Ashley?

Nabs   Some friend you are. You know what he's going to do, new boy? You figured it out yet? Alright, he's gonna rip up his bed sheets, make a noose, wrap it round his neck, choke every bit of life out of him. Do you know what happens when you hang yourself, new boy? Your eyes go all blood red, yeah, then they look like they're gonna pop outta yer head, hundred miles an hour. Then yer bladder goes all mad up inside and you piss yourself. Innit, Ashley? You go quiet now, Ashley? Maybe he's already done it. He's hanged himself.

Delroy   Ashley?

Nabs   We had some kid do it here once, new boy, month after I come here, soppy fool, wouldn't stop crying. They found him next morning, 'bout this time, hanging from the window, dead up! Boom! I have to say though, new boy, I'd thought it'd be you doing it, not him. I woulda placed money if I knew.

Delroy   Ashley, tell me this ain't true, tell me you ain't gonna do it.

Nabs   He's doing it, it all makes sense now, the way he's bin acting.

Delroy   Ashley, no! No, man! Tell me, talk to me.

Nabs   Leave him.

Delroy   What?

Nabs   Let him do it.

Delroy   No.

Nabs   How are you going to stop him? You know how to walk through walls now?

Delroy   Ash? I'll scream the whole building down if you don't speak, Ash!

Ashley   Make friends with Ralf.

Delroy   What?

Ashley   Make friends with Ralf. He's light-skinned, bushy-haired, can't miss him, goatee beard, he's a good laugh.

Delroy   Ash?

Ashley   He ain't top boy or nuttin. But everyone likes him, cos he's funny and that. Hang wid him. Don't trust him with anything, though, he's still a little thief. He loves playing pool, but you gotta watch him, don't let him hustle you now.

Nabs   He's gone.

Ashley   Boy's smart, you see. He loves to stand by and let you pocket a few balls, he misses a few on purpose, praising you, making out you is hustling him. And that's his trap, makes you feel all sweet. If yer not thinking straight, you up the bet. Once you do that, that's it, he's got you. He then turns into a demon man, believe! A demon with a cue, he'll pot his balls right in front of you, trust, you won't know what day it is.

Delroy   That's good to know, mate.

Ashley   Just keep it in your head, man.

Delroy   I got a problem though.

Ashley   Why am I not surprised?

Delroy   I can't play pool.

Ashley   So learn.

Delroy   I've tried to learn, you tried to teach me once, remember?

Ashley   Yeah, yeah.

Delroy   It took me half-hour to pot my first ball.

Ashley   More like two hours.

Delroy   Well, there you go then.

Ashley   Ralf loves playing pool though.

Delroy   So?

Ashley   So if you want to be good buddies with him, you should know how to play . . .

Delroy   I don't want to be buddies with him.

Ashley   Don't cry.

Delroy   I'm not crying.

Ashley   He's a good friend to have, Delroy.

Delroy   I don't care about Ralf. I don't care how good he is at pool, or how funny he is, I care about you. You're funny, yer good at pool.

Ashley   Yes, Delroy, but . . .

Delroy   But what? But what, Ash? Tell me. Are you really going to do it, you gonna rip yer sheets?

Ashley   You wouldn't understand if I told yer.

Delroy   And you don't want to try telling me. You can't do this, Ash.

Ashley *puts the noose around his neck.*

Delroy   You can't leave me.

Ashley   It's always about you. You are so selfish.

Delroy   Me?

Ashley   Yeah, you! Wanting me to look after you again, wanting everyone, the world ain't about you, you nuh.

Delroy   Alright then, it ain't, I'm sorry –

Ashley   If you say sorry one more time, it won't be Nabs beating you, it'll be me.

Delroy   Good, then you won't kill yerself.

Ashley   Jus leave me alone.

Delroy   Sorry! See, I said it again, you gonna beat me now? You can't! You'll have to wait until later.

Ashley   No, I don't.

Delroy   Yes, you do.

Ashley   I'll get Nabs to do it, he's gonna beat you up anyway.

Nabs   Nice, bro.

Delroy   Nabs, don't, please.

Nabs   Yes, new boy, yer learning, beg! I like that.

Delroy   I'm not begging. If you say you won't do it, then he'll have to do it.

Nabs   So?

Delroy   So, he won't hang himself.

Nabs   I don't care if he does or not.

Delroy   You can't mean that.

Nabs   Bwoi, don't tell me what I can't mean.

Ashley   Yer wasting yer time, Delroy, Nabs only cares about number one.

Nabs   Ca thass the only way to be.

Ashley   He's bin Laden's brother.

Delroy   That's out of order, Ash.

Nabs   New boy, I don't need you fighting my battles for me.

Ashley   What's the first thing you're going to do when you get out, Nabs, fly a plane into a building? Go fight with your boys in Iraq?

Nabs   Is that noose nice and tight, Ash?

Ashley   Yes thanks.

Nabs   Good!

Delroy   Nabs, can't you see what he's doing? The more angry he gets you, the less you'll want to help me.

Nabs   Help you with what?

Delroy   Stop him killing himself.

Nabs   How is me not beating you up gonna help him?

Delroy   Then he'll have to do it. You heard him, he's sick of me.

Nabs   Yeah, so sick he'll probably choke himself to get away from yer. You dickhead!

Ashley   He's right, Delroy. Sorry, mate.

Delroy   So that's it, you just give up?

Ashley   You got no idea, man.

Nabs   Believe.

Delroy   Yeah, but that's no excuse, Ash.

Ashley   You'll see.

Delroy   That I'll want to hang myself as well, is that what you're saying?

Ashley   Not if you do as I say. You'll be alright.

Delroy   Yer not.

Ashley   It's too late for me.

Delroy   Oh shut up.

Ashley   Excuse me?

Delroy   You go cry now?

Nabs (*laughs*)   Rah, new bwoi thinks he's man.

Delroy   I can't believe I used to look up to you, you nuh. Ashley Williams, bad-arse. The brer you cross the road to avoid.

Nabs   Yes, Delroy, cuss him!

Delroy   If anyone gets in yer face, you buss them up so bad, they'll think twice about doing it again. But I didn't want to cross the road, I wanted to hang with you, ca I wanted to feel important, yeah. If Ashley's bad, I'm bad!

Ashley   I won't miss yer voice.

Delroy   You ain't gonna do it.

Ashley   I am.

Delroy   You would have done it by now. You've had all night! And you're a waste of space.

Nabs   Tell him, Delroy.

Delroy   I meant you, Nabs.

Nabs   Carry on wid that mouth, new boy. You got twenty minutes.

Delroy   Help me.

Nabs   Let the fool do it, what do I care?

Delroy   Don't listen to him, Ash.

Nabs   No, do listen to me, Ash, make sure you tighten that noose, yeah, tight!

Delroy   Ashley!

Ashley   Ashley, what!

Delroy   Come on, mate.

Ashley   But I'm not yer mate though, am I? You're embarrassed to know me now.

Delroy   I didn't mean it.

Ashley   Don't start turning soff now, Delroy. Not when you're getting brave.

Delroy   Don't do it.

Ashley   Don't you get it? That Ash is gone. He's on the bus! This Ash is all that's left. And this Ash can't take any more. You think I want to do it? I don't.

Delroy   So don't.

Ashley   I have to. I'm soff, man. And no offence, yeah, Delroy, but it's all yer fault.

Delroy   Mine?

Ashley   Hanging round me all this time. Getting off on it, whenever I did summin bad. Me loving it, for what? To let my family down? All because I couldn't handle losing my mum.

Delroy   I'm sorry.

Ashley   You're not sorry.

Delroy   I am.

Ashley   Don't say that to me. I say it nuff times to her.

Delroy   Who?

Ashley   My mum, innit!

Delroy   Yer mum?

Ashley   You don't get it.

Delroy   I want to get it.

Ashley   She's here. I see her here.

Nabs   Yep, he's gone.

Delroy   Shush.

Nabs   Oi!

Delroy   Nabs man.

Nabs   'Bout shush.

Delroy   Go on, Ash.

Ashley   I thought it was just noise at first. You know like when you remember summin, and you play it in yer head, over and over, especially if it's a nice memory. Then it sounds real, so real like it's coming from a radio.

Delroy   What is?

Ashley   *Home and Away.*

Delroy   *Home and Away*?

Nabs *laughs.*

Delroy   What about it?

Nabs   *Hollyoaks* ain't good enough for you, Ash?

Delroy   Ignore him.

Ashley   Whenever we watched it, Mum would always sing the theme tune to it. (*Sings the first lines of the song.*) I wouldn't mind but she was such a bad singer! I didn't mind really though. I loved it actually, I couldn't get enough of it cos it was our time. She'd pick me up from school, I would take off my shoes when I got home, cuddle up to her while we watched *Home and Away*. Mum used to say it was the calm before the storm, before my brothers and sister came home and my dad. We'd make up funny stories about our day, she'd say something like she won the lottery, bought a private jet, flew to Barbados. I'd say I got picked by the England football team, scored two goals, just like Wayne Rooney. Sven made me captain. We'd laugh. Then she would have to stop and make dinner. That is what I started hearing in here, *Home and Away*, and my mum singing. It was nice at first, but then it started getting louder and louder. I didn't need that, you just don't need that. Then I could smell her, I remember what she smelt like and I could smell it in this room, I swear, I ain't lying to yer. I told Andy, I told him to come into this cell and smell it himself, but he couldn't, looked at me like I was mad or summin.

Nabs (*sarcastic*)   Is it?

Ashley   Then one night, just come in for lockdown, I turned round to turn off the light, turn round, to take off my sweater, getting ready for bed, I look up and she's standing right there in the middle of my room, man, my mum. She was standing here.

Nabs   Shut up, you fool.

Ashley   She was.

Nabs   She look at you?

Ashley   Right at me.

Delroy   Did she say anything?

Nabs   I was gonna ask that.

Delroy   What did she say to you, Ash?

Ashley   Not a word. She didn't have to.

Delroy   I don't get yer.

Ashley   The way she looked. I knew exactly what she was saying. I let her down, broke my promise to be good. She knew about everything I'd done.

Nabs   But how could she know though?

Delroy   She's a ghost, innit, they can do what they want.

Nabs   No they can't.

Delroy   Yes they can.

Nabs   Listen, yeah, I saw this film on telly, right, about this boy seeing ghosts all the time, and he was telling Bruce Willis, yeah, that they were all walking around like normal people, they didn't even know they were dead.

Delroy   Yer point?

Nabs   My point, fool, is this, if Ash's mum know all about what has happened to him, then she would have to know she was dead, so that means she can't be a ghost! Case rested.

Delroy   Ghosts ain't even real.

Nabs   So what's my man doing in the cell then? Why you so fast to believe him?

Delroy   I'm trying to help him.

Ashley   You two finished? I coulda hung myself while you two were chatting away.

Delroy   But you didn't.

Ashley   It don't matter what you two think, I saw her. I can still see her.

Delroy   Right now?

Nabs   Yo, Ash, is your mum fit-looking? Ca if she is, tell her to come in my cell, she can keep me company, you know what I'm saying.

Delroy   What makes her think you let her down?

Ashley   Cos I have. She died thinking I was going to do summin good with my life. Look what I done with my life. Now she's here, now she won't leave. Reminding me. I can't have this, seeing her face, being here, no more!

Delroy   She's yer mum, man.

Ashley   She knew me, you didn't know me, you think you do, she knew me. No one else. No one knows anything worth knowing about me.

Delroy   I know.

Ashley   What? What do you know? That I can fight? That I'm a good thief? All the girls on the estate are on it. That Yvonne Straker has been telling me she's wanted to go out with me for a whole year now. None of that matters, man.

Delroy   Yvonne Straker?

Ashley   Yes.

Delroy   You didn't tell me she fancied you.

Ashley   Not now, Delroy.

Delroy   Yes now!

Ashley   Oh man!

Delroy   You were going to set her up with me.

Ashley   Bwoi!

Delroy   You promised.

Ashley   She weren't interested in you.

Delroy   What you mean she weren't?

Nabs   You need to ask?

Delroy   I coulda had a chance.

Ashley   No you couldn't.

Delroy   Why not?

Ashley   I pointed you out to her.

Delroy   And?

Ashley   And? What do you think? 'Bout And?

Delroy   I dunno.

Ashley   Delroy, she saw yer . . .

Delroy   And?

Nabs   And she didn't like what was on the menu.

Delroy   So, she chose you.

Ashley   Sorry, man.

Delroy   It's always you.

Ashley   That ain't my fault.

Nabs   This Yvonne? She nice?

Delroy   Prettier than Neela.

Nabs   You don't even know Neela, you ain't seen her.

Delroy   Yvonne is fine! But I was never gonna get a chance with her, was I? Cos of him. It's always him.

Ashley   That's what I'm talking about, Delroy, that is all you care about, comparing yourself to me, you don't know me.

Delroy   So that's it? All the girls on the estate love you up and yer crying about it?

Ashley   I'm not crying.

Nabs   No, but yer whining like a bitch, calling fer yer mummy.

Ashley   You know what, Delroy? I wish Yvonne had said yes to you. Cos then I'd finally be free of yer, no more hanging round me, no more excuses. You screw up on yer own . . .

Delroy What? Ash, what?

Ashley Brendan Price.

Delroy What about him?

Ashley His eighteenth birthday party. I remember now, I told you in his kitchen that Yvonne wanted to go out with me.

Delroy So?

Ashley So why you acting all surprised now? You knew, you knew for ages.

Delroy So what?

Ashley So why are you carrying on like this now? What you playing at, Delroy? Trying to take my mind off what I want to do.

Delroy You don't want to do it.

Ashley You daring me now?

Nabs I'll dare yer.

Ashley Don't do this to me, yeah, it's bad enough I've got Mum –

Delroy Yer mum ain't there, Ash, she ain't doing nuttin, she loved you. She ain't disappointed in you, yer disappointed in you, it's you.

Ashley Right, I got nuttin going for me, so shut up and let me do it, yeah?

Nabs Yeah, Delroy, shut up.

Delroy I ain't shutting up.

Nabs Man, I can't wait to get my hands on you. Fifteen minutes.

Delroy I ain't shutting up for nobody no more. I don't care what you do to me, Nabs, I don't care, I so don't care.

Nabs/Ashley SHUT UP!

Delroy I ain't shutting up! You shut up! Shut up, shut up, shut up!

Nabs Bwoi.

Delroy I'm sick of everyone looking at me, like I'm shit!

Nabs Oh, he swore. I'm telling.

Delroy I ain't shit, yeah, I ain't.

Nabs You talk it though.

Delroy You say I don't know you, Ash?

Ashley You don't.

Delroy I know yer my friend.

Nabs Soff.

Delroy I know you used to let me copy yer homework.

Ashley Yeah, so what? I used to copy yours.

Delroy That field trip we went on with our school, you put up my tent for me. No one else would help me. You were the only one.

Ashley What was I supposed to do, let you get all cold or summin?

Delroy You're a good person, that is what I know about you.

Ashley It's not enough. I just gotta get out of here.

Delroy Don't do it, Ash, I'm telling yer.

Ashley You're telling me?

Delroy I'm telling yer! What's enough?

Ashley I ain't got the strength to look after you and me.

Delroy You don't have to look after me.

Ashley   I always am though.

Delroy   Not any more you don't, I'll look after myself from now on. Starting now, alright?

Ashley   It's not enough.

Delroy   Then what is enough? Tell me what's enough, Ashley!

Nabs   Yer wasting yer time.

Delroy   Why don't you shut up and help me, Nabs?

Nabs   No one helped me.

Delroy   But you wanted someone to help you though.

Nabs   I do. Neela is helping me. All I have to do is think of her face, yeah, that's all I have to do. And thass it. Nuttin else comes near. I'm gonna ask her to marry me, and she'll say yes. Ca we love each other. One thing, new boy, the one thing yer gonna do as soon as you get out. Just keep that in yer head, everything else don't mean nish. If my man there can't even do that, I say let him go. There's nothing he can do for you now.

Delroy   There's plenty I can do for him.

Nabs   You need to help yerself.

Delroy   Ashley, I'll help you, I swear, let me do this for you, just once, one time, let me do something for you.

Ashley   Tempting thought.

Delroy   Bloody funny, ain't it?

Ashley   You – (*laughing*) looking after yerself!

Delroy   I'll fall on my arse.

Ashley   Believe!

Delroy   You go, you won't see it. You won't be able to say, 'See, Delroy, can't even tie yer own shoe laces without me.' Gonna miss out, Ash.

Nabs   Yes, Ash, yer gonna miss out on the same old rubbish, every day, every night.

Delroy   You want him to do it?

Nabs   I don't care! Just hurry up and get on with it, Ash, you and this fool are doing my head in.

Delroy   Yer going to do what he says, Ash? Yer gonna let this fool win?

Ashley   I'm going, Del.

Delroy   No, you're not! You can't. You ain't finished telling me what I have to do.

Ashley   I'm finished.

Delroy   No, you ain't. How do I get Ralf interested in me? How much am I supposed to tell Andy?

Ashley   Tell him what you like.

Delroy   Don't you do it, don't you bloody do it! Ashley! I won't go to Andy, I won't look out for Ralf. I won't do anything you tell me. The only way you'll know if I do, is that you have to make me do it. I'll scream, Ash. Guards will be here in five minutes to cut you down.

Nabs   He'll be dead in five minutes.

Delroy   Ashley!

Nabs   That's if he ain't dead awready. Yo, Ash? You still wid us?

Delroy   Ashley!

Nabs (*mocks* **Delroy**)   Ashley!

Delroy   Ash?

Nabs   'Im dead.

Delroy   No he ain't. I know he ain't. If you do it, I'll do it. Yeah. (*He rips up his bed sheets.*) I'll string myself up like you. I'll do it, I'll do it.

Nabs   Oh yes, it's on now. (*He shouts out through the window.*) Yo! Yo! I got two suicides in waiting here, two! Ash and the new boy. I'm putting five down on the new boy, any takers?

Sound of other boys from their cell windows, placing bets. **Nabs** *grabs a paper and pen and starts taking bets.*

Nabs (*finding it hard to keep up*)   Hold up, hold up, one at a time, yeah, please.

Delroy   I know you can hear me. Ash?

Ashley   Thank you, Delroy, thank you for ruining this for me.

Delroy   Me?

Ashley   Even if I was gonna change my mind, I'd never live it down. Every brer is gonna run me down now. You made it worse.

Delroy   You wanted to kill yourself. How worse could it get?

Ashley   Yer always copying me, always following me.

Delroy   I don't want to do this.

Ashley   Then stop.

Delroy   No, Ashley, you stop. You stop! You stop, then I'll stop.

Ashley   Alright, man, I heard yer!

Delroy   So, you're gonna stop?

Nabs   Yo, Ash, you ain't done the deed, yeah?

Ashley   Get lost, Nabs.

Nabs   Yeah, yeah, whatever. Just hold up fer a sec, yeah. Don't dead up yet. I'm still tekin bets, man. Just wait till I'm done. Peace.

Ashley (*laughs*)   He wants me to wait.

Delroy   I want you to stop.

Ashley   What you want from me, man?

Delroy   I told yer.

Ashley   What about my mum? I can still see her.

Delroy   She ain't there, Ash.

Ashley   I know she ain't there, I know that. She's in my head, yeah, how you gonna help me with that? Tell me.

Delroy   You think she's gonna be happy you doing this though? If she was here, she'd fling herself at you. Am I right?

Ashley   Yes.

Delroy   So what are you chatting about?

Ashley   I don't know what I'm chatting about.

Delroy   What's the first thing you would like to do when you get out?

Ashley   See Mum's grave.

Delroy   That's what you've got to hold on to. Nabs said.

Ashley   Nabs?

Delroy   One thing. The one thing yer gonna do as soon as you get out. Just keep that in yer head, everything else don't mean nish. Or are you telling me you don't care about that no more?

Ashley   Hey, boy, yer asking fer a slap here.

Delroy   Have to catch me first.

Ashley   I'll catch yer.

Delroy   How?

Ashley (*smiles*)   Delroy turn man overnight.

Delroy   Just keeping thinking, one more day.

Ashley   You don't know what this place is like, man.

Delroy   You'll help me. I'll help you.

Ashley   So what are you thinking about? What's your thing?

Delroy   Go-karting with my little brother.

Ashley   Go-karting? He's worse than you.

Delroy   Don't care.

Ashley   One more day?

Delroy   One more. Ash? Ash, what you doing, man?

Ashley   I ain't doing anything, you happy now?

Delroy   Yeah.

Ashley   You wait till the doors open. See if yer smiling then.

Nabs   Alright, I'm done. Bets are closed. Ash, new boy, when yer ready, yeah. Ash? Him dead awready, new boy?

Ashley   No, he ain't.

Delroy   And he ain't gonna be.

Nabs   Soff.

Delroy   I told him what you said, holding on to one thing.

Nabs   I took bets.

Ashley   So?

Nabs   You know how much this will cost me?

Delroy (*sarcastic*)   Bothered?

Ashley *and* **Delroy** *laugh.*

Nabs   Yeah, laugh now, both of yer. Just remember where you are.

Ashley   I don't need you telling me where I am.

Nabs   How about you, new boy?

Ashley   Leave 'im.

Delroy   It's alright, Ash.

Nabs   You and me gonna have some fun, yeah, in five minutes.

Delroy   I can take it.

Nabs   Yer still scared.

Delroy   I know I am. I can take it.

Nabs   Big bwoi!

Ashley   You got anything else to say, Nabs?

Nabs   Oh listen to the two of yer, carrying on like there's nuttin this place can do to touch you. Everyone gets touched.

Ashley   Except you?

Nabs   Believe.

Ashley   Yer girlfriend is waiting for yer?

Nabs   She's waiting.

Ashley   So where is she, Nabs? She ain't come to visit you for six months, where is she?

Nabs   She's busy.

Ashley   For six months? Are you blind as well as stupid, Nabs? You must be. What do you think Neela and Tariq have been getting up to for the last six months? Chatting about you? Wake up, you fool. I wonder what she and Tariq are up to right now. I wonder where he's taking her.

Nabs   They wouldn't do that.

Ashley   They're doing it.

Nabs   She's my girl.

Delroy   Leave 'im, Ash. It's not worth it.

Ashley   It is worth it. After the way he's been treating you.

Delroy   Can't we just have one day without it? One day. You telling me you don't want it?

Ashley   I want it.

Delroy   So have it.

Ashley   Yer so moany.

Delroy   Ash?

Ashley   What?

Delroy   I'm still scared, man.

Ashley   You should be. One day at a time, yeah?

Delroy (*nods his head*)   One day.

Nabs   Hey, Ashley? Ash? Why you think Tariq is getting off with Neela?

Ashley   I don't.

Nabs   So you were lying?

Ashley   Yeah, I was lying.

Nabs   Don't chat to me like I'm soff, yeah.

Ashley   I ain't.

Nabs   It's me yer talking to, not yer soppy friend here.

Ashley   I know.

Nabs   So you were juss messing wid me, yeah?

Ashley   Yeah.

Nabs   You don't believe she's doing that?

Ashley   No, I don't.

Nabs   You really don't?

Ashley   I really don't.

Nabs   Honestly?

Ashley   Honestly.

Nabs   She's my girl.

Ashley   Yeah.

Nabs *lies on his bed for a moment. Then he jumps up and paces around his cell, looking increasingly distraught. He finds the picture of Neela, places it on his desk and addresses it.*

Nabs   You should hear what they say about you. Nasty things, ca they don't know how to treat a woman. Love them, respect them, like my dad wid my mum. Ain't got a clue, wid their dirty minds. But it's alright, ca I'll kill anyone who badmouths you, I'll beat up on anyone that even thinks about you in that way. Ca thass how much you mean to me. I know it. Every fool in here knows it, and if they don't, they soon will. I would do all that, and twice over for you. That's why I know, you wouldn't do what he said. You wouldn't get off with Tariq, dump me, nuh, you wouldn't do that. Tell me what your sister wrote ain't true. You wouldn't do that to me. Tariq ain't yer husband, she's chatting rubbish, yeah, yeah. I've blocked it for so long now, I'm the king at blocking things out, but it keeps coming back, yeah, and I don't want it to keep coming back, I want you to come here, tell me it ain't true. PLEASE! I knew. I knew. That Tariq had better treat you right, you nuh, oderwise him and me are gonna have words. (*Tearful.*) Those who do it, those who take it.

Sound of keys rattling. The three boys rise to their feet and wait. **Ashley**'s *door unlocks, he step forward.* **Delroy**'s *door unlocks, he steps forward.* **Nabs**'s *door unlocks, he steps forward. The boys glance at each other.* **Delroy** *gives* **Ashley** *a reassuring pat on the shoulder.* **Ashley** *and* **Delroy** *exit, followed by* **Nabs**. **Nabs** *walks past* **Ashley**'s *cell, and stops when he sees the noose* **Ashley** *made.* **Nabs** *walks in, picks up the noose. He stares at it.*

Days of Significance

Much Noise
On the Side of the Angels
A Parting of the Ways

Days of Significance was first performed at the Swan Theatre, Stratford-upon-Avon, in a production by the Royal Shakespeare Company, on 10 January 2007. The cast was as follows:

Bouncer	Jason Barnett
Lenny	Nigel Cooke
Tony/Sean	Daniel Dalton
Ben	Jamie Davis
Dan	Trystan Gravelle
Steve	Simon Harrison
Vince	Richard Katz
Drunken Man	Robin Lawrence
Jamie	Ashley Rolfe
Brookes/Bouncer	Mark Theodore
Hannah	Claire-Louise Cordwell
Gail	Amanda Daniels
Trish	Pippa Nixon
Clare	Michelle Terry
Donna	Ony Uhiara

Director Maria Aberg
Set/Costume Designer Lizzie Clachan
Lighting Designer David Holmes
Sound Designer Carolyn Downing

Much Noise

Cast of characters

Dan, *early twenties*
Jamie, *late teens*
Ben, *early twenties*
Trish, *early twenties.*
Hannah, *late teens*
Lenny, *late forties*
Donna, *early twenties*
Clare, *early twenties*
Gail, *mid-thirties,*
Vince, *early thirties*
Steve, *late teens*
Tony, *early twenties*
Bouncer

A pedestrian square in the middle of a city centre somewhere in the south-east of England. It is night-time. Two uniformed police officers, **Gail** *and* **Vince***, find themselves surrounded by a drunken youngish mob (average age twenty) while trying to interview two suspects involved in a drunken brawl.*

Gail   Can you hear me, love? Can you hear me?

The boys behind **Ben** *huddle up close behind him, egging* **Vince** *and* **Dan** *on, hoping to see some action here tonight.*

Vince   Step back.

Gail   What is your name?

Jamie   What?

Gail   Name!

Jamie   Ain't got one.

Gail (*points at* **Dan**)   So, what were you doing fighting with him, Mr I-Ain't-Got-One?

Jamie   Spilt my beer.

Dan   You spilt mine.

Jamie   I'll split you in your head.

Gail   Yes, alright, girls.

Ben   Looks like Britney!

The boys laugh again.

Gail   You must be pissed.

Vince   I said step back.

Ben   Little doggie loves to bark.

Tony   Is little doggie gonna bite?

Gail   These your mates then, are they, Steve?

Steve (*protests*)   What?!

Jamie (*sings*)
  'Give me a sign, hit me, baby, one more time.'

Gail   He's winding me up, this one.

Jamie   Why don't you take me to bed?

Ben   Spank his arse!

Gail (*to* **Dan**)   Oi, smiley, come here!

Dan   Oh, yes!

Steve   Go, Dan!

Dan   Well, why go for hamburger, when you can have streak, innit, Brits?

Gail   Do you want to press charges against him? Yes or no? Don't be scared. What you want?

Ben (*sings*)
  'I'll tell you what I want, what I really really want . . .'

Jamie (sings)
  'No I'll tell you what I want, what I really really want . . .'

Gail   Oh for crying out loud.

Vince (*his radio crackles*)   Yeah, this 3–7.

Gail   Fancy a ride, do yer?

Ben   Oh, yes!

Jamie   Bring it on!

Steve   Lucky bastard!

Gail   To the nick!

Vince   We gotta go.

Gail   I'm in the middle of summin here!

Ben   Yes, Vince, she's in the middle of summin, here!

Jamie   Run along now.

Vince   We've got an Emergency. It's kicking off on the other side of town.

Gail   It's kicking off here.

Ben (*grabs his crotch*)   It's bursting in here.

Vince   Nuffink but pissheads, fuck 'em.

Ben   Oh, line up now, boys.

Jamie   Gang bang!

Gail   You're skating on thin ice now, the lot of yer.

Vince   Gail, we're needed!

Gail   Alright! You boys, behave. Steve, tell them.

Ben   What's the hurry, Brits?

Gail   Get out of my way.

Ben (*sings*)
  'Let me . . .'

Boys (*continuing*)
  '. . . entertain you . . .'

Gail   Get out of my way.

Vince   Do it now!

Steve   But we're having such fun.

Gail   Well I'm not . . . hey! Who just grabbed my arse?

Vince   Oi!

Jamie   Whoa!

Gail   Who was it?

Ben   Yeah, who was it that grabbed Britney's arse? Come on, I'm waiting, who grabbed the arse! Whoever it was, I'm disgusted with yer, I'm ashamed.

He mouths quietly to the boys it was him. The boys chuckle.

Gail   The thinnest of ice.

Jamie   Do you do head, Brits?

Boys roar with laughter. They start jostling **Gail** *and* **Vince**, *who as a last resort pull out their batons.*

Ben   Whoa! What you got there, Britney?

Steve   Longer than yours, Ben.

Jamie   What's that, am I scared?

Gail   I bet I know how you like to take it, long and hard.

Boys laugh. Sound of sirens.

Gail   Now, back off.

Vince   Come on, Gail.

Jamie   Go on, Vince.

Steve   Ride him, Gail.

Ben   We want details!

Gail *and* **Vince** *exit. The boys gather outside a nightclub, joining the queue.*

Jamie   Shoulda taken him.

Steve   Little boy thinks he's in the desert already.

Jamie   Less of the boy, fat man.

Ben   Yeah, alright, J.

Steve   Wass the matter with yer, we respect yer, alright? That's what we was saying. We all do.

Jamie   Right.

Dan   Go fight by all means.

Jamie   Cool.

Dan   Yeah. (*Aside.*) Little boy.

Jamie   You fuck.

Dan (*chuckles*)   Yeah, come on, you feeling strong?

Ben   Yes, yes thank you one and all. Half-time, half-time! Easy! You muppets, come on! It's our last weekend here. Yeah? So entertain us, you bastards!

The boys roar.

Ben   Juss ignore him, J. He's scared of going himself.

Dan   Do I look like a mug?

Jamie   Go march.

Ben   Already did, the cunt.

Dan   Little boy.

Jamie   Nothing little about serving your country.

Dan (*laughs*)   Oh, fuck off with that.

Ben   You got a problem with that, cunt?

Dan   No, mate.

Ben   I want more alcohol! Is someone going to help me out or what? (*Shouts at the nightclub door.*) Come on!

Dan   I just want you to think about what you're doing.

Ben   Boring.

Jamie   Smart-arse.

Ben (*calls*)   Bladdered?

Steve (*aside to* **Dan**)   You gonna take that?

Ben   Has no choice, do yer, cunt?

Jamie   So what are you going to do, Danny boy?

Ben   Going to college, the ponce.

Dan   To get my mind educated.

Ben   You stay wid the women.

Dan (*brags*)   You make that sound like a bad thing!

Steve (*roars*)   Danny bwoi! Go put it out?

Dan   Who's around to stop me? Eh?

Jamie   Get him.

Ben (*bangs door of the nightclub*)   Come on, mate, let us in! There's only four of us!

Jamie   Is this queue moving?

Dan   Look, Ben, I just wanna –

Ben *belches in his face.*

Dan   Nice, really nice.

Ben   Can I have some alcohol please?

Lenny *enters, he begins opening up his chip van.*

Hannah *and her friends come running out of the nearest McDonald's in hysterical laughter.*

Hannah   Come on!

Clare   Trish!

Hannah   Trish!

Clare   Oh my God! Oh my God!

Donna   That is just nasty.

Clare   Oh my God, he's coming!

Hannah   Trish, run, will yer.

Trish *runs out to join her friends.*

Trish   Oh, fucking hell!

Clare   He's coming.

Tony *comes running out after the girls, he is holding his penis in his hand. The girls are screaming in fits of horror and laughter.*

Clare   Oh my God!

Tony   You want some?

Trish   Hold, please.

Trish *gets up close to take a picture with her mobile phone of* **Tony** *holding his dick.*

Tony   You want it?

Trish   Yeah, I want it.

Licks her lips. The girls are in pains of laughter)

Hold still.

She takes the picture, the girls applaud.

Trish (*takes a bow*)   I thank you!

Tony   Don't be shy, Trish, come closer.

Trish *shows the girls the picture. They all roar with laughter.*

Donna   Oh my God!

Tony *continues to flaunt his penis in front of them.*

Donna (*points*)   Get him.

Hannah   You can put it away now, love.

The girls roar as **Tony** *begins undressing.*

Clare   Go on, my son!

Girls (*chants*)   Off . . . off . . . off . . . (*Etc.*)

Clare   Have it!

Tony   You want some more?

Trish (*roars*)   Yes, darling, we want some more!

Tony *shows off his penis from the side. The girls scream again. The girls are laughing inanely, then they scream to warn* **Trish** *when* **Tony** *leans forward and tries to kiss her.* **Trish** *pushes him away.*

Trish   I don't think so.

Clare   As if!

Donna   Can you imagine?

Tony   She . . . she said . . .

Donna   Who?

Clare   Who said?

Tony   Trish!

Trish   Yeah?

Donna   She said what?

Tony   You want see my cock.

Trish   I said, you want to see my cock?

The girls chuckle.

Tony   You fucking slag.

Trish   Save me!

Tony   Can't handle the cock, love.

Clare   Your cock?

Tony   My cock!

Donna   That cock?

Tony   Come on!

Trish   Sweetheart, that ain't no cock.

Clare   That's a pencil.

Tony   Stupid fucking slags.

Trish   Stupid?

Donna   Fucking?

Clare   Slags?

Donna   Well, get him.

Trish   Have a wank, Tone.

Tony   I'd wank over you.

Trish   Try.

Hannah (*gets between them*)   Oi!

Tony   Lucky cunt.

Trish   You're the one who's lucky, Tone.

Clare   Bye! Bye!

Tony *slopes away to join his mates.*

Trish   Tell me something, why is it always ugly men that like to do that shit?

The girls laugh.

It's always bare, ugly men that love to get all nasty like that. Now if it was some fine fit-looking boy man, we're talking Brad Pitt, six-pack, firm arse, bedroom eyes, the works, I wouldn't complain. Whip it out by all means. I will suck it right off!

The girls roar with laughter.

But don't give me Tony 'I'm so ugly' Harman who couldn't get it up if he tried, no!

Clare   Don't think so.

Donna   Believe.

Trish   Of course. Hannah?

Hannah   What?

Trish   Explanation? Watcha stop us for?

Clare   Right little Girl Scout, you.

Hannah   There's no such thing as Girl Scouts. They're called Brownies.

Clare   Face? Bovvered?

Trish   He got his cock out.

Donna   Not allowed.

Hannah   You were this much from lamping him.

Trish   And she's off!

Clare *and* **Donna** *yawn.*

Hannah   You wanna get nicked again? You and yer temper are going to get sent down, Trish, guaranteed.

Trish   Come here. It's dick night, Hannah. (*Kisses her.*) Give yer brain a rest.

The girls join the queue for the club.

Hannah *notices* **Jamie** *staring at her.*

Hannah   Yes?

Jamie   What?

Trish   Is that you up there, Ben?

Ben   You want summin, Trish?

Trish   Yer head on a stick. So big, I can see it coming a mile away.

Ben   I can smell you coming a mile away.

The boys laugh.

Trish   So Ben knows how to cuss now. Well, fuck me.

Ben   I did.

Trish   You tried. Move yer arse up.

Ben   We'll need a forklift truck to move yer arse.

Trish   Oooh, save me!

Bouncer (*shouts*)   Right, that's it, no more!

The crowd of revellers protest.

Steve   Oh, what are you saying, mate?

Bouncer   We're full up, that's what we're saying.

Ben   Shut up.

Bouncer   Back off.

Jamie   Now he's starting.

Bouncer   Do it now.

Ben   This is a conspiracy to fuck up my night, innit? Has to be.

Trish   Gonna go crying to Mummy, Ben?

Jamie   Don't tell me you're full up.

Bouncer   Are you drunk?

Ben (*belches*)   No.

Jamie   Fat fuck.

Bouncer   Oi!

Jamie   What?

Ben   We're going.

Bouncer   Go now.

Ben   Just don't touch my friend, yeah. Don't do that.

Bouncer   On your way.

Trish   Still acting hard, Ben?

Ben   It was nothing.

Trish   Like yer dick.

Ben   You loved my dick, I could hear you groaning.

Trish   To keep me from laughing in yer face.

The girls roar.

Ben   If only my motor could go as fast as yer mouth.

Trish   Face? Bovvered?

Ben   Let's head back to Yates's.

Hannah   Still not looking?

Jamie   No.

Hannah   Div.

The boys stride over towards Yates's. **Jamie** *keeps staring over at* **Hannah**.

Tony   Oi, oi, the boy's in love.

Dan   Eyes off, mate, slapper ain't the word for it.

Ben   Still crying, cunt?

Dan   You telling me she ain't, Ben?

Ben   I'm telling you that you were whining like a bitch, cos she blanked you.

Dan *slopes away.*

Steve   Where you going?

Tony   Dan? (*Follows* **Dan**.) Hold up.

Ben   Yes, Tony, go follow yer wife. Right, are we done now? Bladdered? Alcohol? Over there! Come on, J, let's see if we can help you vibe wid this girl.

The boys step into Yates's.

Clare *and* **Donna** *share a joke. They roar with laughter.* **Donna** *accidentally spills her drink over* **Hannah**'s *top.*

Hannah   Jesus, Donna!

Donna   What?

Hannah   Do you wanna get hit?

Trish   Ladies?

Hannah   Where did you find this bitch from, Clare?

Donna   Well, smell her.

Hannah   Don't stare me out.

Donna   I'll do what I like.

Hannah   I'll cut yer face.

Donna   Oh, yes?

Trish   We are not doing this, girls. Not on a Friday. Not on my watch. Eyes front, look at me! Fingers on lips! The weekend is here, we're on a forty-eight-hour pass. Bring some beef, you lose some teeth. We're going to get bladdered up, loved up, drugged up, whatever is up, so you two, put the nails away. Cos I want some dick! And I think you all know how angry and upset I can be, if I don't get no dick! So, are you feeling me? Hannah?

Hannah   I'm feeling you.

Trish   Donna?

Donna (*talks black*)   Mi feel you!

Hannah   I can't look like this.

Donna   A little stain.

Hannah (*warning*)   You wanna slap?

Trish   Excuse? Did you two hear?

Hannah   Am I allowed to put some water on it, please?

Trish   Clock is ticking.

Hannah (*approaching* **Lenny**)   Len?

Lenny   Not a penny.

Hannah   What?

Lenny   Spent all of your money already?

Hannah   No, Mr Arsey, I ain't.

Lenny   You will by tomorrow.

Hannah   It's what weekends are for.

Lenny   Just don't come running to me.

Hannah   Can I please use your sink?

Lenny   The stain?

Hannah   See, you can see it. Gonna kill that Donna.

Lenny *lets her in.* **Hannah** *removes her top,* **Lenny** *looks away in embarrassment.*

Lenny (*protests*)   Do you have to?

Hannah   Chill, Dad.

Lenny   Shouldn't call me that.

Hannah   Yeah, yeah, you don't like it.

Lenny   I don't deserve it.

Hannah   Whatever. Can I have some . . .

Lenny (*hands her chips*)   . . . chips.

Hannah   You got a . . .

Lenny (*hands her a fork*)   . . . fork.

Hannah   Am I that . . .

Lenny   . . . predictable?

Hannah   I'm staying round Trish's tonight.

Lenny   Call your mum.

Hannah *protests.*

Lenny   You know she worries. She wants you to be safe.

Hannah   She wants me under a bus.

Lenny   Don't be silly.

Hannah   Nagging cow.

Lenny   Excuse, that's my wife yer laying into there.

Hannah   Well, tell her. I'm finally going to college, I'm getting out from under her feet, is she happy, is she fuck?

Lenny   She worries.

Hannah   She doesn't think I can do it, don't lie for her. One day, she is going to trust me that I know what I'm doing with my life.

Lenny   We only want what's best.

Trish   Hannah!

Hannah   Shut the fuck up.

Lenny (*protests*)   Oi, oi, what do you think this is?

Hannah   Stop being such a stroppy bollocks.

Lenny   Well, you try working here all nights, without going home to yer mum, smelling of grease –

Hannah (*knows what's coming*)   – smelling of grease from head to toe.

Lenny   Yer think yer funny?

Hannah   I do as it goes.

Lenny   Yeah, let's see how funny it is when that new chippie opens next week . . .

Hannah   Len?

Lenny   Open all hours, nicking my trade.

Hannah   Bloody hell.

Lenny   Back on the bleeding scrapheap, that'll be me!

Hannah   Have you finished?

Lenny   Just forget it.

Hannah   I think someone needs cheering up here.

Lenny (*knows what's coming*)   Don't even think.

Hannah   Sorry, Lenny, you've given me no choice.

Lenny   You, get away from me.

Hannah   I have to.

Lenny   You don't have to.

Hannah   Yes I do.

Lenny   I'll fight yer.

Hannah   Playing hard to get, I like that.

She grabs her stepdad and tickles him ruthlessly. He laughs.

We happy?

Lenny   No.

Hannah *continues to tickle him.*

Lenny   Alright – yes, yes!

Hannah   Yes, what?

Lenny   We are happy.

Hannah   Be told.

Lenny   Thank you, love.

Hannah   It was only a tickle.

Lenny   Never underestimate the power of your actions.

Hannah (*cringes*)   Oh, Len.

Lenny   I'm just saying, darlin'.

Hannah   You say a lot of things, I never know what they mean though.

Lenny   Just, don't waste yerself, yeah?

Hannah   You're so sweet.

She gives him a peck on the cheek.

Lenny   Go on, go and get lashed.

Hannah   Intend to.

She sees that the girls have gone.

Fucking slags!

Lenny   Hannah!

Hannah   Only went in without me.

Lenny   Call yer mum.

Hannah *blows* **Lenny** *a kiss.*

Lenny (*sighs*)   Oh Christ.

Hannah *walks over to Yates's.* **Jamie** *comes crashing out of there, escorted by a bouncer.*

Jamie   Get yer fucking hand off me.

The **Bouncer** *goes back inside.*

Jamie   Yeah, move from me. Yer wankers! Wankers! (*Notices* **Hannah**.)

Hannah   You just can't stay out of it. What you looking at?

Jamie   You got a stain.

Hannah   I got nothing. Why do you like fighting? Every weekend you're at it. You won't have enough left for Iraq, if you carry on.

Jamie   Bring it on, I got plenty of fight.

Hannah   Big man.

Jamie   Yep.

Hannah   See yer then.

Jamie   Stay, if you want.

Hannah (*chuckles*)   I ain't getting off with yer.

Jamie   To talk.

Hannah   Talk?

Jamie   Yeah.

Hannah *stays.*

Jamie   So?

Hannah   So, what?

Jamie   So, talk.

Hannah   About what? I just want to rave.

Jamie   Me as well.

Hannah   Why aren't you?

Jamie   Some black geezer's in there, has a big mouth. Everyone thinks they've got an opinion.

Hannah   On the war?

Jamie   He calls me a thug in uniform, I'm not having that.

Hannah   Coulda ignored him.

Jamie   I smacked him good. Woulda glassed him.

Hannah   Lucky.

Jamie   Lucky?

Hannah   Woulda got arrested. No army for you.

Jamie   What you saying?

Hannah   You are lucky. That is what I am saying. Can I go in now?

Jamie   Yeah, be like the rest of them.

Hannah   Like what?

Jamie   Don't give a toss about what we're doing.

Hannah   I've got a Smirnoff Ice waiting.

Jamie   Just telling yer.

Hannah   Right. You're not scared.

Jamie   No.

Hannah   Despite what they all say?

Jamie   Who?

Hannah   Geezers on the telly. The papers. Another soldier getting killed.

Jamie   Was it a bomb?

Hannah   Think so. I just hope it's not Basra you're going to. Nuri al-Maliki has declared a state of emergency now.

Jamie   Nuri who?

Hannah   Iraqi Prime Minister.

Jamie   What have you been reading?

Hannah   Just telling you what I see, what I hear. I'm going to college.

Jamie (*scoffs*)   You go on that march then, you and yer college mates?

Hannah   Are you on crack? I just said I'm going to college.

Jamie   Look, I have to go. I don't have a choice.

Hannah   Thought you said you wanted to go. Are you alright? I'll get Ben and Dan.

Jamie   Don't get them.

Hannah   They're your mates.

Jamie (*pleads*)   I said, don't get them.

Hannah (*realises*)   Oh shame.

Jamie   Look, if you're gonna start, piss off.

Hannah   I'll start on yer head if you keep this up.

Jamie   Hannah the slapper.

Hannah   Bye.

Jamie   Wait?

Hannah   For what? For more cussing?

Jamie   No.

Hannah   Good, cos I'll cuss you right under the table, mate.

Jamie *chuckles.*

Hannah   If you don't want to go . . .

Jamie   Who said I didn't want to go? I didn't say I didn't want to go. Telling me I don't wanna go.

Hannah   See yer.

Jamie   No, wait.

Hannah   For what? What am I waiting for? Are you even going to try to make a move on me?

Jamie   Can't.

Hannah   You gay?

Jamie   Fuck off.

Hannah (*approaches*)   So, come aboard, and fasten yer seat belt (*Tries to kiss him.*).

Jamie   I see you out and about, every weekend.

Hannah   I see you. The point?

Jamie   You always look nice.

Hannah   I am nice.

Jamie   Yates's, a couple of weeks back, trying to get to the bar, all the lads were staring, tongues hanging, trying to vibe with yer, especially Dan, you weren't having any of it. They got outta yer way, it was like you were parting the Red Sea and no one could touch yer. You got to the front, they were playing Kylie, you were wearing a white strapless top. Couldn't take my eyes off.

Hannah   Perv.

Jamie   You were bopping yer shoulders to the song, you had no idea how nice you looked. I thought, no one that lovely could be cruel, just not possible. Like yer God's gift. An angel. My mum got this from an old song she liked, part of it goes, 'Dreams are like angels, they keep bad at bay, love is the light, scaring darkness away.'

Hannah (*chuckles*)   What are you going on with?

Jamie   I've seen you about. You look . . . You've got a lovely face, Hannah. It's trusting.

Hannah   Like an angel?

Jamie   Believe.

A memorable romantic love song is being played from inside Yates's.

Oh yes! I love this one. Dance with me.

Hannah (*laughs*)   Get the fuck . . . (*Can see that* **Jamie***'s feelings are hurt.*) Jamie, I gotta go in.

Jamie (*holds her hand*)   Dance.

Hannah *takes* **Jamie** *by the hand as they dance together throughout the duration of the song.* **Jamie** *clings to* **Hannah***, like his life depended on it.* **Hannah** *is a little embarrassed at first, but gradually seems to like the way* **Jamie** *is holding her. They stare at each other, then kiss as the song comes to an end.*

Jamie   Thanks.

Hannah (*quoting* **Lenny**)   Never underestimate the power of your actions.

Jamie   Will you see me?

Hannah   I'm seeing you now, you div.

Jamie   Before I go.

They kiss again. **Hannah** *goes inside Yates's.* **Jamie** *remains outside.*

Enter **Dan**, *followed by* **Tony**, *then* **Steve**, *who comes out of Yates's to join his mates by* **Lenny**'s *chip van.*

Steve   Yo! Yo, burger man.

Lenny (*aside*)   Feeding time at the zoo.

Tony   Cheeseburger.

Steve   Burger man!

Lenny   Please?

Steve   Oh, don't play the big un.

Lenny   I've never played anything in my life.

Tony   Big man.

Steve   The big burger man.

Dan   Three cheeseburgers.

Lenny (*slams the sauce bottle down*)   Sauce?

Steve   Oooh!

Tony   What's that look for?

Steve   Burger man?

Tony   Got summin to say?

Steve   Burger man?

Tony   Teach you a lesson.

Lenny   What the fuck you got to teach me?

Steve (*leans over*)   How much money you make?

Lenny   Don't even think.

Steve   Chill, Len.

Lenny   I'll snap you in half, boy.

Steve   Oh yes?

Dan (*snaps*)   Shut up, Steve!

Lenny   Yes, Steve, shut up.

Steve   As if.

Dan   You go on and on, you do.

Steve   What?

Tony (*trying to lighten the mood*)   Oi, he's a whiny little runt that Jamie, though, ain't he? Acting like he's the big I-Am.

Steve   Loves up Ben, though, he's only going to help him get off with that Hannah.

Dan   Hannah's a slag. Ben's a mug.

Tony   Can't say that.

Dan   And why is that, Tone?

Tony   Well, he's going Iraq now.

Dan   And your point?

Tony   Well, he's army. He's a proper.

Dan   Army – you wanna know why he signed up, truthfully? They had some woman soldier handing out leaflets on the high street, the only time him and J weren't looking at her arse is when they staring at her tits.

Tony   Oi, oi!

Steve   That's my boys!

Dan   She reeled them in.

Steve   She can reel me in.

Tony   I'm going!

Dan   Fucking army, fucking war!

Steve   Alright, Dan, calm it down. He'll be lucky he fires a shot, him.

Tony   He'll have six months in the desert, working on his tan.

Steve   Summa that!

Dan   You twats.

Steve   Dan?

Tony   Mate?

Lenny (*chuckles*)   What I wouldn't give?

Tony   You say summin?

Steve   Burger man?

Lenny   You lot, in the army.

The boys heckle.

Lenny   Six days, let alone six months, you'll be crying for yer mums.

Tony   What's he going into now?

Steve   Just hurry up with the food, yeah.

Lenny   How appropriate.

Dan   What do you mean by that?

Steve   Don't encourage him.

Dan   Shut up.

Lenny   You lot. I mean you're nothing but fast food yourselves.

Tony   Yes, mate, whatever.

Lenny   It's tragic.

Steve   Oh, fuck me.

Lenny   There's just no lines drawn with you lot, is there?

Steve *and* **Tony** *heckle.*

Lenny   You're all the bleedin' same.

Tony   Talking shit!

Lenny   Don't know yer born, what you believe.

Steve   That's not true, I believe in summin.

Lenny   What you believe in?

Steve   Enormous tits.

Lenny   And the point is made. Stacked, packed and racked.

Steve   I'll stack you in a sec.

Lenny   It's tragic.

Tony   Shut up, yer boring!

Lenny *hands the burgers over.*

Lenny   Eight quid.

Steve (*sees* **Dan**)   Yer not eating, Dan?

Dan *throws his burger to the ground.*

Steve   Easy, mate.

Tony   Where's he going?

Steve   Dan! Hold up?

Tony   Where you going?

Steve *goes after* **Dan**.

Trish *comes out of Yates's, carrying a drunken* **Donna***, who has been throwing up. She takes* **Donna** *to a corner, where she is sick again.*

Trish   Are you done now? Get up. Donna? Get up. I'll fucking leave you here. Get up!

Donna *retches.*

Trish   On my shoes!

Donna (*slurring her words*)   Just leave me, man.

Trish   Stupid cow.

She decides to leave **Donna** *where she is, and walks back to Yates's, when she almost crashes into* **Ben***, who is coming out.*

Trish   Yes?

Ben   You alright?

Trish   Do I look?

Ben   Forget it.

Trish   Div.

Ben   Shit.

Trish *goes back inside.* **Ben** *goes to find* **Jamie***.*

Steve *is bringing* **Dan** *back towards the van.*

Steve   Come back 'ere, you moany sod, put yer face back. Wass all this? I know what will cheer you up.

Dan   Is that right, Steve?

Steve   I'm always right.

Tony *grabs one of* **Lenny***'s sauce bottles to squirt* **Steve** *with.*

Steve   Fuck off, Tone!

Lenny   Oi! Find somewhere else to fuck about. Yer bad for business.

The boys move.

Steve   So, you want to hear it then?

Dan   Come on, genius.

Steve   You know I've been banging Clare, yeah? Trish's mate.

Dan   And?

Steve   Girl's a walking tap, bro, I can turn her on and off whenever I like. I left her panting in Yates's man . . .

Dan (*restless*)   Yeah, and?

Steve   She was coming out with all kinds of shit to me, how she heard Hannah telling that Trish in the toilets that she and Jamie are loved up now, that they were out here dancing, that he's scared about going. Truly.

Tony   Pussy boy.

Steve   So get Jamie, tell them you got proof Hannah's a dirty little big-mouth slapper.

Dan   And that's it?

Steve   It'll be a laugh.

Dan   That's your master plan, is it, Steve?

Steve   What else we gonna do?

Dan (*sighs*)   Absolutely nothing.

Dan *goes.* **Jamie** *enters with* **Ben**.

Ben   Dancing?

Jamie   She wants to see me again.

Ben   You were dancing?

Jamie   Yeah.

Ben   Out here?

Jamie   I'm mad up for her, Ben, I am.

Ben   You're flying out on Tuesday.

Jamie   And when I do, I'll be thinking of her. Big smile on my face.

Ben   Yer drooling.

Jamie   And you. Trish? You still wanna sex her?

Ben   She's a loudmouth sket.

Jamie   Who wants to sex you.

Ben   No. Yeah?

Jamie   The way you were looking at each other, not looking at each other. Like everyone else is stupid, we can't see it. Why'd you dump her?

Ben   Shut up about her. Look, this is our last night. So get jiggy with it. Let's get on with summin.

Jamie *empties his can of beer all over* **Ben**.

Jamie   Shower!

Ben   You bastard.

He wrestles **Jamie** *to the ground.* **Dan** *enters, he stands over them, looking jealous.*

Ben   What, you come back?

Dan   No, I'm still at home, Ben. Bin looking for yer.

Ben   Found me.

Dan   Calling me cunt all night, wass that about? Eh? Ben?

Ben   What?

Dan   Do you hate me?

Ben   No more drugs for this man.

Dan (*snaps*)   Look, it was a poxy little march.

Ben   So why'd you go on it then? Why?

Dan   Cos I believed in it.

Ben   Pussy is what you believe in, and plenty of it. You don't know what you believe.

Dan   So what do you?

Jamie   Have him, Ben.

Ben (*at* **Dan**)   You stinking student lamo.

Dan   Here we go.

Ben   Go get a job.

Dan   Every time!

Ben   Stop robbing us of our taxes.

Jamie   Robbing cunt!

Dan   What do you believe, Ben?

Jamie   Slap him.

Dan   Tell me.

Ben   Saddam's a cunt, alright?

Dan   And that is it? Saddam's a cunt?

Jamie   He is a cunt!

Dan   Why is he a cunt?

Jamie   Cos he's got a big moustache.

Dan   Ben?

Jamie   You grow a tache that big, yer up to summin.

Dan   What was he arrested for? What are his crimes? How was he in breach of UN regulations? (*Sighs.*) You don't even know.

Ben   Do you?

Dan   Yeah, as it goes.

Jamie   Have him!

Dan   If you want, I'll tell yer.

Ben   Don't do that.

Dan   At least know what you're fighting for.

Ben   Don't look down at me like I'm thick.

Dan   I'm not, mate, that's in yer head!

Jamie   Thinks yer stupid.

Ben   You think I'm stupid!

Dan   I think you're going there to get bitch slapped. Ain't you scared?

Ben   Ain't scared of anything.

Dan   Talk to me.

Ben   I want beer!

Dan *grabs* **Jamie**'s *can, he gulps most of it down.*

Jamie (*grabs it back*)   Oi, oi, put the brakes on.

Dan   This is how you wanna play it, Ben, wid yer little boy here?

Jamie   Excuse?

Dan   Giving it large?

Ben   Piss off, why don't yer!

Dan   When I'm ready.

Ben   Fucking student.

Trish, *followed by* **Hannah** *and* **Clare**, *come out of Yates's to try and lift* **Donna** *up.*

Dan   A little bird's been saying you loving up Hannah, J.

Jamie   Mos def!

Dan   You wanna lower yourself with that slag?

Ben   Shut yer mouth, Dan.

Dan   Dan now, is it, not cunt?

Jamie   Say slag again, I dare yer.

Ben   Why don't you just go?

Dan   Just thought he had a right to know.

Jamie   Know what?

Dan   I couldn't it believe it when I heard.

Ben   Don't fuck about.

Dan   Bitch bin flapping her mouth. Telling everyone how shit-scared you are about going. Dancing together, out here. Bin telling Trish. Laughing their tits off in Yates's they were.

They stride over towards the chip van. **Steve** *and* **Tony** *are there, eating their burger and chips, playfully throwing their chips at each other.*

Trish   Come on!

Ben (*sees the girls trying to lift* **Donna**)   Oi, oi, lezzer show!

Trish   Wank somewhere else, you turd.

Hannah (*sees* **Jamie** *approaching*)   Jamie?

Jamie   You skank-faced bitch!

Hannah   Jamie?

Trish   Excuse!

Jamie   I told you things.

Hannah   I know you did.

Jamie   So why you open yer mouth to her? Yer lucky I don't drop yer!

Lenny   Hey!

Jamie   Bitch.

Trish (*threatening*)   Say that one more time.

Jamie   What, bitch?

Lenny   Hold yer tongue, boy, do it now.

Ben   Leave it, J.

Lenny   You don't talk to my girl like that, not in front of me.

Hannah   Why are you doing this?

Jamie   I told you things.

Dan   She's bin telling everyone how scared he is, bin broadcasting it.

Hannah   I never.

Dan   So how come she knows?

Hannah   Trish?

Trish   I never breathed a word.

Jamie   You love to laugh at me.

Hannah   Don't blame me cos yer scared.

Jamie   Slapper.

Hannah   Wanker.

Lenny   Don't, love.

Hannah   Why?

Lenny   Come on.

Lenny *takes* **Hannah** *away*.

Jamie (*calls*)   Hannah the slapper.

Trish   Oi!

Jamie   I danced wid her! I bloody danced.

Ben   Yeah, alright, J.

Jamie   You calling me a liar, Ben?

Ben   What?

Jamie   You calling me?

Ben   Shut up, you fool.

Trish   Talking shit about my cousin, I'm not having that.

Ben (*sees* **Dan** *grinning*)   What you grinning at?

Dan   You just didn't wanna know. (*Sneers.*) Fast food.

Ben   What?

Dan (*calls*)   Tell him, Len.

Ben   What?

Dan *leaves, followed by* **Tony**.

Clare (*aside*)   Did you fucking tell him?

Steve   Tell him what?

Clare   Steve!

Steve   Shut up.

Steve *goes.* **Clare** *follows.*

Ben (*bemused*)   What, what the fuck? (*Sees* **Trish** *staring.*) What?

Trish (*mimics*)   What?

Ben   What?

Trish   What!

Ben   Well . . .

Trish   Well?

Ben   You know.

Trish   Do I?

Ben   Yeah.

Trish   Right. I know.

Ben   You know?

Trish   I know.

Ben   You know. What do you know?

Trish   I know how you feel.

Ben   You know how I feel?

Trish   Yeah.

Ben   Good.

Trish   Right.

Ben   I know how you feel.

Trish   Good.

Ben   Right.

Trish   I always knew.

Ben   Always knew too.

Trish   Oh for fuck . . .

She lunges at him. They kiss like animals. **Ben** *tries to put his hand up her skirt.*

Trish (*stops*)   Easy, tiger.

Ben   You love to tease.

Trish   Calm it.

Ben   I'll calm you. Cussing me down in front of my mates, what was that?

Trish   Foreplay.

Ben   It does my head in.

Trish   Cos I know how you think.

Ben   How do I think?

Trish   Yer too easy, too horny. What, more?

Ben   Much more. (*Holds her hand.*)

Trish   Yer talking bollocks. Last chance to get yer end away before you go.

Ben   I'm going to Basra.

Trish   I know.

Ben   Mother of all rucks over there.

Trish   So I hear.

Ben   When the shit goes down, I'm getting more than a bloody nose, guaranteed.

Trish   Probably are, yeah.

Ben   I'm not that lucky, never have been.

Trish   You are not getting into my knickers, Ben.

Ben   You don't wear any. I'm leaving Wednesday.

Trish   My problem how?

Ben   Come on, you gotta give summin.

Trish *giggles*.

Ben   You know how long it's been? How long it's gonna be? I am gasping.

Trish (*grabs his crotch*)   Here, that's something.

Ben   For starters.

Trish   I'll spank yer arse for yer? You know what I'm like.

Ben   I know what yer like.

Trish   Good.

Ben (*grabs her*)   Come here.

Trish   Down, boy.

Ben   Don't prick-tease.

Trish   Fight Jamie.

Ben   What?

Trish   Beat the shit out of him.

Ben   I can't.

Trish   You will.

Ben   Why?

Trish   Talking to my cousin like that, thinking he can get away with it, you all do. Like yer big men, yer wankers!

Ben   He's off his head.

Trish   So give him a slap.

Ben   You're a right sort.

Trish   I could say it was the Smirnoff Ice, but I'll be lying. Look at me. You need someone – (*taps side of his head*) in here. Cos you ain't got no one else. That's what yer asking me, yeah? Isn't it? Ben?

Ben   What?

Trish   I'm saying yes to you. Look at me, don't laugh. I'm saying yes. That proves yer worth it, now you prove I'm worth it.

Ben   He shouldn't have said it.

Trish   And he's gonna know about it.

*A still drunken **Donna** has woken up, she staggers over to **Trish** and **Ben**.*

Donna   Wass 'appening? What? What?

Trish *and* **Ben** *walk away.*

Donna   What? Trish?

*They exit. Enter **Steve** and **Tony**, who find a corner to throw up in.*

Steve   'Ere, Tony, fancy having a nice greasy dripping kebab afterwards?

*The thought of this makes **Tony** throw up even more.*

Tony   Bastard.

Steve (*sees something*)   Oi oi, eyes front.

Tony *and* **Steve** *see an attractive-looking young woman passing their way.* **Steve** *whispers something in* **Tony***'s ear. He laughs.*

Steve   'Scuse us, love, me and my friend were wondering if you could help us out here.

Tony   We were both wondering if you could give us marks out of ten.

They both unzip their flies, but the woman darts off before they can whip out their dicks.

Hold up, you ain't even sampled the merchandise.

Steve   Come on, lick the stick!

The two friends laugh their heads off, then find a wall to piss on. **Tony** *deliberately pisses on* **Steve** *'s shoes.*

Steve   Fuck off!

Enter **Gail***, followed by* **Vince***.*

Tony   How about Jamie, eh, losing it like that.

Steve   Crying like a bitch, he was. Clare too. Going on about me betraying her. I goes, 'Shut up,' give her a slap.

Gail   Evening, gents.

Tony   Britney!

Steve   Come on, Gail – (*pulls his trousers and pants down*) spank my arse.

Gail   Oh, nice.

Vince   I hate weekends.

Gail   Trousers up, big boy.

Steve   What?

Vince   We're nicking yer.

Tony   Little bitta arse, man.

Gail   It's indecent exposure.

Vince   Not allowed.

Gail   And that's not all you've been showing, is it? Two men, matching your vitals, have been seen in this area, getting their cocks out for the ladies.

Tony I bet you'd love a nice big cock, innit, Britney?

Gail Yes, keep digging.

Tony I wished I had a black cock!

Steve You mean you wish you had a cock.

Gail Who were you calling a bitch just now? Who did you slap? I hope it wasn't Clare, Steve.

Tony You know Clare?

Gail I know her brother.

Tony Has Clare's brother got a big cock? Is my cock as big as his?

Gail You'd wish.

Tony Britney's getting nasty here.

Vince Stand still.

Gail Why don't you tell Britney all about it?

Tony Dan was up for it.

Gail Dan?

Tony Wanted to get back at Ben?

Gail And what's that got to do with Clare?

Steve It's got nothing to do with Clare.

Tony It's about pussy boy.

Gail Who is pussy boy?

Tony Jamie.

Gail Who's Jamie?

Steve Soldier boy.

Tony The pussy!

Vince Move.

They all exit. Enter **Jamie** *followed by* **Ben**.

Ben   You gotta take it back, J.

Jamie   No.

Ben   Trish is offering herself on a plate here.

Jamie   My problem how?

Ben   If I don't get any sex tonight, I'm gonna shoot meself. On my life! Look, what if I juss give you a little slap, won't hurt.

Jamie   You can try.

Ben   Don't make me hurt you, J.

Jamie   Excuse?

Ben   I am gasping.

Jamie *(scoffs)*   Don't mug yerself.

Ben *(lunges at him)*   Take it back.

Trish, **Donna** *and* **Clare** *enter*.

Trish   Is he still breathing?

Jamie   Oh hear it?

Trish   Wass he say?

Ben   J?

Jamie   No!

Ben   Last chance.

Trish   What you waiting for? Kick his arse!

Enter **Gail**, *followed by* **Vince**.

Gail   Hey, do you all want to step back now, please? Come on.

Ben   Britney!

Jamie   Wass up!

Clare   What you doing, Gail?

Gail   My job? Now, now, what's all this?

Jamie   She's a slapper. Hannah, the slapper!

Ben   Take it back.

Gail   Excuse me! Now, I'm just guessing here, but this wouldn't have anything to do with Steve, now would it? Clare?

Clare   What . . . what you looking at me for?

Gail   A little bird tells me that you're the one who can shed some light on this.

Clare   No.

Gail   Clare?

Clare   Girl mad.

Gail   Clare!

Trish   What do you know?

Clare   Nothing.

Trish   I will knock yer teeth out.

Gail   Oi!

Clare (*to* **Gail**)   I don't know what my brother sees in you.

Trish   What do you know?

Clare   Alright, it was me, I heard you and her talking in the loos – (*points at* **Jamie**) 'bout him.

Trish   And you kept yer mouth quiet all this time?

Clare   I didn't want you starting on me, yer always starting on me.

Trish (*to* **Jamie**)   Oi, Dumbo? You got summin to say?

Jamie   I just got mad.

Trish   Tell her that.

Jamie   Fuck off.

Jamie *goes,* **Ben** *follows.*

Trish (*to* **Clare**)   I'm so gonna kill you.

Gail   Excuse me, love.

Trish   And they call this one Britney?

Gail   Careful, sweetheart.

Trish   Girl love herself.

Gail   You really wanna try summin?

Vince   Leave it out, Gail.

Trish   Yes, leave it out, Gail.

Gail   Start walking.

Trish *and the girls walk.*

Clare   I said I was sorry!

They exit. Enter **Jamie** *and* **Ben**.

Ben   Yer losing it! Yer nuffink but a little boy. What you trying to do to me?

Jamie   I was telling her things.

Ben   And I was this much from getting some tonight, thank you.

Jamie   So what now? Ben?

Ben   I don't fucking know! I ain't Jesus! Jamie, I don't wanna think about where we're going, alright?

Jamie   You like Trish?

Ben   J, I need her. So go on, piss yerself, have a giraffe. Way it is, there you go.

Jamie   You think Hannah's pretty?

Ben   Yes, Hannah's pretty.

Trish *and* **Hannah** *approach.*

Hannah   She's only bin taking on Britney.

Trish   She's a bitch.

Ben   Bad girl, Trish.

Trish   I can be good.

Ben   Is it?

Trish   No more games.

Ben   Trish . . . I need . . .

Trish   Me as well.

Jamie *nervously approaches* **Hannah**.

Lenny (*to* **Jamie**)   You mind yer manners!

Jamie   I'm sorry, yeah. Hannah?

Hannah *clips* **Jamie** *around the head. She does it again, then again, each hit gets harder and harder.* **Jamie** *shields himself.*

Jamie   What?!

Hannah   You think dem Iraqis are bad, J, try me.

Jamie   I still want to see you.

Hannah   Yer seeing me now.

Hannah *takes* **Jamie**'s *hand.* **Jamie** *stares over at* **Ben** *who is with* **Trish**. **Ben** *stares back.*

Blackout.

On the Side of the Angels

Characters

Ben, *early twenties*
Brookes, *late twenties*
Sean, *early twenties*
Jamie, *early twenties*

Scene One

Darkness, except for a large video screen showing static.

Voice from screen come on! You fucking piece of . . .
come on . . .

The screen continues to flicker, until the audience can see **Ben** *standing
(in uniform) facing the screen, talking to his video camcorder.*

Ben Is it on? (*Checks.*) Yes! (*Speaking directly to the camera.*)
Right, right.

Ben *starts walking backwards, to reveal the army barracks.*

(*Speaking to the camera*) How yo doing, Trish? You alright?
So, here I am, my first week, not so bad. Everyone's bin
saying, it really kicks off here, but I can't see it. Keep this
up, it'll be a piece of piss. (*Beginning to get distracted by some
noises coming from the barracks.*) We're out on patrol most
hours. (*Aside.*) Oi, will you shut up, I'm talking . . . Fucking
kids here, sorry, babe . . . (*Aside.*) Shut the fuck up! (*Takes out
a photo from his pocket.*) Got yer photo. (*Chuckles.*) You are a
dirty bitch, you know that. Who took this picture? Better
not be Dan, or Steve, it better be one of them timer things
. . . (*He hears more noise, this time Rap music.*) For fuck's sake . . .
Anyhows, I'm putting it to good use, every night, toilets, you
know what I'm saying? Course you do. (*Blows kiss, laughs
again.*) Dirty bitch.

Brookes, **Sean** *and* **Jamie** *appear on screen, dancing. They are
slowly creeping up behind* **Ben**. **Sean** *grabs* **Ben***'s head and plants
a kiss on his cheek.* **Brookes** *swipes the photo out of* **Ben***'s hand.*

Ben Jesus . . .

Brookes (*sees picture*) . . . Whoa! . . . Fucking hell!

Ben Pass my picture back!

Jamie (*speaking to camera*) Yo, people of the UK! Wass up!

Sean Wass up!

Ben *is now chasing* **Brookes** *around the barracks, coming in and out of view of the screen.*

Brookes   This is Trish?

Ben   Brookes!

Brookes (*faces camera*)   Trish? You dat?

Sean   This is Sean, C-boy, Curtis broadcasting to the nation!

Ben   C-boy?

Brookes   Cunt boy!

Sean   Now don't you go worrying about a thing, UK, we're looking after your interests here, on the side of the angels, telling the Arabs, to their faces, yeah, 'Oi, we're British, behave yerselves!'

Ben   Pass my picture, Brookes!

Brookes   Pass my picture, Sarge, you lickle rass.

Jamie *is passed the photo.*

Jamie (*shows* **Sean**)   Say hello to Ben's woman.

Sean   Whoa! Well, hello there, Ben's woman. What's a fine, big-titted woman like you doing with pussy boy here?

Brookes *is playfully gagging* **Ben** *with his hands.*

Sean   You wanna piece of this, Trish? (*Places a rolled-up sleeping bag between his legs.*)

Brookes   You call that a piece? (*Shoves* **Sean** *out of the picture.*) Move! See, Trish.

Sean *starts dancing, then sits his arse on* **Ben***'s face.*

Brookes   Fart on him . . .

A muffled **Ben** *tries to break free.*

Brookes   As I was saying, his piece was nuttin, ain't worth time or effort, but this however . . . (*Unzips his trousers.*) Now you see, Trish, what we have here is a magnificent thick specimen of pure Harlesden prime, ripe blacksnake. Please, observe, don't fain't now . . . (*Smells the fart.*) . . . Oh man!

Ben (*waves the air*)   Jesus!

Jamie   Jesus, Sean!

Sean (*giggling*)   You said fart on him.

Ben   . . . 'S that curry . . .

*He breaks free of **Sean**'s grasp and pulls **Brookes** backwards before he can get his dick out. They continue to roll around playfully on the floor.*

Sean (*faces camera*)   Makes you proud to be British, don't it? Anyhow, don't worry about them two, Trish, nuttin but kids, C-boy will look after you.

Ben/Brookes   Cunt boy!

Sean   I'll show you a cunt . . . Hold him down . . .

Brookes   Hold him down, Sarge!

Sean (*to **Ben***)   You my bitch now.

Sean *puts the sleeping bag between his legs, stands behind **Ben** who is now bent over, he simulates having anal sex with him. **Ben** is trying to break free but is laughing.*

Brookes   Scream, bitch!

Sean   Too big!

Ben   Too small.

Sean   'How very dare you.'

Ben   'Me, dear? No, dear.'

Jamie   Look at that. I bet you didn't know he loves taking it up the 'arris, Trish!

Ben *manages to break free. He stands up, takes a kung fu pose.*

Brookes   Yes, you want some?

Sean   You want some?

Ben (*adopts terrible Chinese accent*)   Wat yu say, black boy? You take piss!

Brookes   Take this, you boomba!

Sound of a distant explosion from outside.

Sean   Whoa!

Jamie   Fucking mortars!

Brookes   Hey, chill.

Sound of another explosion.

Brookes   Right, come on. On yer feet, man!

Ben *goes, followed by* **Sean**.

Ben   Sorry to cut this short, babes, but it looks like we're gonna be seeing some action already. Oh, yes!

Brookes (*off camera*)   Yo, Ben!

Ben   Coming! Love yer, don't worry, my luck's in. (*Waves photo.*) Got you, dirty bitch!

Brookes   Pearce!

Ben   Hold yer water.

Ben *blows a kiss, turns the camera off. Video screen is blank.*

Scene Two

Five months later. Basra, southern Iraq. An alleyway. Early evening.

Sounds of massive gunfire. **Ben** *and* **Jamie** *come running. They take cover behind a wall.*

Ben   You alright, Jamie?

Jamie   I'm alright! Jesus!

Ben   Well, fucking answer me then.

Jamie   I juss did.

Ben   Them Ali Babas are summin else, ain't they? Fuck! They've got balls, I'll give them that. Coming at us. We can't stay here for long, we gotta go, you ready?

Jamie   Sarge was behind.

Ben   Sarge is dead.

Jamie   He was right behind us, Ben. He musta seen us head here.

Ben   So where is he?

Jamie   I dunno. But he was right behind, Sean as well, we can't just –

Ben   Alright, we'll wait. Two minutes. Load. Load!

Jamie   I'm loading.

Ben   Over there.

Jamie *slowly crawls over to where* **Ben** *was pointing.*

Ben   Quietly.

Jamie   Nuh, really?!

Ben   Don't get arsey, J, time and place, alright? It's too quiet.

Jamie   I like it this way.

Ben   Why?

Jamie   They're as wired as we are.

Ben   You think so?

Jamie   Must be.

Ben *squats down. Then he slowly crawls along the ground like a snake to reach the edge of the wall, and very slowly lifts his head up to see. Then he lowers his head and begins crawling slowly and quietly back towards* **Jamie**.

Ben   Alone at last, eh, J?

Jamie   Yeah.

Ben   You and me side by side again, eh? Bin a while.

Jamie   You got me mistaken for someone else?

Ben   You've bin at it for days, mate.

Jamie   At what?

Ben   I come in a room, you go out, every time.

Jamie   No.

Ben   Yes. Don't lie.

Jamie   I don't know what yer saying.

Ben   You gonna look at me. Even now, are you ever gonna look at me?

Jamie *slowly turns his head to look at* **Ben**.

Ben   That's it. Show us your handsome! Beginning to forget.

Jamie (*looks away*)   What you going on about, Ben?

Ben   You ain't looked at me proper for days, J.

Jamie   I reckon all this heat is turning you gay, mate.

Ben   Look at me, J.

Jamie   I juss did.

Ben   So look again.

Jamie   You really know how to pick yer moments.

Ben (*snaps*)   I said, fucking look. (*Kicks.*)

Jamie *turns to look at* **Ben** *again*.

Jamie   Happy? Now, can we get on with saving our lives?

Ben   Dan was right about you.

Jamie   Dan?

Ben   Yer nuttin but a little runt, always hanging around, playing the bad man. Ain't playing now, are yer? Don't know what yer doing.

Jamie   Are you gone?

Ben   Pissing yerself! Need me now, eh, watch yer sodding back for yer!

Jamie   What is yer problem?

Ben   No, what is *yer* problem, J? Why did you freeze back there?

Jamie   I didn't.

Ben   Fucking saw yer.

Jamie   Fucking cracked.

Ben   What was yer problem, J?

Jamie   I don't have a problem.

Ben   You think I'm blind? Do you think yer better than me? Than all of us?

Jamie   No.

Ben   So, what?

Jamie   Jesus!

Ben   So, what, J? You a soldier or what?

Jamie   You call that being a soldier?

Ben   Oh, so what are you now, some fucking liberal?

Jamie   I ain't no liberal, I ain't like that.

Ben   Good, cos I'll put a bullet in you right now, save them the trouble.

Jamie   I'll kick the head of any cunt that's coming at me, Ben, you know that.

Ben There you go then.

Jamie But he weren't coming at yer.

Ben Yes he was.

Jamie He was a kid.

Ben He was coming at me like the rest of them, like these are now.

Jamie Like that geezer in the cell?

Ben Oh, fucking knew it. How many more times?

Jamie I'm juss sayin'. None of this . . .

Ben What?

Jamie It ain't what I thought.

Ben No shit?

Jamie Friday night it ain't.

Ben You think too much. They're all the same. That's how you got to see them, that's all that matters, use yer head. Don't pussy out on me, cos I ain't watching the back of no pussy.

Jamie What you saying?

Ben You want out of here alive? Go back to Hannah? When I tell you to shoot, you shoot, when I tell you to hold an Iraqi down, you . . . Don't ever say no to me again, not out here.

Jamie Ben?

Ben Don't Ben me!

Jamie What's happened to yer?

Ben Yer thinking again. Stop it. Now, what was that kid doing, J? Answer me.

Jamie (*gives in*) He was coming at yer. He gave them the signal.

Ben   Yer learning!

Sean *and* **Brookes** *come running on.* **Sean** *is clutching the side of his neck.*

Jamie   Oh man, I thought that was it, I swear!

Brookes   Where'd you go?

Ben   Here of course.

Brookes   Thought you were dead.

Ben   Me as well.

Brookes   Shame that.

Ben   What, you gonna cry now?

Brookes   You best back off, Ben, cos I've had a really shitty day. (*To* **Sean**.) You hit? Are you hit? Sean, are you hit?

Sean   It fucking hurts.

Brookes   Ah, shit.

Sean   Oh God! I'm dying.

Brookes   Hey!

Sean   I'm gonna fucking die. I know.

Brookes   Hey, yungsta, you don't know shit, so just hold on to yerself, yeah? Peace!

Sean   Oh, why don't you just fuck off with all of that black talk, Brookes?

Brookes   No, it's fuck off with all that black talk, Sarge!

Sean   We're gonna die, innit?

Ben   Not today.

Sean   I got blood on me. I'm hit.

Jamie   You ain't dead yet, Sean.

Sean   Fucking dying.

Brookes   You don't know shit. Now look at me, look at me, Sean, that's an order. You don't know shit. Say it.

Sean   You don't know shit.

Brookes   No, no, you say it, you don't know shit.

Sean   I just did.

Brookes   'I don't know shit.'

Sean   I know you don't.

Brookes   Don't wind me up, bwoi.

Sean   I ain't.

Brookes   I'll rephrase.

Sean   You what?

Brookes   Say what I say, exactly what I say! 'I don't know shit.'

Sean   I don't know shit.

Brookes   'I ain't gonna die.'

Sean   I ain't gonna die.

Brookes   Believe.

Sean   Believe.

Brookes   You didn't need to say that bit.

Sean   You didn't need to say that bit.

Brookes   You can stop now.

Sean   You can stop now.

Brookes   Sean?

Sean   Sean?

Brookes   Don't wind me up. (*Sighs.*) Fuck it, where are we?

Ben   You know we can't stay here.

Brookes *nods.*

Sean   Did you see Lee? Did you see him call for backup?

Brookes   Dunno.

Sean   Did he call for backup? Before he –

Brookes   I said I don't know. Are you deaf?

Ben *can feel* **Brookes** *staring at him.*

Ben   What!

Brookes (*to* **Sean**)   Still hurts? Let me see.

Sean   Iraqis, man, cheeky fuckers.

Ben   We were juss saying, innit, J? Fuckin' lowlifes.

Sean (*panting*)   I wanna go home.

Brookes (*examines his wound*)   You wanna slap.

Sean   Easy!

Brookes   It's just a nick you got, a cut! Little piece of sodding shrapnel. You need a microscope to see it.

Sean   But I got blood.

Brookes   It's not yours.

Sean   Kevin's? Oh God, it's Kevin's all over me –

Brookes   Will you just shut up and let me think, please!

He is breathing heavily.

Sean   What are you doing?

Brookes   I'm thinking!

Brookes *glares over again at* **Ben** *and* **Jamie**.

Ben   Is he gonna propose?

Jamie   Leave it, Ben.

Ben　What, Brookes?

Brookes　It's what, Sarge, you stupid motherfucker.

Sean　I can see blood.

Brookes　It's not yer blood, how many more times?

Sean　I meant you. Yer bleeding. Oh man, you got hit, didn't yer?

Ben　You got hit, Sarge?

Sean　And there's me crying.

Brookes　Look, don't worry yerselves, I'm alright. Get off me.

Sean　This is fucked up. They fucked us up, big time.

Jamie　You don't say, Sean.

Brookes　Anyone see that kid? Anyone? You know you saw it.

Jamie　We know we saw it.

Ben　We just don't wanna talk about it.

Brookes　How old you reckon he was, Sean? Ten?

Sean　Twelve.

Brookes　How can you be so sure?

Sean　He was the same height as my brother. Looked like him as well – he was always running around with a bloody football in his hands, wearing that stupid Arsenal top.

Brookes　Eh, you have a problem with Arsenal now?

Sean　I do, as it goes.

Brookes　Oh Jesus, you are, innit, a Spurs man, you are, a fucking Spurs man, I can smell it.

Sean　Eat shit and die.

Brookes *winces with pain.*

Sean   Sarge?

Jamie   Ah man, he's a mess.

Brookes (*slaps his hand away*)   Don't.

Sean   Just let me see, will yer?

Brookes   A Spurs supporter! Don't tell me God ain't got a sense of humour.

Sean   We can't stay here.

Brookes   Did you see Lee radio for backup? Did he have time?

Jamie   Yes, he did.

Brookes   Well, deh you go, problem solved. That was ten minutes ago, they'll be here any sec. We just hang tight here, till they come.

Sean   What if the fucking sand-niggers come before then?

Brookes   Hey!

Sean   I didn't say 'nigger'.

Brookes   A white boy don't say the 'N'-word in front of a brudda from Harlesden, not unless he wants a slow, painful death.

Sean   What are we waiting for? Let's just go.

Brookes   Just be quiet.

Ben   The sarge is right. We should wait.

Sean   The sarge's gut is all shot up.

Ben (*sees*)   Well, that's it, we can't move him in that condition.

Brookes   Fuck you, and your mum.

Ben   What's your problem?

Brookes   This, this is all your bloody fault!

Sean Hold it down!

Brookes You open fire when I give the order, do you understand?

Sean (*worried he'll be heard*) Sarge!

Brookes You cease fire when I give the order, do you understand? Are you hearing me?

Ben The whole of Basra can hear you.

Sean (*panicking*) Shush!

They look around, nervous that someone may have heard them. **Ben** *crawls along the ground to the edge of the wall again and tilts his head up. He turns to the others, shakes his head – no one is there. He crawls his way back.*

Sean Lie back, Sarge.

Brookes Piss off.

Ben Maggots.

Brookes Excuse me?

Ben Those kids, they're nothing but maggots. Their fucking dads are maggots. It was probably their same fucking maggot dads that jumped us. They're not people, they aren't human, they are the enemy, alright? I bin here six months, I ain't losing my life here, they can fuck off with that. Right or wrong, J?

Brookes Yer bleedin mad.

Ben (*presses*) J? Tell him.

Jamie (*cowers*) That kid was signalling to them.

Brookes Who asked you to speak?

Jamie I saw him.

Ben Thank you, J.

Jamie   When he dropped that ball, that was their sign to open fire. Ben got in there first.

Ben   Thank you!

Brookes   Now, when you've quite finished sucking him off, how about the truth?

Jamie   It *is* the truth.

Brookes   My arse!

Ben   Cry all you like, boy, I saved yer life.

Brookes   Did you just call me boy? Pass my gun.

Sean   Sarge?

Brookes   I'm gonna shoot him.

Sean   Be quiet!

Ben   Look, I told them to get out of the way, three times, I told them. You fucking blind or what, Sean? You saw it as well.

Sean   He did, Sarge.

Brookes   Oh, that makes it alright?

Sean   Will you just be quiet?

Ben   If they had done what they were told, they'd still be out there, playing with their ball.

Brookes   Kids!

Ben   Maggots.

Brookes   Pass my gun.

Sean   Here then, go on, shoot him, tell them where we are, bring a whole fucking tribe down on us, Brookes.

Brookes   You call me Sarge.

Sean   Oh, have a day off, will yer?

Brookes Every time you lot don't listen to me, you know
. . . It's one more thing I'm reporting in back at base, I'm
making a list, so, watch it, all of yer.

They sit in silence for a while and wait, jumping, especially **Sean**, *at
the slightest sound being made.* **Ben** *decides he cannot take much more
of this. The waiting is killing him. He crawls his way back to the edge
again.*

Ben Come on, come on , where's the cavalry!

Sean Backup is on its way, isn't it? Yes?

Jamie Lee made the call. I saw him.

Sean But we got jumped, what, fifteen minutes ago? So
where the fuck are they? They should be here by now.

Ben They're coming, so calm it, yeah?

Brookes *groans in pain.*

Ben Shut him up.

Sean He needs a medic.

Brookes Bloody Spurs man!

Sean 'You'll never win the title.'

Brookes Changed my mind, I'm shooting you. (*Winces in
pain.*)

Sean You gotta be quiet, Sarge.

Brookes Do you have any idea how painful this is?

Ben Talk to him about summin, take his mind off it.

Sean Hey, Sarge, did I ever tell you about my girlfriend,
Sarge? Did I tell you?

Brookes Yes, Pearce, you've told me.

Ben And me.

Sean Justine.

Brookes   Yeah, Justine.

Sean   She's a fucking whore.

Ben   The biggest whore.

Brookes   The queen of whores.

Sean   Dumping me. I'll dump all over her when I get back.

Brookes   Yes, Sean, you see? Not if we get back, but when we get back, yer learning.

Ben   Any one of those bastards come through here, I'm gonna kill them.

Brookes   Yes, cos yer such a big man, innit, Pearce?

Ben   Keep him quiet, Sean.

Sean   Wanna see her picture, Sarge – of Justine?

Brookes   Gwan den.

Sean *shows him.*

Sean   Nice, ain't she? (*Checks* **Brookes**'s *face.*) What? What?

Brookes   Nothing.

Sean   Say it.

Brookes   I'm not sure you want me to, mate.

Sean   I know what you're going to say.

Brookes   Is it?

Sean   I get it all the time. Or should I say, she gets it.

Brookes   Oh yeah, I bet she gets it.

Sean   Used to make me feel sweet, you know. I'm out with my woman, guys are all staring, checking her.

Brookes   Nice one, Sean.

Sean   Come on, say it.

Brookes   I ain't in the mood for wind-ups.

Sean   No wind-up. Say it. I know what you want to say. I can tell. She looks just like her, yeah?

Brookes   No.

Sean   No?

Brookes   No.

Sean   You telling me she don't look like her?

Brookes   I ain't telling you she don't look her, I'm telling you it is her.

Sean   Yes, Justine, my girl.

Brookes   That's your girlfriend?

Sean   Telling yer.

Brookes   Yer telling me bollocks.

Sean   Look, if you don't want to believe me, that's up to you. You can fuck off, do what you want, I don't care. I'm just telling you this, sharing with you, pass the fucking time.

Brookes   Calm down.

Sean   You calm down, you fuck off.

Ben   Shut up, what's the matter with you?

Brookes (*snatches picture*)   Gimme that. Tell me who that is.

Ben and **Jamie** *crawl back to see.*

Ben   Victoria Beckham.

Brookes   Thank you.

Ben   For what?

Brookes   Geezer's mad.

Sean   Telling him about my girl.

Ben   Are you saying this is your girl, Sean?

Sean   Yeah.

Jamie   This is Justine? The one you've bin boring the arse off us with for the last six months?

Sean   See, already I know what you're going to say as well.

Jamie   Justine, is Victoria Beckham, your girl?

Sean   Nah, don't be stupid. I'm telling you, she looks like Victoria Beckham.

Brookes   She *is* Victoria Beckham.

Sean   Nah, man.

Brookes   Nah, Sarge!

Sean   She gets it all the time, that's what I'm telling him.

Brookes   Cut it out, Sean.

Sean   What? I show you a picture of my girl, and you get all arsey.

Brookes   It's Victoria fucking Beckham!

Sean   She *looks* like her. Honest to God. That's how we got together. We were at school, I said she looked like Posh, she was well happy, she thought she was ugly, I goes, nuh, you mad? I bought her Posh's first album on CD.

Jamie   But now she's freeing it up for some other man.

Sean   The whore. I'll stop it.

Brookes   Talking shit, is what you should stop.

Sean   I hear summin.

The boys get down as they can hear distant voices. **Ben** *crawls back to the edge.*

Sean   Is it them? Ben?

Ben   Shut up! (*Looks.*) Ain't them.

Sean   Where the fuck are they then?

Brookes   They're coming!

Sean   Our lot ain't coming, are they? Are they?

Brookes   Sean?

Sean   They should be here by now.

Brookes   They're looking for us.

Sean   Fuck it, I say fuck it, let's go!

Brookes   Hey, in yer dreams, yungsta.

Sean   That's a fucking mob coming for us, isn't it?

Brookes   If yer get lost, you don't make yourself even more lost. You sit yer arse down, make it easy for our lot to find you.

Sean   How are they going to find us? How are we gonna tell them?

Brookes   I dunno, alright, I don't know.

Sean   Well, fuck it then, we go. Make a run for it.

Brookes   I make the decisions.

Sean   Ben? J?

Brookes   Sean, I'm warning you . . .

Sean   Fuck's sake, come on.

Ben   Sarge can't be moved. He'll be dead before we make ten yards.

Brookes   Since when you get all compassionate?

Sean   Or he could die just lying there.

Brookes   What did you say?

Sean   Nuttin.

Brookes   You fucking gutless little prick.

Sean   I ain't wrong though.

Brookes   You ain't leaving.

Ben   Meaning we ain't leaving you.

Brookes   You shut yer mouth.

Ben   You don't wanna die here by yerself, just admit it.

Brookes   You want fight?

Ben   Sarge?

Brookes   You want do it now, Pearce?

Ben (*chuckles*)   With yer guts hanging?

Brookes   You tink that'll stop me? You shot that kid in half!

Ben   So grass me up, make a report. I dare yer.

Brookes   Is my name Jamie?

Ben   Here we go!

Brookes   You think I'm keeping quiet like him?

Ben   There's nothing to keep quiet about.

Brookes   Jamie? Jamie! What happened in those cells last week?

Ben   Nuffink.

Brookes   I'm talking to him.

Jamie   Nuffink, alright!

Brookes   I saw those blokes carried out to the hospital. They looked worse off than me. What the fuck did you do to them, Pearce?

Sean   Calm it, will yer!

Brookes   Why do you think they went for us today? Think about it. Cos they're pissed, cos of what he did last week.

Ben   Listen to it, coming off all noble. You were getting a bit naughty yourself last week, Brookes.

Brookes   Any Iraqi who mouths off is entitled to a couple of slaps, but what you did was above and beyond.

Ben   To prolong the shock of capture. You were there as well when they said it.

Brookes   I don't give a boomba! Yer fucking mad.

Ben   This whole fucking thing is mad. Dunno what I'm doing any more.

Sound of Arab voices in the distance.

Sean   You hear that? They're getting closer.

Brookes *winces again in pain.*

Sean (*puts his hand over* **Brookes***'s mouth*)   Shut up. What you fucking trying to do, eh?

Brookes   Get off me!

Jamie   Shut up, all of yer.

Ben *looks up.*

Ben   Oh, this ain't 'appening.

Sean   What? What?

Ben *crawls his way back over to them.*

Ben   They're coming this way, six of them.

Sean   That's it, we can't stay here.

Ben (*to* **Brookes**)   Can you walk?

Brookes   You having a laugh?

Ben   No, as it goes.

Sean   He's shot up, he can't be moved.

Ben   What you want us to fucking do, Sean? The way it is, Sarge, yer gonna die either way. Yeah?

Brookes   I can't.

Ben   You can, you bloody will. Least with us you stand a chance, yeah? Now, come on. Sean!

Sean helps Ben get Brookes on his feet. Brookes screams in pain and collapses, taking Sean and Ben with him.

Sean   Get up! Fucking get up, will yer! (*Kicks him.*)

Ben   Get off him. Come on, Sarge.

Brookes   I can't.

Ben   Get up!

Brookes   Leave me.

Ben   Fuck's sake!

Sean   Right, come on, Ben, let's go. Let's go.

Ben ignores Sean and tries to lift Brookes up again. Jamie helps him.

Sean   Fucking leave him, he told us to do. They are coming to kill us!

Ben   We ain't leaving him.

Brookes realises what he must do. He crawls his way back to the wall. He removes his dagger from a side pocket and takes a deep last breath before stabbing himself in the stomach with it.

Ben (*sees*)   Oh shit!

He tries to take the knife off Brookes, but Brookes pushes him away.

Ben   Oh, you stupid fuckin . . .

Brookes   I said go!

He drops his head on the ground. He dies. **Ben** *is shaking; he cannot believe what has happened. Sound of approaching footsteps, followed by gunfire.* **Ben** *again crawls over to see.*

Ben   The cavalry, over by that road.

Sean   Sarge was right.

Ben   Just keep low – you with me, alright?

Sean   Don't you worry.

Jamie *looks over at* **Brookes**'*s dead body. His eyes become fixed on him.*

Ben   J?

He slaps J's face to make him come to.)

Ben   J! (*Shaking him.*) He died from his wounds in the shoot-out, alright? Fucking Arabs got him, just like the others. Alright?

Ben *signals to the others that they are on their way. He whispers to* **Sean** *and* **Jamie** *that on the count of three they will move.* **Ben** *counts to three, and they run out. Sound of rapid gunfire and of* **Sean**, **Ben** *and* **Jamie** *screaming.*

Scene Three

Six weeks earlier. Video screen comes back on. **Ben**, *more jaded than before, faces the screen.*

Ben   So how you doing, baby girl, my Trish? Thought you were gonna send me new pictures, it's bin three months now, you letting me down. Or are you too busy, going out every weekend, getting some new dick, eh? Are you? Wanna show you summin. (*Holds up a pair of bolt cutters.*) I got bolt cutters . . . (*Shows a dagger.*) Knife . . . (*Flashes a torch.*) Torch . . . Word is we're going on a raid later, bust down the doors of a couple of houses we suspect are housing insurgents. Cheeky fuckers. Don't know who they are, what they look

like. Could be smiling at you one day . . . planning to do you
over the next. You remember that kid I was telling you
about – Mickey? He was on patrol yesterday and . . . face,
boom, all over . . . side of the road . . . I mean you just don't
need it. 'Dass wat you get, motherfucker, get ready to die!'
Out here, wouldn't fucking believe . . . Friday night out, it
ain't, you know it's just . . . (*Shakes his head.*)

*He tries hard to find the strength to say any more, but cannot. He just
sits there and stares out, shaking his head at times.*

Do me a favour, tell Dan that I . . . fuck it, don't tell him
anything. (*Pause.*) Look, I'm sorry, yeah . . .

He turns off the camera. The video screen goes blank.

A Parting of the Ways

Characters

Hannah, *early twenties*
Trish, *early twenties*
Dan, *early twenties*
Lenny, *mid-forties*
Jamie, *early twenties*
Steve, *early twenties*
Clare, *early twenties*
Donna, *early twenties*
Darren, *mid-thirties*
Gail, *mid-thirties*
Tony, *early twenties*
Wedding guests

All of the characters, including the ones who do not speak, remain onstage throughout.

A wedding reception.

Dan *addresses the* **Guests**.

Dan I would like to set the record straight here, ladies and gents, by saying how pleased I am, Steve asked me to be his best man. Me, him, Tony and Ben, God rest, go way back as teenagers. Steve, I tell yer, is a best man's dream groom. I mean, he's had more accidents than Mr Bean, more booze in him than this bar, and according to his missus, at night, he's goes faster than Google. Being handsome teenagers such as we were, neither of us could walk into a bar without some gorgeous woman annoying us all night. Probably cos they wouldn't talk to us. Yeah, we've been through a lot together, me, him and Ben, God rest, lager, haircuts, porno mags. We shared a lot, Steve, me and Ben. But we never let our rivalries spoil our friendship. So, by marrying Clare, Steve, you really do have the last laugh, mate. Here's to yer, mate, to yer both, and of course to Ben, God rest. The bride and groom!

Guests Bride and groom!

Trish So, Jamie ain't coming then?

Hannah If he's smart, he'll stay at home.

Trish Just as well cos I'll have any dick that's going tonight, Hannah, I ain't lying.

Hannah Are you arseholed already?

Trish (*belches*) No.

Hannah Jesus!

Trish What? Better out than in. Staring me out.

Hannah Sorry I spoke.

Trish Will be.

Hannah Yeah, alright!

Trish Gonna be making tracks soon. You still up?

Hannah   Stay here, free booze.

Trish   Not for long. We'll have to pay behind the bar in a sec.

Hannah   Wass the plan?

Trish   We dash for the club of course. It's Ladies Night, two for one.

Hannah   In other words, same as usual.

Trish   Well, why change the habit? I ain't seen you in bleedin months, girl. You alright?

Hannah   Fine.

Trish   Yer still going wid him tomorrow, and yer still up for a piss-up?

Hannah   It's only a court hearing.

Trish   Right, as soon as poss, Maxine's gonna drive us.

Hannah   No Donna?

Trish   You see a sign on my head that says, 'I hang out with dirty skank bitches'?

Hannah   Alright, what's happened?

Trish   Don't worry yerself. Donna, fuckhead that she is, ain't coming. She'll only bring that knob Darren.

Hannah   He's alright.

Trish   He's married.

Hannah   Oh, the stupid cow.

Trish   Nice pair.

Hannah *takes off her shoes.*

Trish (*tries them on*)   Oh! Hello, lover. Borrow?

Hannah   No.

Trish   Cheers. Tellin yer, best place for Jamie right now is home. Trust me. You got some serious catching up to do.

Hannah   Bring it. Feel as though I ain't bin out for months.

Trish *and* **Hannah** *watch a drunken* **Clare** *on the mike trying to sing 'I Will Always Love You' badly.*

Trish   Will you just look at the state of her?

Hannah   You really think Clare has done the right thing? I mean, Steve?

Trish   Yeah, I know. Whatever flicks her switch.

Hannah   Floats her boat.

Trish   Climbs her rope.

They laugh. **Trish** *stares over at where* **Donna** *is sitting.* **Darren** *leaves the table to go to the loo.* **Trish** *squeezes his arse as he passes by.*

Hannah   You are shameless.

Trish   Look at her, giving me the eye, the bitch.

Hannah   Look, why don't I go over and have a chat wid her?

Trish   Sit down.

Hannah   You gonna tell me what's happened?

Trish   Beatrice.

Hannah   Excuse?

Trish   She keeps calling me Beatrice.

Hannah   It *is* yer name.

Trish   Love yer top.

Hannah   Trish, hello?

Trish Borrow?

Hannah Ain't yer size.

Trish You calling me fat?

Hannah Mwah?

Trish I'll cave your head in.

Hannah Donna calls you Beatrice, and?

Trish We had a fight about it, I knocked her spark out, got arrested for me trouble, the slag!

Hannah Arrested?

Trish Put yer face back. I warned her nuff times. Clare's bleeding sister-in-law, over there, Gail, tries to break it up, throwing her weight about like she always does. She shoved me, I cut her face with a beer bottle. No way does she look like Britney now, if ever.

Hannah I was wondering how she got that cut on her face.

Trish Now you know. Look at her. Still staring. (*Calls.*) Yes, darling, what else you got?

Hannah Jesus, Trish.

Trish Come on, you know how it goes.

Hannah Just reel it in a little.

Trish Still playing the nun?

Hannah You could have gone inside.

Trish Yeah, could have, Hannah. I got a two-year suspended sentence. (*She sees* **Hannah***'s face.*) What?

Hannah How many lives have you got, girl?

Trish People lose it, shit happens.

Hannah Both eyes on you tonight.

Trish   Well, it's bin a while since you've done that as well, hasn't it?

Hannah   I know.

Trish   I know you know.

Hannah   I've missed you.

Trish (*surprised*)   You missed me?

Hannah   Yeah.

Trish   Dyke.

Hannah   Fat.

Trish   Oh, hello.

Hannah   What?

She tuns round to see **Jamie** *arriving. Most of the other* **Guests** *have seen him arrive and are staring over at him.*

Hannah   Oh for fuck's sake.

She approaches him.

What are you doing?

Jamie   Just fancied a walk.

Hannah   In yer suit?

Jamie   I was invited. They all seem pleased to see me.

Hannah   They're surprised to see you. Go home, J.

Jamie   Steve's my mate. I've done nothing wrong.

Hannah   Not now, please.

Jamie   You saying I have?

Hannah   Christ!

Lenny (*approaching*)   Hannah, you alright, love?

Hannah   I'm fine, Len.

Jamie   Yes, we're both alright, Len. Thanks for asking.

Lenny   Good to see you, son.

Jamie   'Hannah, you alright, love?'

Hannah   Keep your voice down.

Jamie   What did he think I was going to do?

Hannah   Nothing.

Jamie   Giving me that look.

Hannah   What do you expect?

Jamie   Alright, I should have stayed in, but I can't sleep, just wanted to know.

Hannah   What?

Jamie   You are still coming tomorrow, yeah?

Hannah   Not now, J.

Jamie   Yes or no?

Dan *approaches.*

Dan   Jamie? Good to see yer, mate. How you keeping?

Hannah   He's fine.

Jamie   Cheers, Dan.

Dan   Missed you at the stag do. I suppose you had other things.

Hannah   You suppose right.

Dan   We had a blinder over at Wetherspoons – you know, across the road from the centre?

Jamie   Yeah, I know.

Dan   There was no drink left in that bar, we had it all, God's honest.

Jamie   Right.

Hannah   He's leaving now.

Dan   But he's only just arrived. What you having, J?

Jamie   Dunno.

Dan   You dunno?

Jamie   Beer!

Dan   Tone, chuck us a beer.

Tony *throws a can in* **Dan***'s direction, which he catches and hands to* **Jamie**.

Dan   Really good to see you, mate, wouldn't be the same. You missed my best-man speech. I mentioned Ben a few times, I know it's weird and that, wedding an all, but Ben was one of us, you know, wouldn't seem right going through this day without mentioning him, you know what I mean? After what he's done. He's a hero.

Jamie   No.

Dan   What, no he ain't a hero?

Jamie   No, I mean what you said, it wouldn't be right.

Dan   Course. Ben was a proper.

Jamie   Yeah.

Dan   So here's to him, our friend, our hero. To Ben!

Jamie *slams his can onto the ground and heads for the exit.*

Dan   Jamie, mate?

Hannah   Oh, nice.

Hannah *glares at* **Dan***, who blows her a kiss.*

A drunken **Darren** *comes out of the loo. He recognises* **Jamie** *and blocks his path.*

Jamie   You wanna move outta my way?

Darren   It's you, innit?

Jamie   Here we go.

Darren   The one in the paper.

Donna (*calls*)   Darren!

Darren   One they're talking about, him.

Donna   Fingers on lips.

Jamie   Got a problem?

Darren   You're the one with the problem, mate, a serious problem.

Jamie   Oh yes?

Hannah   Donna, will you have a word please?

Donna   I'm trying to. Over here!

Darren   You are one sick man, you know that?

Donna   Darren!

Darren   What?

Jamie *shoves* **Darren** *aside.*

Darren   Oi, manners! (*He joins* **Donna** *back at the table.*) What?

Donna   What part of 'shut the fuck up' do you not understand?

Jamie *is outside with* **Hannah**.

Hannah   What? What is it?

Jamie   Fucking going on about Ben, every chance he gets, you hear him?

Hannah   Ben was his best mate.

Jamie   So what was I? Some no-mark who dragged him to war? Is that what he thinks, what everyone in there thinks?

Hannah   Of course not.

Jamie   'Poor sweet, innocent Ben, the hero' – is that what you think, Hannah?

Hannah   No.

Jamie   What's made you so nice? You'll be telling me it's gonna be alright next.

Hannah   I would have to be stupid.

Jamie   Excuse?

Hannah   Never mind.

Jamie   Talk to me, Hannah.

Hannah   About what?

Jamie   Anything.

Hannah *isn't sure where to begin.*

Hannah   Did I tell you about Lauren?

Jamie   Lauren?

Hannah   My friend from college. She's a little stressed out.

Jamie   Yeah – and?

Hannah   Cos of her essay.

Jamie (*not really listening*)   Yeah.

Hannah   Because, you see, her essay was due on Thursday, but I knew she wasn't going to finish it. So, to save some time, she lifted a couple of passages from a book that wasn't on our reading list. She would have got away with it, if our lecturer didn't know the book in question.

Jamie   'The book in question'?

Hannah   He told Lauren to do it again, and have it done by Monday, or he's failing her. There goes her weekend.

Jamie   That's it? You wanna tell me that?

Hannah (*sighs*)   You said anything.

Jamie (*snaps*)   Summin else then!

Hannah (*snaps back*)   Like what? What do you want me to do? I told you not to come here.

Jamie   I didn't want to be alone.

Hannah   I know, but you can't keep running away.

Jamie   Hearing starts tomorrow. They've taken my passport. Where the fuck am I going to run away to?

Hannah   Please don't swear at me.

Jamie   'Please don't swear at me . . .' What's happened to you?

Hannah   What's happened to you?!

Jamie *leaves.* **Hannah** *holds her head in frustration.*

Darren *continues to stares over at* **Trish**, *who deliberately drops a knife on the floor, so that she can bend over, allowing* **Darren** *to look up her dress.*

Darren (*grinning*)   Jeez!

Donna (*turning round*)   What did you say?

Darren   Nothing.

Trish   Having fun, Donna?

Donna   Blinding, Beatrice.

Trish *grabs a champagne bottle, with the intention of smashing it over* **Donna**'s *head but stops herself when she sees* **Gail** *rising from her seat.* **Trish** *joins* **Hannah** *outside to cool off.*

Trish   Bitch is asking for it, Hannah, bitch has no idea who she's dealing with. Watch me steal her boyfriend before the night is out, gonna have him drooling, if I haven't already. Where's laughing boy?

Hannah   Gone for a sulk. Gimme that.

She takes a swig of **Trish**'s *drink.*

Trish   You don't think you should go after?

Hannah   Fucking tired of it.

Trish   Just as you like.

Hannah   We going clubbing or what?

Trish   Yeah.

Hannah   Well, let's go then.

Trish   Maxine is dropping her mum off home. Put the brakes on.

Hannah   I want to leave now, I've got some serious catching up to do.

Trish   Sweetheart, you would have had to have made a start last year, to try and catch up with me.

Hannah   What makes you think I haven't?

Trish   Cos your new best mate Lauren don't seem the type.

Hannah   Lauren's alright.

Trish   But?

Hannah   She ain't you. Or Clare, or Donna.

Trish   Do not mention that cow's name to me any more.

Hannah   I've always thought Beatrice suits yer.

Trish   You think she'd be getting on my tits this much if it was just cos of that?

Hannah   So?

Trish   Forget it, yeah.

Hannah   No. What?

Trish   Few months back, she was going on about Ben getting killed, saying it was the government's fault, shouldn't have sent them, usual bollocks. It only turns out she had a thing for Ben. Fancied him for months, by all accounts, stupid cow.

Hannah   You're right, she's a mouthy skank bitch.

Trish   You don't agree with her then? About the war?

Hannah (*surprised*)   The war?

Trish   Yes, Hannah, the war.

Hannah   What have you been smoking? Since when do you care about the war?

Trish   You're right. What could I possibly know, eh?

Hannah   Trish?

Trish   Don't worry about it. Let's go out, eh? Get the boys drooling, some nice hard dick! Yes?

Hannah   Look, why don't you just give it to me, whatever you want to say?

Trish   Was out with Clare, a couple of weeks back, checking out that new bar in Newton's? Saw you in there, hanging with Lauren.

Hannah   And you didn't say hello?

Trish   I was in the Ladies, one of the cubicles, heard you come in. Going on about the war, how much you hate it, Blair-bashing, all that shit.

Hannah   You stalking me?

Trish   How awful it was, seeing those pictures. Those nasty vicious soldiers. Does Jamie know you think like that? Does Lauren know about Jamie? 'No' would be my bet.

Hannah   It ain't what you think.

Trish   I think it is what I think, Hannah.

Hannah   All I was doing was seeing things from their point of view.

Trish *sneers.*

Hannah   We were having a debate.

Trish   Having a debate? Is that why you blew me out?

Hannah   Read my lips, Trish –

Trish (*snaps*)   Six months, Hannah!

Hannah   Well, I'm here now, aren't I? So why don't you go to bed and get up again? Jesus!

A drunken **Tony** *comes out of the Gents.*

Tony   Alright, girls? Do not go in there. (*He waves the air.*) Whoa!

He staggers back inside.

Trish   You think the rest of us are stupid? You think I'm not angry about Ben? I can't feel what you feel?

Hannah   Fuck's sake.

Trish   Is it?

Hannah   Don't embarrass yourself.

Trish   Smug little bitch.

Hannah   Oi! There's a lot you don't know.

Trish   Fucking squaddies, going mental . . .

Hannah   It's not their fault.

Trish   No one forced them.

Hannah   You can't say that.

Trish   Come on, Hannah, your turn.

Hannah   You telling me you blame Ben for dying?

Trish   I blame him for blaming me.

Hannah   I'm going back in.

Trish   Hannah?

Hannah   Gimme a shout when you're ready.

Trish   I wanna talk about the war.

Hannah   Well, I don't.

Lights on **Steve**, *drunk.*

Steve   Alright. Bit nervous. Sorry. Just like to say, this ain't the first time today I've gotten up from a warm seat with a piece of paper in my hand. Don't worry, everyone, my speech will be as short as one of Clare's skirts. Long enough to cover the essentials, but short enough to hold your attention. I feel like one of them Arab sheikhs going into his harem – you know what you gotta do, you just don't know where to start. (*To himself.*) Shut up with the jokes, Steve. Anyhow, it's supposed to be my job to thank everyone. So, thank you all for coming tonight, it wouldn't have been the same, and neither would my bank balance. Seriously, it's nice to see you all. Don't the bridesmaids look great, eh? Love 'em! Cheers to Lenny, for all the catering, it's pukka, mate. Cheers, Mum, cheers, Dad, love you both. Clare's mum, honestly, Mrs Rowan, you don't look that old to me. Thank you, I mean this, thank you for making me feel like the son you never wanted . . . I mean had. The son you never had. What? Yer brother? Yeah, I know you got a brother, Clare, I can see him – sorry, mate – I just thought it sounded funny. Last but not, my best man, Dan. What a pukka gent, eh? Where are yer, where's he gone? Oi, oi, Danny bwoi's on the scent, I can tell. We got all the bridesmaids here? Give her one for me. What, Clare? It was a joke! Anyhow, thanks again one and all, cheers.

Dan *and* **Hannah** *have locked themselves in a passionate embrace.*

Hannah   Better stop now. Did you hear?

Dan *grabs her arse.*

Hannah   Hands!

Dan   Come here.

Hannah   That is your lot, naughty boy.

Dan   Ain't even taken you home yet.

Hannah   Down, you!

Dan   I'm hungry.

Hannah   Someone will see.

Dan   Let them.

Hannah   Some mate you are.

Dan   What have you got me down as?

Hannah   A fucking bastard?

Dan   You telling me you'll be waiting for Jamie? It'll be five years before he's out.

Hannah   Not necessarily.

Dan   Did you see those pictures?

Hannah   He was following orders.

Dan   Bollocks.

Hannah   Now they're screwing him.

Dan   It was an illegal order.

Hannah   You really think Jamie knows the difference?

Dan   Forget him.

Hannah   Do yer?

Dan   How do you get this off?

Hannah   (*slaps his hand away*)   I'm talking.

A drunken **Clare** *comes out from the reception.*

Clare   Baby!

Hannah   Alright, my darling?

Clare   Where the fuck is Trish?

Hannah   She's inside somewhere. Can't you find her?

Clare   Slag has fucked off to Yates's, I bet.

Hannah   No, babe.

Clare   Without saying goodbye!

Hannah   Go find her, she's inside.

Clare   Yer here, ain't yer?

Hannah   No, I'm back home, Clare.

Clare   Ca you love me, innit?

Hannah   Girl, I'm mad for yer.

Clare   Bogs!

She opens the toilet door, but not before squeezing **Dan***'s arse on the way. The smell of a used toilet comes wafting out from the loo.*

Clare   Jesus, who was in here last? Bit unnecessary.

Hannah   Open the winder then.

Clare   If I'm not out in five, call an ambulance. The dirty bastard.

She goes in.

Hannah   Well?

Dan   Alright, my opinion is, if he's got half a brain, he should know the difference. But then again, this is Jamie we're talking about. Let's go back to mine.

Hannah   You telling me you don't care?

Dan   Does it look like I care?

Hannah   You blame him for Ben, don't yer?

Dan   Don't try and be clever, Hannah. Not when yer looking this sexy.

Hannah   Why won't you answer my question?

Dan   Shut up.

Hannah   Do you blame him?

Dan   Come here.

Hannah   Cos you're ashamed of the way you left things with Ben?

Dan   What? What are you doing?

Hannah   You can say.

Dan   You really think yer smart enough now to ask me that?

Hannah   I just wanna talk.

Dan   Ain't got yer bleedin degree yet, Hannah. Lauren would be pissing herself.

Hannah   No.

Dan   You think yer so worthy now?

Hannah   Calm down.

Clare *comes out of the toilet. She grabs hold of* **Dan***'s arse again.*

Hannah   Easy, Clare.

Clare   Arse like a peach! Seriously though, Dan, seriously, I loved yer speech.

Dan   Cheers, Clare.

Clare   I'm serious, serious, lovely speech, blinding it was, blinding. From the heart, you know, from the heart. Steve loves you, you know, he really does.

Dan   Yeah.

Clare   Not in a gay way.

Dan   There's a relief.

Clare   Come here.

Dan *leans forward.* **Clare** *gets him in a clinch and proceeds to snog his face off. Then she squeezes his arse again.*

Clare   Love it!

She goes back in.

Dan (*grabs* **Hannah***'s arm*)   Where you going?

Hannah   Get off me.

Dan   Little Miss Smart-arse, thought you wanted to talk?

Hannah   Just forget it.

Dan   Nuh, I don't wanna forget it. Think yer it now, all-knowing.

Hannah   No.

Dan   Let's have a talk, let's talk about the war. I'm Lauren, we're back at college. So tell me, Hannah, do you think that the killing of Abu al-Zarqawi has reinforced fears that the country is sliding towards all-out civil war, bearing in mind, of course, that this week's death toll also included day-labourers in a Shia district of Baghdad and pre-dawn executions of Shia men in the provincial town of Taji?

Hannah   What?

Dan   Too complicated? Never mind, how about this? Do you believe the Iraqi government took a historic gamble last year when the ruling Shia and Kurdish coalition bulldozed over the objections of Sunni Arabs to complete a new constitutional charter? Hannah?

Hannah (*unsure*)   Well, it depends.

Dan   One final question, Hannah, please. Do you share the same viewpoint as the Americans and the British that if the Iraqis adopt a democratically written constitution for the first time in their history and if the Sunnis are convinced to join the political process –

Hannah   Bastard.

Dan   – they will deprive the insurgents of their main base of support, help bring back home the troops and ease the mounting pressure on Blair and Bush?

Hannah   Fuck you.

Dan   Think you can fuck around then blow me off. Don't ever say Ben's name to me again. You ain't earned the right. Dunno where you are, girl. Go to that courtroom with Jamie. Hold his hand, like some sad divvy cow.

Hannah (*slaps his face*)   This sad divvy cow will fuck you up, if you come it.

Steve *enters, also drunk.*

Steve   Oi, oi, what's all this?

Dan   Nuffink, we're alright, Steve.

Steve   Felt that from here. Am I sensing some tension?

Dan   It's nuffink, mate.

Steve   Where'd Jamie run off to?

Hannah   Had stuff to do, you know.

Steve   Tell him good luck for me, yeah, on my life, dog's bollocks. 'Ere, Dan, come 'ere, got a minute? Just wanted to say . . . blinding speech, mate, it was pukka! Dead proud, couldn't have asked for a better . . . (*He trails off.*)

Dan   Speech?

Steve   Mate. Yer my best mate. I know what Ben meant to yer, and I ain't replacing him or nuttin. Could never replace Ben.

Dan   Correct.

Steve   But you and me, it's you and me now, mate. But you can't have me all the time, not in a gay way. Gotta save some for Clare, you know what I mean? Fucking love her, mate, ain't lying. It's what it's all about, ain't it? Love. Beats fighting a war, any time. You know what my old man just said to me?

Dan   Mine's a double?

Steve   No, before that. He goes, you don't marry the person you're with, you marry the person you can't live without. Poetry, mate. Right, time I sexed my wife, don't you think? Where is she? (*Calls.*) Clare?

Steve *leaves.*

Hannah   Ain't my fault you dropped out of college, Dan.

Dan   Never said it was.

Hannah   Then why you doing this?

Dan   Doesn't matter.

Hannah   Liar.

Dan   It doesn't matter, Hannah, cos we don't matter.

Hannah   Stop saying that.

Dan   Come on.

Hannah *gives in. They kiss again.*

Jamie *comes in.*

Dan   Jamie! You alright, mate?

Hannah   Thought you'd –

Jamie *goes for* **Dan**. **Dan** *gets the upper hand and he twists* **Jamie***'s arm around his back.*

Dan   Feeling strong, are yer, J? Playing army boy. Like it's a game. It's what I told everybody when we saw your face on the news, it's silly little Jamie, playing about, as usual. You've well and truly fucked yourself now, ain'tcha? 'Gonna be heroes, Ben, made for life.' On at him, all the time, couldn't leave him alone.

Hannah   Alright!

Dan (*releases* **Jamie**)   I was only keeping her warm. Had to be you that came back, innit?

He leaves.

Hannah   Let me see your face.

Jamie *pushes her away.*

Hannah   Don't start.

The same song that **Jamie** *and* **Hannah** *danced to together in 'Much Noise' is being played.* **Steve** *and* **Clare** *are first to step onto the floor and slow-dance to it.*

Hannah   That's our song. Jamie?

Clare   You do love me, don't yer, Steve?

They eat each other's face off right in front of everybody.

Hannah   What, are you just going to stand there all night? Ignoring me? (*She waits for him to say something.*) Jamie?

Jamie   Why?

Hannah   I got tired of everyone telling me I can handle it. I can't handle it.

Jamie   And that made you want to get off with him?

Hannah   I needed to forget.

Jamie   To be Hannah the slapper again.

Hannah   Yeah, I wanted to be her. No one cares what that Hannah thinks. That Hannah does not have an opinion, on anything. But I can't help it, Jamie, it's haunting me. The more I think about what you did to those people, the more I . . .

Jamie   Hate me? I can see it in people's faces what they think of me. Even when they try to hide it, I can see it.

Hannah *goes to touch him.*

Jamie   Fuck off out of it. You shag him?

Hannah (*chuckles*)   I used him.

Jamie   I could kill you right now.

Hannah   Yes, show everyone again what a big man you are.

Jamie   That's it, that's the look. Do you think I'm a monster?

Hannah   I don't want to think about any of this. This fucking war!

Jamie   So what you want?

Hannah   Come back to me. You musta known it weren't right.

Jamie   It was an order! To prolong the shock –

Hannah   – shock of capture. Boring!

Jamie   Don't turn against me as well, Hannah. Don't look at me like I'm some monster.

Hannah   How should I look at you, J? People won't care. They won't believe you.

Jamie   We got tough with them, like they wanted.

Hannah   That's not what they wanted.

Jamie   Like they said.

Hannah   Who is they?

Jamie   You sound just like Dan.

Hannah   You should have known it was wrong, you shoulda said no.

Jamie   So what you want me to do?

Hannah   Tell them you were scared.

Jamie   But that wouldn't be true.

Hannah   Like you were before you left. You were scared shitless.

Jamie   No I weren't.

Hannah   Jamie?! I was there!

Jamie   I can't go there crying like a bitch, I had a job to do.

Hannah   They were innocent –

Jamie   Innocent? Oh for fuck . . . this ain't you talking, it's yer fucking college mates. What do they say about me? That I'm evil? Is that what they say, Hannah?

Hannah   Yes.

Jamie   And I bet you just sit there, taking it all in, not opening your mouth, like it's gospel.

Hannah   Prove me wrong then.

Jamie   Fuck them, like I care. Least I know where I stand. But not with you though . . . playing the slapper. I'd have more respect if you just said, fuck off, Jamie, you're an evil monster. But don't tell me to act stupid, and say I'm scared, right, that I don't matter!

Hannah   Fuck off, Jamie . . .

Jamie (*pleads*)   No!

Hannah   You're an evil monster.

Jamie (*screams*)   Hannah?!

Hannah   Well, what then? I'm trying to understand, I'm trying so hard not to hate you, but yer giving me fuck all here. Can't you at least tell them it wasn't just you?

Jamie   Grass on my mates? Dishonour myself as well as my unit? You really don't know me, Hannah.

Hannah   No, I don't. Why'd you do it, and don't give me you were following orders?

Jamie   I was.

Hannah (*pleads*)   Jamie! Why'd you do it? You can tell me, please, will yer? I don't wanna hate you, so don't make me. Why'd you do it? Why'd you do it?

Jamie   Dunno. I dunno, Hannah, I dunno. I dunno, I dunno why I did it, I didn't think, right, wrong, I dunno, I dunno, I don't fucking know. We juss lost it. (*He shrugs his shoulders again.*)

Hannah   Tell me what you felt.

Jamie   Nuffink.

Trish *comes out, snogging the face off* **Darren**.

Trish   See, Hannah, what did I say? Never, in yer life, bet against a girl who's on heat!

Hannah   Are we going?

Trish   Excuse?

Hannah   Clubbing, now!

She brushes **Darren** *aside.*

Darren   Oi, manners, darling!

Hannah   Piss off, before I call yer wife.

Darren *goes back inside.*

Trish   This you giving it large, Hannah?

Hannah   Text Maxine we'll meet her at Yates's. Text her, Trish! Right now. We're going.

Trish   You had me.

Hannah   Trish!

Trish   You really had me, right up until you said you missed me, you bitch. I really felt you cut me off.

Hannah (*pleads*)   One night, away from it, that's all I want, fuck the war.

Trish   We live two streets apart, and I've barely seen you.

Hannah   I didn't think you'd miss me.

Trish   Do you wanna get hit? Like I'm really gonna see much of Clare after she's married? As for Donna . . .

Hannah   Skank bitch.

Trish   Right. There ain't no one left. Who knows how I feel.

Hannah   Feeling what? Feeling this? It's overrated. It's a pain in the arse.

Trish   How often did you write to her, J? Was that place getting to you?

Hannah   Leave him alone.

Trish   Ben wrote, every week, sent me videos. Full of mouth at first, but I could feel the change. Like he was dead inside.

Hannah   Whatever.

Trish (*snaps*)   Say whatever again, see what I do to you. Trying to be flash and mug me off. I got things to say.

Hannah   So hurry up, let's go out.

Trish   He had to go and die though, didn't he? Be a sodding hero! He should be here, so I can cuss him down like I always do, then he'd have a lame go at trying to cuss me. Then we'd go and shag each other senseless. Like fucking animals.

Hannah   I don't want this. You two, doing my head in.

Trish   J, you understand, don't yer? J? You gonna talk to me?

Jamie *turns away.*

Trish   What's yer problem, J? For fuck's sake. You know, you wanna grow up a bit, J. Blanking me . . . it didn't just happen to you.

Hannah   Will you keep your stupid mouth shut, just for once?

Trish   I loved him as well.

Jamie   Same here.

Trish   Well, for fuck's sake then.

Jamie   I miss him. I'd give anything for him to be here, right now.

Trish   He wouldn't want us going at it.

Jamie   So I can stamp all over his head.

Trish   What is the matter wid you?

Hannah   He's stressed.

Trish   He's wired. He wants to be put to sleep.

Hannah   Go to Yates's, Trish.

Trish   And don't tell me about you stamping on his head, he'd kick yer arse, son, if he knew.

Jamie   If he knew!

Trish   He'd think you were sick.

Jamie   If he knew!

Trish   He's cussing you, from up there.

Jamie   Doubt that.

Trish   Meaning? Explanation?

Hannah   Will you please leave?

Trish   I wanna know what he meant.

Jamie   Go to Yates's, Trish. You don't want to know.

Trish   That he hated me?

Jamie   Not even near.

Trish   Well, let's have it, big man! Whatever it is. Tell me what he felt. What did he say about me? What was he going through?

Jamie   Before or after that Iraqi had a broomstick up his arse?

Trish   Shut the fuck up!

Jamie   On my life.

Trish   You are out of it.

Jamie   I was there.

Hannah   J?

Jamie   She wanted to know, so did you. Ben ever tell you about our mate Mickey, about him getting half his face blown off? I know he sent you a vid. Too much for yer was it, Trish? Well, it was too much for him not hearing from you. No more photos with yer tits out. No more showing them to the rest of the unit. The midnight wank was what we used to call you. When Mickey died, Ben went steaming into that cell, on and on he was, 'You wanna have fun with someone else's mate, you had fun with Mickey, now have fun with me, have some fun with me, don't be shy, have it!' Not that the geezer had much of a choice – after all, Ben was holding a knife against his neck the whole time. Poor cunt was praying overtime to Allah to get him out of there. All I did was a few kicks, a couple of slaps, some dickhead of a corporal gets his camera out, and now I'm the one that's in the dock tomorrow. So don't come to me about you loving poor heroic Ben!

Trish *feels sick. She finds a corner and throws up.*

Steve *and* **Clare** *come back.*

Steve   Here she is.

Clare   Where you bin hiding yerself, you slag!

Steve   Face down as usual.

Clare   Maxine wants yer.

Steve   Trish? Never had a chance to say, Ben, he was alright, Trish, a proper.

Clare   Sodding off to the club with Maxine without telling me! 'Ere, I'm fucking married, Trish, can you believe? (*Screams.*)

Steve   So, wass all this? Party's in there, people, look lively! Jamie, you bastard, come here. (*Hugs him.*) Glad you came. Yer a top man, a proper, no matter what they say, you fought for yer country, nuffink more prouder than that. I say fuck them, fuck them . . .

Clare *is showing off her ring to* **Trish** *and* **Hannah**.

Clare   Have a look!

Trish   Nice.

Hannah   It's lovely.

Clare   It's the dog's, innit? I'm never taking it off. He really loves me, innit?

Steve   Fuck's sake, Clare.

Clare   I mean, you don't shell out this much for someone you don't love, yeah?

Steve   Already told you I love yer, you stupid bitch. Untold times. You never listen.

Clare   Juss wanna be sure.

Steve (*yells*)   Clare, I love you! Fucking do.

Clare (*moved*)   Oh, Steve!

Steve   Love yer, love yer, love yer! (*Kisses her.*) Oi, what's this, a peepshow? Come on, everyone, enough of the long faces, fuck's sake. Music's playing – inside, now.

Steve *and* **Clare** *go back inside.*

Trish *leaves, heartbroken.* **Jamie** *clocks* **Hannah**'*s face.*

Jamie   You got that look again.

Hannah *goes back inside.* **Jamie** *is left alone. Then he goes.*

Lenny *comes out from the reception, drink in hand. He rolls himself a cigarette.*

Hannah *comes out a short while later, drinking from a bottle of Smirnoff Ice. She throws up in the same corner as* **Trish** *did a moment ago.*

Lenny   What are you doing, sweetheart?

Hannah   It ain't me, it's those sausage rolls.

Lenny   Oi, I made those.

Hannah *chuckles.*

Lenny   Cheeky mare.

Hannah   Give us a drag, Len.

She takes a drag of his roll-up. She offers it back.

Lenny   I don't want it now, do I?

Hannah   So, you enjoying yourself then?

Lenny   I'd be enjoying myself a lot more if Steve's dad would keep his eyes off you for more than five seconds.

Hannah   Oh he's harmless.

Lenny   He can't take his eyes off your legs.

Hannah   So? I've got nice legs.

Lenny   It's disgusting.

Hannah   Gawd!

Lenny   Man his age.

Hannah   You'd give aspirin a headache, you.

Lenny   Hannah, why don't you put the brakes on and sit down for five minutes, eh? Can't have you showing up in court tomorrow with a hangover.

Hannah   Fine, then don't have me, don't have me showing up in court tomorrow with a hangover, cos that's exactly what I intend to have.

Lenny   That's silly talk.

Hannah   What's it have to do with me? It's Jamie.

Lenny   You're going.

Hannah   Maybe.

Lenny   There is no maybe. He needs you.

Hannah   Oh, Lenny, go and fry something, will yer?

Lenny   Thanks.

Hannah   It was a joke! Like I'm a joke.

Lenny   Don't ever say that, darling.

Hannah   Look at me. I'm not up for this.

Lenny   No, but you're up for messing around with that Dan. I saw yer. He's no good for you, love.

Hannah   So?

Lenny   Hannah, don't.

Hannah   Why shouldn't I shag him? And don't say cos I'm better than that, cos I'll come over there and stab yer.

Lenny   Cos you know he's a piece of shit. And he knows you're right.

Hannah   I don't want to be a good girl. It's hard work. I don't want to think about these things at all. I don't want that war to matter to me. I want to get so fucking drunk.

Lenny   Well, mission accomplished. So what's left then, eh?

Hannah   Yer funny.

Lenny   Sweetheart?

Hannah   Don't call me that.

Lenny   Life only throws at you what it thinks you can handle.

Hannah   And stop talking bollocks. Yer always doing that, saying things, confusing the fuck.

Lenny   I say it cos you're special.

Hannah   Special? Special how, Len? I got my boyfriend and best mate hating me in one night, what is so special about me? I mean, what you got me down as, some sort of crusading angel, who's gonna make the world alright?

Lenny   Why not?

Hannah *laughs.*

Lenny   Why not? The whole bleedin world's crying out for one.

Hannah   The words cuckoo, land and cloud spring to mind.

Lenny   Just care, Hannah. That's all I want, it's what we all want . . .

Hannah   To care?

Lenny   Is that so bad?

Hannah   So lame . . .

Lenny   My old man would say sometimes, the worth of our lives comes not in what we do or who we know, or what we say, but by who we are.

Hannah *scoffs.*

Lenny   Oi, I'm serious.

Hannah   Ain't so simple.

Lenny   But what if it is, though? What if it is that simple?

Hannah (*cringes*)   Oh, Lenny, stop it.

Lenny   Please, Hannah.

Hannah   Yer killing my buzz, man.

Lenny   Don't do this to yourself.

Hannah   Do what?

Lenny   You're not throwing away your life.

Hannah   You wanna lay off the Strongbow, mate.

Lenny   You make me feel that I matter. All the time.

Hannah   Seriously?

Lenny   Yes. And I love you for it.

Hannah *leans forward and kisses* **Lenny** *on the lips. He pushes her away in disgust.*

Hannah   What?

Lenny   What do you mean, what? What the fuck was that?

Hannah (*giggles*)   Only a kiss.

Lenny   Do you think this is funny?

Hannah   I can do a lot more if you like.

Lenny   Go back home, Hannah.

Hannah   Excuse?

Lenny   I said go back home, you need to sleep it off.

Hannah   Is that a no then?

Lenny   Don't you dare.

Hannah   Dare what? It's not illegal.

Lenny   That's enough.

Hannah   Come on, you're telling me there's nothing going on here?

Lenny   I'm telling you that you're arseholed.

Hannah   Don't believe yer.

Lenny   So, this your answer for everything? Acting like some cheap little tart?

Hannah   It's what everyone says.

Lenny   You were never like that.

Hannah   But I've seen the way you look at me, Len.

Lenny   How dare you.

Hannah   I've caught yer eye, more than once, don't deny it.

Lenny   Don't do this.

Hannah   Look at me, right now. All those years, hugs and kisses, you telling me you've never –

Lenny   No. No!

Hannah   I can see it, it's in yer eyes, mate.

Lenny   Hannah!

Hannah   Every geezer's eyes, for as long as I've grown a pair. Why should you be any different?

Lenny   I'm yer father.

Hannah   But you ain't though.

Lenny   I'm the closet thing – don't you forget it.

Hannah   I'll make it easy, shall I, get my tits out?

Lenny   Don't be disgusting.

Hannah   I'll lie on the ground, spread my legs.

Lenny   Stop it.

Hannah   Go on, get yer dick out.

Lenny *grabs her.*

Lenny   Stop it, stop it now. I don't want to hear any more of this filth coming outta yer mouth, stop it! Now you are going to listen to me.

Hannah   Kiss me first.

Lenny (*screams then shakes her*)   Hannah! You're breaking my heart. Can't you see it? Can't you see how lovely you are? How special? I've seen you grow into this blinding young woman. A diamond, who's capable of doing so much with her life and I adore you. That's all. I could never . . . I love you too much. You make me proud. You make me smile. You're no slag. I want to kill anyone who says that about you, rip their fucking heads off, I do! You understand everybody, you want to make them matter and you want to make it right. Cos, you see, it's people like you, that don't do the obvious. It's people like you, who know where the line is drawn, that change things, always has been. That's a gift, a precious gift. You're going to be amazing, my girl, whatever it is you do, it's gonna be amazing. I know it. I do love you. And I know you. You'll do what's right for Jamie, and for yourself. You can't help it, despite the chat. It's in you. It's in yer nature. You inspire me, my angel. You make me feel better. You.

Hannah *breaks down. She buries herself in* **Lenny***'s arms.* **Tony** *comes out, to find the toilet door is locked. He waits.*

Hannah   Those pictures, Len.

Lenny   I know.

Hannah   They make me sick. I was sick. How could he? How? But I can't hate him. You should hear them at college with all their PC shit, those poor Arabs, blah blah blah . . . When I disagree, want them to see it from Jamie's point of view, they look at me like I'm taking shite, so I believe it.

Tony *is getting impatient. He bangs on the door.*

Hannah   I shoulda known better, right from the off. It was the faces that told me.

Lenny   What faces?

Hannah   First time I saw their college prospectus online. First page had these faces. Students, lecturers, black, white, all colours. All happy walking through campus without a care, grinning at me, like they were saying, 'We've got art courses, business courses, computer courses, language courses, media courses, hair & beauty courses, sports courses, music courses, film courses, and none of them are for you, so fuck off out of it, estate girl! Jog on back to Yates's, go drown yourself in vodka straights.'

Tony   Come on! I got an emergency here.

Hannah   Shoulda listened.

Lenny   No.

Hannah   They were right.

Lenny   Bollocks to that.

Hannah   I don't know what to do.

Tony *is tired of waiting. He finds a corner to piss in.*

Tony   Awright, Len?

Lenny   Yeah, smashing, Tone.

Tony   Laters.

He zips up his flies and goes back in.

Lenny   Don't go under. You keep shouting. You keep raising your voice. That is what you do.

Hannah   You saying I should go with Jamie tomorrow? You are, innit? (*She sighs.*) Alright, I'll go. I'll go. Every day. I'll hold his hand. I'll listen as he gives evidence. Taking all of the blame. Sit and watch, as they all take turns crucifying him, march him off to prison for five years. Yes, Lenny, that is what I should do.

Lenny   I'm proud of you.

Hannah   I best go and find him, eh? We gonna be alright?

Lenny   Course.

Hannah (*feeling ashamed*)   Stuff I said, I never meant . . .

Lenny   I know.

Hannah (*pleads*)   You are like my dad, Len, you are my dad.

Lenny   It never happened.

Hannah *gives* **Lenny** *a peck on the cheek. She sees* **Jamie** *across the stage, looking like a little boy lost. She extends her hand to him. He takes it.*

Blackout.

Absolute Beginners

Adapted from the novel by Colin MacInnes

Absolute Beginners was first performed at the Lyric Theatre Hammersmith, London, on 26 April 2007. The cast was as follows;

Photo Boy	Sid Mitchell
Crepe Suzette	Joanne Matthews
Wiz/Hoplite	Tom Stuart
Dad/Venice Partners	David Sibley
Dean Swift/Ed the Ted/Verne	Richard Frame
Carl	Darren Hart
Marcus/Student	Tosin Olomowewe
Mum/Big Jill	Rachel Sanders
Henley/Mickey P	James Clyde
Mr Cool	Micah Balfour

Director Liam Steel
Designer Lizzie Clachan
Sound Designer Nick Manning
Music Soweto Kinch

Characters

The Teens
Photo Boy
Wiz
Crêpe Suzette
Mr Cool
Ed the Ted
Fabulous Hoplite
Big Jill
Dean Swift
Ted 1
Ted 2
Carl
Marcus
African Student

The citizens
Mickey P
Mum
Dad
Verne
Vendice Partners
Henley
Admiral Drove

Other parts to be played by members of the company.

Act One

In June

A group of excited kids enter the coffee bar. They select a track on the jukebox. 'He's Got the Whole World in his Hands' by Laurie London is playing. Some of the kids dance, the others sing along. **Photo Boy** *and his mate* **Wiz** *watch.*

Photo Boy   I should have known they'd play that. Come on, Wiz, let's split, go somewhere else.

Wiz   Go where? They're ain't nowhere else. The kid is all over.

Photo Boy   Fourteen years old, that absolute beginner.

Wiz   It is a sign of decadence, my boy! This teenage thing is getting out of hand.

Photo Boy   It's alright for young sperms like you, you've still got a lot of teenage living to do. As for me, nineteen summers old, I'll very soon be out there among the oldies.

Wiz (*shouts over at the waiter*)   Oh, I suppose you're underpaid, mate, that's what's the matter with you. Don't like your work down here with us mere sucklings.

Waiter   You best settle up and hop it.

Wiz   'Op it, he says, just listen. This serf speaks authentic old-time *My Fair Lady* dialect.

Photo Boy   You're fearless.

Wiz   You're paying. (*Sings.*)
  'He's got the whole wide in his hands!
  He's got the beardless little microbes in his hands.
  He's got – '

Photo Boy   Easy, boy.

Wiz   Get off.

Photo Boy   Alright, big man, I'm not by nature given to interference, it's just that I think the way you're going on you'll kill yourself, which I'd regret. I got to see Suzette. I hear she has a client for me.

Wiz   You should like that, after you've spent so much paying bills for *me*.

Photo Boy   You're a horrid little creature, you know that, Wiz? It's a wonder to me they don't use you for some experiment.

Wiz   Give my hate to Suzette. (*Sneers.*) Ask her if she's had her hundredth spade yet.

Photo Boy   Careful.

Wiz   Taxi!

A taxi arrives. **Wiz** *jumps in.*

Wiz   Any chance of leaving a door open, citizen? So that the summer breeze can ruffle my greased-back DA hairstyle on my journey?

Taxi Driver   You want a breeze, stay on the street.

Wiz   Charming. Home please, citizen.

Wiz *and the taxi drive off.*

Suzette *enters, dancing with a black youth. They kiss passionately. The black youth thrusts his hands up her skirt.* **Photo Boy** *watches from the sidelines.*

Photo Boy   The first time I ever met Suze was in a coffee bar in Belgravia. I watched as she was lovingly allowing her cappuccino to grow cold, and nibbled at a cream-cheese sandwich as I took her picture. From that second on, I was loved up with her. Suze never eats at midday, as she's inclined to plumpness, which I rather like, but makes up for it at evening time with huge plates of chicken and peas she cooks for her spade visitors.

Finally, **Photo Boy** *cuts in. The black youth slopes away.*
Suzette *straightens her clothes.*

Suzette   Hi, darl.

Photo Boy   Had your hundredth yet?

Suzette   No, not yet.

Photo Boy   You ever thought of marrying one of them?

Suzette (*laughs*)   If ever I marry, it will be exclusively for distinction.

Photo Boy   Not with a spade then?

Suzette   Depends what he's offering.

Photo Boy   What could a spade offer you? They're as skint as I am.

Suzette   You'd be surprised. There's quite a few I know with style, distinction –

Photo Boy   Money?

Suzette   Well, that's something you could never give me.

Photo Boy   Ouch. Tell me about this client then. The who and when.

Suzette   He's a diplomat. Or so he says.

Photo Boy   Any special country?

Suzette   Not exactly. He's over here for some conference. So she told me.

Photo Boy   She who?

Suzette   His woman. She came into the shop with him to buy dresses.

Photo Boy   How do you go about raising the matter, that you're an agent for my camera studies?

Suzette   Quite simple really. Sometimes of course, they know of me, I mean, recommended by other clients. Or else

I just size them up and show them some from my collection. Hands!

Photo Boy   I've missed you.

Suzette   Business, darl.

Photo Boy (*stops*)   What kind of snap does he need?

Suzette   I didn't go into details.

Photo Boy   Don't come the acid drop, you're taking 25 per cent, ain't yer?

Suzette   I don't suppose you have it for me in advance? Thought not.

Photo Boy   I'll go out looking for this character then.

Suzette   Make the most.

Photo Boy   Come again?

Suzette   We need to call time on these jobs.

Photo Boy *protests*.

Suzette   Just for a bit. My boss is getting suspicious.

Photo Boy   Your clients' money is the only dough I got coming in.

Suzette   Poor little darl.

Photo Boy   What do I do now?

Suzette   Why are you asking me? Why is it always me that has to sort us out?

Photo Boy   Suppose I can always get a proper job.

Suzette (*scoffs*)   Be a taxpayer?

Photo Boy   It will be regular money for once. Could get hitched.

Suzette   To who? (*Realises.*) Oh babe!

Photo Boy   Why not? We love each other.

Suzette   Love ain't enough, darl.

Photo Boy   Says who?

Suzette   And then what? After a hard day's graft, you hurry back to the world of *What's My Line?* and England's green and pleasant land, relaxing in yer beloved armchair whilst eating yer dinner off yer tray?

Photo Boy   Alright, forget it.

Suzette (*chuckles*)   What are you thinking? If I ain't got time for a bloke who has less than five hundred in his pocket at any given, what makes you think I'm gonna marry one who's lucky if he earns that in a year? I don't want to be no drudge.

Photo Boy   I don't want you sleeping with the spades.

Suzette   Then do something about it for once.

Photo Boy   Alright, what if I had five hundred notes, in my hip pocket, right now? What would you do?

Suzette   I'd say, 'Show me the colour of your money, and you'll see what I can do.'

Photo Boy (*turned on*)   Girl, you are on.

Suzette   No, you are. (*She grabs his crotch.*)

They kiss.

Photo Boy   And you, no more sleeping with the spades.

Suzette   You wanna rob me of every pleasure?

Photo Boy   That's the deal. I get the money, you don't take every spade you meet and drag him between the sheets.

Suzette   Alright, big boy, it's a deal. Let's see what you're made of. And your time starts – now.

Photo Boy   You watch me.

Suzette *gives him another kiss before leaving.*

Photo Boy *gets up to spin a record. He sees* **Mr Cool**.

Cool   Hey, young one! What are you looking so cheerful about?

Photo Boy   Sun is shining, my friend.

Cool   But the summer can't last!

Photo Boy (*feeling revved up*) Yes it can, Cool! It can last till the calendar says stop.

Photo Boy *is in* **Mickey P**'s *flat. He listens with pleasure as a track of Billie Holiday is playing on the record player.*

Mickey P *enters, wearing a bathrobe.*

Mickey P   Ah, you like Billie?

Photo Boy   Sends a shiver. She's suffered so much in her life, Lady D, it's like she carries all your pain for you. One spin of hers, and I'm a cheerful cat again. So, where are you from, Mickey, Latin America?

Mickey P   I come from these parts, but I live in the United States. You have a drink?

Photo Boy   No, ta.

Mickey P   You don't drink?

Photo Boy   Never.

Mickey P   Then how do you get by?

Photo Boy   I get all the kicks I need from me. What kind of print might your wife be needing?

Mickey P   She would like you to photograph me.

Photo Boy   Doing what?

Mickey P   Athletic pose, in my gym uniform.

Photo Boy   Alone?

Mickey P *disrobes to reveal himself wearing a pair of white-laced navy-blue basketball shoes, black ballet rehearsal tights, a nude chest thatched like a Christmas card and on his head a small round racing swimmer's cap.*

Photo Boy (*like he's used to it*)   Right.

Mickey P   You may begin.

Photo Boy   How many poses do you want?

Mickey P   About one reel's worth?

Photo Boy   Alright, walk about, do what comes naturally.

Photo boy *clicks away as* **Mickey P** *poses. Each one becoming more and more narcissistic.*

Mickey P   Perhaps you can help me?

Photo Boy   I thought I was.

Mickey P   It is like this. I have a study to complete for the UN on British folk ways in the middle of the century.

Photo Boy   Oh yeah?

Mickey P   I have observed the British, but I've got very few interesting ideas about them.

Photo Boy   How long you been observing them?

Mickey P   Six weeks, which I know is not a very long time, but even so, I cannot get perspectives. Even the weather is wrong. It's reputed to be cold in the English summer, but look at it.

Photo Boy   Yeah, I know what you mean. An old sun from the Sahara crept up on us, unawares, one we weren't at all ready for. Hold it – nice.

Mickey P   Take the two main political parties.

Photo Boy   I'd rather not. You can smile, if you like that kind of snap.

Mickey P   They do not interest you?

Photo Boy   How could they? Good one.

Mickey P   But your destinies are being worked out by their initiatives.

Photo Boy   Whoever is working out my destinies, you can be sure it ain't any one of those parliamentary numbers.

Mickey P   You despise politics? Somebody has to do the housekeeping.

Photo Boy   If they'd stick to their housekeeping, and stopped playing Winston Churchill and the Great Armada when there's no tin soldiers left to play with any more, then no one would despise them, because no one would even notice them. Lovely! Try lying down.

Mickey P (*lies down*)   The bomb – what would you do about that?

Photo Boy   No one in the world under twenty could give a single lump of cat's shit for the bomb. Bend over.

Mickey P   How do you know that?

Photo Boy   It's only you adult numbers who want to destroy each other. Use this broom, that's it. I mean, you don't have to travel to know what it's like to be young, any time, anywhere. Youth is international, just like old age. We're both very fond of life. Do you want yer belly showing?

Mickey P *sucks in his stomach. He pouts his lips.*

Photo Boy   Very nice.

Mickey P   That only leaves us with one topic: Her Majesty the Queen.

Photo Boy   Oh please! I can't even work up the interest to have any ideas about that. Very nice. That's it.

Mickey P *hands him a cheque.*

Mickey P   Thank you.

Photo Boy   Thank you, guv'nor. Ten down, 490 to go.

Mickey P *places the record back in its sleeve, then shoves it under the boy's arm.*

Mickey P   Why don't you take this as well, please?

Photo Boy   Cheers!

Mickey P   So you have not much to tell me about Britain and her position?

Photo Boy   Her position, Mickey, is that she hasn't found her position. Fare you well.

Photo Boy *arrives home. He bangs on the door several times. A middle-aged woman, wearing nothing but underwear underneath her dressing gown, appears by the balcony.*

Mum   Oi, oi, oi, what's all the noise? Hold yer horses, I'm coming, where's the fire? Oh, it's you! Hello, Blitz baby.

Photo Boy   Hello, Ma.

A half-naked man creeps up behind **Mum** *and fondles her breasts. She giggles.*

Mum   Careful now, Turkish. Oi, hands!

Photo Boy   Are you going to open up, or shall I climb in through your front-parlour window?

Mum   Yes, alright, Mr Stroppy Bollocks. I'll send yer father down. (*Shouts to someone downstairs.*) Bert! (*To the man.*) And as for you, come here!

Mum *and the man giggle as she leads him back inside.* **Photo Boy**'s **Dad** *lets him in.*

Photo Boy   Hello, Dad.

Dad (*solemn*)   Hello, son.

Photo Boy *enters his darkroom. He notices something is moving underneath a pile of old rags. He chooses to ignore this and get on with* *his work, but he is distracted by the noise of somebody belching. It is coming from the rags.*

Photo Boy Alright, Jules, so how's my favourite yobbo, then?

A shabbily dressed man, mid-twenties, appears from underneath. He looks like he hasn't washed for a month.

Verne Stop calling me Jules, it's Verne.

Photo Boy (*looks at him*) Not another King Kong performance? Dear oh dear.

Verne You can talk, with your short-arse Italian jacket. I didn't spend a penny on this. It's my demobilisation suit. When you've done your military service you'll be given one too. And a decent haircut for once.

Photo Boy Oh, Verne, somehow you've just missed the teenage rave, ain't yer?

Verne The war was Britain's finest hour.

Photo Boy Which war was that? Cyprus? Suez? Korea?

Verne The real war, don't you remember?

Photo Boy I'm glad I don't. All you form-filling taxpayers certainly try to keep it well in mind. Every time I open a newspaper, go to the Odeon, it's war, war, war!

Verne You're just ignorant.

Photo Boy That's OK by me.

Verne Let's see you laughing when you have to go.

Photo Boy (*scoffs*) I've no intention of playing soldiers for anybody, mate.

Verne You'll have to go. What we done, you gotta do.

Photo Boy Jeez, one minute talking to you and I'm exhausted already. Subject's closed. Now be a *half*-good brother and let me work. What you doing in my darkroom anyway?

Dad *comes into the darkroom, carrying cups of tea and a tatty notebook under his arm.*

Dad   He's been quarrelling with the lodgers. Here's yer tea, son.

Photo Boy   Cheers, Dad. 'Ere, so how's the book of yours going?

Dad   I'm on Chapter 23, as we speak.

Photo Boy   Nice one. Where are you up to then?

Dad   The 1930s, terrible time to be young then, son.

Verne   And he's off!

Photo Boy   Ignore it, Dad.

Dad   We had poverty, mass unemployment, no chance, no opportunities, no sunlight at the end of the corridor. Just a load of hard, frightened, rich old men sitting on top of a pile of dustbin lids, keeping the masses from spilling over. I tell you, boy, it's better now, even with the bomb.

Photo Boy   If you like the fifties so much, why don't you enjoy yourself a bit? Ain't too late you know, ain't even forty yet. Get a job, travel around, see where the sights are?

Verne   Too afraid to leave, ain'tcha, 'Dad'?

Photo Boy   Mouth shut, Jules.

Verne   It's true. She keeps him here, to make the place look respectable.

Dad   I don't know why I put up with you, I mean, you've nothing to do with me, have yer?

Photo Boy   Just ignore him, it's easy.

Verne   At least I ain't a traitor to the working class!

Photo Boy   I ain't a traitor to the working class, because I do not belong to the working class, you prehistoric monster. Come on, Dad.

They both step outside.

Mum *appears, leaning over the balcony.*

Mum   Bert!

Dad   Oh, what now?

Mum   There's a mile-high of dishes in here – they won't wash themselves.

Dad   Yeah, I know.

Photo Boy   Fancy going on a boat trip for your birthday, Dad?

Dad   Does the Pope live in Rome?

Mum   Bert!

Dad   I'm coming.

Photo Boy   It will do you good to get out.

Dad   So come on, quickly, what's the news, how's your lady friend? Still gorgeous?

Photo Boy   You better believe it.

Dad   Time you started thinking about putting a ring on her finger.

Photo Boy *laughs.*

Dad   What?

Photo Boy   Ain't her scene, Dad, the old dinero is her scene, and plenty of it.

Dad   You mean she says that's what she wants. All birds want their fellas to go on their bended knees.

Photo Boy   Not my Suze.

Dad   Bring her round one Sunday for tea. It's time we met the girl, don't you think? Or are you ashamed?

Photo Boy   No.

Dad   You lie like yer mother, you do.

Photo Boy   It's complicated.

Dad   So, you are ashamed?

Photo Boy   Times change, Dad. (*Scoffs.*) Sunday tea? That ain't us.

Dad   Just tell me you love her, or don't you kids do that any more?

Photo Boy   I'm crazy for her.

Dad   Well, at least that's one thing good that hasn't changed. Just don't you let her go now.

Photo Boy   No intention.

Mum (*screams*)   Bert!

Dad   Alright. Be lucky, son. Live for me, yeah?

Dad *goes back inside.*

Photo Boy   Well, hello, Madame Blanche. So how's the harem in reverse then?

Mum   You're getting too big for your boots, my lad.

Photo Boy   Shoes actually. I gotta split.

Mum   Not so fast, I wanna talk to you.

Photo Boy   I'm in a rush.

Mum   It's about yer dad.

Photo Boy   What about?

Mum   He's dying, son.

Photo Boy (*laughs*)   What? Leave off.

Mum   I'm serious.

Photo Boy   You're cracked. I'm gone.

Mum   Listen to me. It's the truth.

Photo Boy   He don't look like he's dying one bit.

Mum   Well, the doctor says different.

Photo Boy   Sick joke, Ma.

Mum   If it was a joke, but it ain't. I'm sorry, love.

Photo Boy   Oh yes? Are yer?

Mum   Don't be such a baby, Blitz baby.

Photo Boy   You serious? What's he got?

Mum   It's his chest, of course, him and his pipe.

Photo Boy   Does he know?

Mum   Course he knows.

Photo Boy   I'm gonna talk to him.

Mum   He'll deny it, you know him.

Photo Boy   Not to me.

Mum   Just let him have his pride, will yer?

Photo Boy   What would you know about his pride?

Mum   Just listen to what I have to say, cloth ears. If something should happen to your father, I want you to move back here.

Photo Boy   Oh yeah? Why? To keep this place respectable? Cos Verne is such a drip-dry drag that no one would ever take him for the male of the establishment? You're unbelievable, I'm out of here.

Mum   Yes, run away, like there's no tomorrow. What about yer dad?

Photo Boy   I'll take my instructions in that matter from
Dad, and Dad alone. And if he dies, I'll take my instructions
from myself. Why don't you go back to your gigolo lodger.

Mum   You're a little monster.

Photo Boy   Mother should know.

Photo Boy *rides his scooter. He arrives at Napoli.* **Ed the Ted**
and his thugs are throwing a young black man out.

Ed the Ted   Take all yer crap, and all yer little *Schwarzers*
out of here! You deaf!

Cool *enters. He stands between* **Ed the Ted** *and his friend. He
holds* **Ed***'s gaze, warning him to back off, which he does.*

Cool   Hey, young one?

Ed the Ted   You talking to me, Mr Cool?

Cool   Today is a good day.

Ed the Ted   For what?

Cool   To die!

Ed the Ted (*to* **Cool***'s friend*)   You'll keep.

Photo Boy   You'd not live in our Napoli if you could live
anywhere else. That is why there are, to the square yard,
more boys fresh from the nick, and national refugee
minorities, and whores and queers, than anywhere else, I
should expect, in London town. If you come in, they take it
for granted that you know the scene. If you don't, it's true,
they'll throw you out in pieces.

Photo Boy *removes his shirt to have a wash.* **Cool***, in the flat
above him, is cleaning his clarinet.*

Photo Boy (*calls*)   Hey, Cool, play us a tune, man!

Cool   Patience, young one, gotta have the vibe!

Fabulous Hoplite *enters.*

Hoplite (*showing off his outfit*)   Well? Opinion?

Photo Boy   Smashing, Hoplite. It gives you a rugged, shaggy, Burt Lancaster appearance.

Hoplite   I'm not sure it's me.

Photo Boy   It's you, alright. You're one who can wear anything, even a swimsuit, and look good.

Hoplite   I know you're one of my fans, but don't mock.

Photo Boy   No mockery, man, you've got dress sense.

Hoplite   Oh, it's not dress sense I need, it's horse sense!

Photo Boy   Spill.

Hoplite   Believe it or not, my dear, but your old friend Fabulous, for the first time in his life, the very first time, in nineteen years, is deep, deep in love. Ask me who?

Photo Boy   Who?

Hoplite   Sadist! An Americano.

Photo Boy   Ah!

Hoplite   And what does that 'Ah' mean?

Photo Boy   Several things, but tell me more.

Hoplite   Misery, that's it.

Photo Boy   Doesn't care for the angle, Hoplite, or doesn't care for you, or just doesn't care either way?

Hoplite   The angle. Not bent at all. Though I had hopes he might have dabbled. And he's so understanding, which makes it worse.

Photo Boy   Oh, you poor old queen.

Hoplite   I only hope it doesn't turn me anti-American.

Photo Boy   It's a sure sign of total defeat to be anti-Yank.

Hoplite   I thought you didn't approve of the American influence. You don't care for Elvis, and you do like Tommy.

Photo Boy   Listen, glamourpuss, because I want English kids to be English kids, not North Ken Yanks. Doesn't mean I'm anti the US thing. We just gotta produce our own variety.

Hoplite   Oh, you're such a clever boy. And deep down, I do believe, a patriot.

Photo Boy   Yeah, a patriot, that hates his country.

Hoplite   There's a party tonight at Chez. You interested?

Photo Boy   What kind?

Hoplite   Oh, the usual SW3 trash! Ad people, TV people, showbiz, all the parasites. Suze is going, with her new man.

Photo Boy   What new man?

Hoplite   Sorry, I meant the other one, whoever he is, this month.

Photo Boy   There is no whoever. Not any more. I'm her man. The one and only.

Hoplite   Since when?

Photo Boy   Since she and I came to an understanding. I keep her happy with her expensive tastes, she stays loyal, to me.

Hoplite   Darling, you will need the deficit of a small country to keep Crêpe Suzette in expensive tastes. Do you actually believe she will keep up her end?

Photo Boy   She promised, Hop, no more sleeping with the spades.

Hoplite   Who said it was a spade? Not I.

Photo Boy   Who else can it be?

Hoplite   You know I don't like to gossip.

Photo Boy   But for me, you'll make an exception.

Hoplite   I don't know his name, but he's an older gent.

Photo Boy   A citizen! Shut up! You are talking out of it.

Hoplite   I tell you what I see, not what it is.

Photo Boy   It's probably nothing. It is nothing.

Hoplite   I'm sure you are right.

Enter **Big Jill** *from her basement flat.*

Big Jill   You studs up there, are you coming down to see yer doll?

Hoplite   I do wish that enormous lesbian wouldn't shout so.

Photo Boy (*shouts*)   One second, Jill. Coming, Hop?

Hoplite   No, please.

Hoplite *blows him a kiss and leaves.* **Photo Boy** *joins* **Big Jill** *downstairs.*

Big Jill   You're late, you horrible little studlet.

Photo Boy   I didn't know we had an appointment.

Big Jill *grabs him and lifts him from the floor.*

Big Jill   Oh, if you were a chick, I'd eat you.

Photo Boy   Easy, ladykiller.

Big Jill   So how's yer sex life, Junior, since we last met?

Photo Boy   We only last met a couple of days ago, Jill.

Big Jill   What, nothing to report?

Photo Boy   You can't say how's yer sex life like you say how's the weather.

Big Jill   Well, pardon me for existing. What's the matter, you skint again? You need a bit dinero? Couple of quid do yer?

Photo Boy   I need a lot more than that.

Big Jill   You got troubles then? Bailiffs? Syphilis?

Photo Boy   No, none of that.

Big Jill   Oh, let me guess. Still playing around with the spades, is she?

Photo Boy   No. Suze is done with that.

Big Jill   Who's she on with now then, the Sikhs?

Photo Boy   She's not on with anyone, she's on with me. You really don't think I have what it takes to hold on to her, do yer?

Big Jill   This ain't about you, my love. I've known Suze longer, and I'm telling yer, she's not going to change.

Photo Boy   She will for me.

Big Jill   Oh, doll.

Photo Boy   Don't call me that.

Big Jill   You lie with the worst of them, you do.

Photo Boy   I ain't lying.

Big Jill   You'll only do yourself an injury, you're too young for that.

Photo Boy   Then what are you doubting me for?

Big Jill   Could never doubt you, stud. Because you are a romantic, a second-feature Romeo. But there's plenty of other kicks out there, you know. World ain't all about Crêpe Suzette. Enjoy yourself, doll, until it don't mean a thing. Trust me, she is.

Photo Boy   I gotta fly, Jill.

Big Jill   So fly, and hey?

Photo Boy   Yep?

Big Jill   Take it easy, breezy.

Photo Boy *gets back on his scooter.*

Music plays. **Photo Boy** *enters the jazz club, Chez Nobody.*

Photo Boy   Now you can think what you like about the art of jazz. Quite frankly, I don't care what you think, cos jazz is a thing so wonderful that if anybody doesn't rave about it, all you can feel for them is pity. In here, no one cares who you are, what you do, as long as you dig the scene, leave all of that crap behind. Provided you don't meddle, it's really a safe place. It's not in Soho, where a sex maniac leaps out of a hedge and violates you.

Dean Swift *enters.* **Photo Boy** *waves to him.*

Dean   Fuck off, you fascist.

Photo Boy   Dean Swift. A sharp modern jazz creation and, by far, my favourite model. Porno snaps of him sell like hot ice cream among vintage women with too many bosoms and time on their hands. But Dean ain't interested in all that, on account of him being a junkie. Hail, squire, you seen Suze?

Dean   Nope. You printed those pictures of me and my bird, yet?

Photo Boy   I've developed the stuff, Deano my man, but your chick has come out too indistinct by far. She must have moved. We gotta do it all again. Client won't pay until then, and I need the cash, man. Can you raise your partner?

Dean   I'll bell yer later. Doesn't this place stink?

Photo Boy   The air or the atmosphere?

Dean   The both. (*Looks around at the kids in the club.*) Look at all these teenage products. Beardless microbes!

Photo Boy   Easy, Dean, you look like a commandant from Auschwitz.

Dean   They're driving scooters and bubble cars now. Couple of years back, they were pushing toy ones on the pavement. Younger and younger, especially the chicks.

The kids in the club cheer as the musicians play 'He's Got the Whole World in his Hands'.

Dean   I don't believe this! What's the matter with you? – it's jazz club, you sheep. See what I mean, boy?

Photo Boy   Hard not to, Dean.

Dean (*shouts*)   You're nothing but a bunch of mindless butterflies.

Vendice Partners *enters. He is handing out business cards to the kids.*

Photo Boy   Is that who I think it is?

Dean   In the flesh! Laurie London is one thing. But I draw the line at fucking Vendice I-am-the-Devil Partners. I'm outside for a fix.

Photo Boy   If you see Suze, tell her I'm looking for her.

Dean   What's she done?

Photo Boy   Just tell her.

Dean *leaves.* **Photo Boy** *takes pictures.*

Vendice   Ah, you must be that famous boy behind the lens.

Photo Boy   You know me?

Vendice   Mickey Pollorosso had been telling me all about you.

Photo Boy   Fab.

Vendice   He tells me you have integrity. Just the kind of man I am always looking for. (*Hands him his card.*) Vendice Partners.

Photo Boy   The Media Mogul. Yeah, and so?

Vendice   You should come and see me, show me your photos, maybe I can help you.

Photo Boy   Yeah?

Vendice   I have a TV series coming out. It's called *Lorn Lovers* and we are looking for persons deeply in love whom fate has sundered. But you're too young for tears. Maybe among your somewhat older companions.

Photo Boy   You could go for Hoplite, I suppose.

Vendice   And who is he in love with? We want to confront the frantic pair in front of the cameras, without either knowing beforehand what's going to hit them.

Photo Boy   He's in love with a Yank.

Vendice   A good angle – though we'd have to pay the fee in dollars. Yes, confront the pair, get them in a clinch! It'll be sensational. It's my aim, my achievement, to bring quality culture material to the pop culture masses. Today, any man, woman and child in the United Kingdom can be made into a personality, a star! Whoever you are, we can make you live for millions.

The kids gather round as **Vendice** *gives out cards.*

Photo Boy *meets* **Wiz**.

Photo Boy   Oi, Wiz, you seen Suze?

Wiz   You're not going to harp on about her all night, are yer? Has she had her hundredth yet?

Photo Boy   Just forget it.

Wiz   Intend to. Come on, ask.

Photo Boy   Ask you what?

Wiz   What's new.

Photo Boy   What is new?

Wiz   I have news, boy.

Photo Boy   Go on.

Wiz   I'm thinking of going into business with a chick! Smile?

Photo Boy   Clever, Wiz. I'll visit you in Brixton.

Wiz   Is that you not approving?

Photo Boy   Give it up, Wiz, you ain't no hustler!

Wiz   Try anything once.

Photo Boy   What's next, breaking and entering? Tell me one ponce you know who's got real brains?

Wiz   I know of several.

Photo Boy   I don't mean craft or cunning, I mean brains. Constructive brains.

Wiz   I could introduce you to several club owners, bookies and car salesmen who've built up their business by loot they've made when on the game.

Photo Boy   I could introduce you to several Saturday midnight at the chemist's and several in-and-out boys and several corpses who've had the same idea.

Wiz   This from a kiddo known around the town for flogging porno pictures.

Photo Boy   You really gonna compare poncing to what I do?

Wiz   Not really, it's better paid.

Photo Boy   Should be ashamed.

Wiz   Ashamed? Oh, you taxpayer.

Photo Boy   You've got brains, Wiz. If you had a fragment of education, you'd have done big things. Ain't too late. Why don't you study?

Wiz   I am studying – school of life.

Photo Boy   Brixton class!

Wiz   Each occupation has its risks. I'm as safe as houses, look! Imagine me in the dock. What jury is going to believe a baby face like me could be a ponce?

Photo Boy   Wiz, if you could see yourself in the mirror now, you'd realise you don't look young any more. Yer old, mate.

Wiz   This game is old. Since A and Eve, there's always been the woman, the visitor and the local male.

Photo Boy   Be the visitor then. Christ, what is happening to us all, eh? What's going on? (*Checks his watch.*)

Wiz   She's really keeping you hanging. Like some horny little spade.

Photo Boy   Button it.

Wiz   What have I been telling you, for months? Holding on to a brass like that. 'Ere, you reckon she'll be interested in coming into business?

Photo Boy   Thin ice, Wiz.

Wiz   You know she'd make a bundle. Come on, crack a smile, you know you adore me.

Photo Boy *slaps* **Wiz**.

Wiz   Not only do you sound like a citizen, you hit like one of them. Once and once only will I let you get away with that.

Wiz *leaves*.

Suzette, *followed by* **Henley**, *enters*. **Photo Boy** *approaches them*.

Photo Boy   Hi, doll.

Suzette   I didn't think you'd be here tonight.

Photo Boy   Had to meet Dean.

Henley   Suzette, my dear, aren't you going to introduce us?

Suzette   Of course. This is Henley. Henley this is –

Henley   Your young man, of course. How do you do?

Photo Boy   Well, if I'm the young man, then you must be the old man.

Suzette   Don't.

Photo Boy   I've barely started.

Henley   Well, if you wouldn't mind starting now, old boy? We're having dinner later.

Photo Boy   But you thought you'd hang out here first, have a glance at how the lowlifes live before you stuff your faces with expensive wine and dead fish. Is that what this place has come to? A tourist attraction? What you playing at, Suze?

Henley   Darling, please enlighten the gentleman.

Suzette   How about a dance?

Photo Boy   A what?

Henley   We mustn't be late for our table, dear.

Suzette   We won't.

As **Suzette** *takes* **Photo Boy** *to the dance floor, he grabs her arm.*

Henley (*sees someone he knows*)   Vendice!

Photo Boy   What are you doing going out with your boss? You didn't tell me.

Suzette   Obviously someone did.

Photo Boy   Yer bleedin shameless.

Suzette   Excuse me, are we married? You didn't think I was going to wait on you?

Photo Boy   I'm working on a couple of things, it takes time.

Suzette   You should have that written on your forehead. 'It Takes Time.'

Photo Boy   We had a plan though.

Suzette   Every plan must carry a contingency, hon.

Photo Boy   You promised me no messing around.

Suzette   With the spades. Does he look like one to you?

Photo Boy   I'll tell you what he looks like.

Suzette   And you'd be right.

Photo Boy   So, he's bent.

Suzette   As a butcher's hook.

Photo Boy   What are you going to get from him?

Suzette   He's loaded. Work it out. He pays me to be seen with him, it's his cover.

Photo Boy   It's disgusting.

Suzette   It's business. You want to stop living your life through that lens.

Photo Boy   But you're my girl.

Suzette (*mocks*)   I'm your girl, you're my boy. What are we, possessions?

Photo Boy   Don't write me off as a pensioner.

Suzette   Well, don't act like one.

Photo Boy   I can see what's good. But can you? Can you see what the pensioners are doing?

Suzette   Don't start that.

Photo Boy   This is our time. They've had theirs. Now they want ours.

Suzette   Boring.

Photo Boy   They give us sequins, when we think we're getting diamonds.

Suzette   Get off the soapbox. Take it down Hyde Park. Henley's asked me to marry him.

Photo Boy   You can't.

Suzette   Says who? He lives in Cookham, you ever bin there? It's so lovely – he's got this gorgeous big house right on the Thames.

Photo Boy   Does this look like a face that's interested?

Suzette   We're thinking of announcing our engagement, end of next month.

Photo Boy   Don't.

Suzette   We'll send out wedding invites beginning of next year.

Photo Boy   Suze?

Suzette   Followed by a spring wedding, in a church, can you imagine?

Photo Boy   I won't let it, I'll stop yer.

Suzette   So stop me. Get those pockets filled, five hundred crispy notes with pictures of the Queen's face on it. Make it happen for once, then watch me drool.

Photo Boy   It takes ti—

Suzette   'It Takes Time.'

Photo Boy *hands her ten pounds.*

Suzette   Wass this?

Photo Boy   A start.

Suzette   And the rest?

Henley *waves.*

Suzette   I have to go. The clock is ticking.

Suzette *leaves with* **Henley**.

Wiz (*approaching*)   See what I mean, boy? It's all about money. The old dinero. Still feel like pissing on my plans for prosperity?

Photo Boy   Nothing wrong with being rich, Wiz, I wanna be rich. But I ain't gonna be hooked.

Wiz   We'll see who gets there first then.

Photo Boy   You're on.

Act Two

In July

Photo Boy *is in* **Vendice**'s *office*.

Photo Boy   So, you in the media game? Load of bollocks, if you ask me.

Vendice   Lucky for you, I am asking.

Photo Boy   So tell me then, Mr Partners –

Vendice   Vendice, please.

Photo Boy   – what's it all for? I mean, what use is it?

Vendice   That is one question we must never pause to answer.

Photo Boy   What's with the coloured folders then?

Vendice   It's about Christmas.

Photo Boy   I don't dig.

Vendice (*holds up folder*)   This is a pitch for a series that will be flooding the airwaves, we hope, at Yuletide.

Photo Boy   But this is July.

Vendice   We must plan ahead, must we not?

Photo Boy   Feel sorry for yer.

Vendice   Thank you. So tell me, what are you? Are you a man with a plan?

Photo Boy   I am a man in search of a plan.

Vendice   Did you bring your photos?

Photo Boy   Here. (*Gives him his folder.*)

Vendice (*flipping through*)   Two words, not commercial.

Photo Boy   I know they're not, that's why I'm here.

Vendice   I don't hold people's hands for a living. I'm a busy man, son, why should I do anything for you? Gimme a reason.

Photo Boy   Hold up, you gave me your card.

Vendice   Still doesn't answer my question.

Photo Boy   Cos you want to?

Vendice   Why do I want to?

Photo Boy   I dunno.

Vendice   Yes you do. And so do I.

Photo Boy   So why ask the question?

Vendice   Because you need to say it.

Photo Boy   If you ask me, you rich cats are the only ones that really keep this nation sliding off its arse.

Vendice   You think so?

Photo Boy   Don't do that.

Vendice   Don't do what?

Photo Boy   Giving me that smile, that amused smile you seniors turn on whenever something intelligent is said by one of us. Naturally I think it, if I just said it.

Vendice   Not many would agree with you.

Photo Boy   You don't have to tell me. Turn on your telly, your radio, do you ever catch anything about businessmen? And yet, don't we all live off what you do? Let's face it, without you tycoons, there just wouldn't be the money for the rent.

Vendice   You're very flattering.

Photo Boy   England was an empire, right, now it isn't any more, so all it's got to live on will be brains and labour and you lot. Now I'm not saying business is difficult, it's not

difficult to coin loot, provided it's your number-one
obsession.

Vendice   Is it yours?

Photo Boy   I'm here, aren't I?

Vendice   Let's have it, son.

Photo Boy   London is changing, finally, for the better!

Vendice   Continue.

Photo Boy   In all of its history, there's never been
anything like us teenagers!

Vendice   Continue.

Photo Boy   No more war, no more grey, just colour. We
are the future. The way it will be from now on.

Vendice   I like it.

Photo Boy   I can be your boy, Vendice. Your own
professional teenager. With my snaps, I can tell it as it is.

Vendice   I can use this. Yes, I'm thinking newspapers, I'm
thinking magazines, short stories, long stories, movies, plays,
radio – just imagine it, on the air with this, twenty-four
hours a day.

Photo Boy   Just telling the truth, yeah, as it is, yeah?

Vendice   Of course, the truth. I see jeans, I see shoes, I
see jackets, T-shirts, perfume. My very own teenage brand.

Photo Boy   You won't find it better anywhere.

Vendice   Or realer. I can make you a very rich man, but
it has to be real, son.

Photo Boy   It will be, I'm the one.

Vendice   Good enough reason. I'll do it. Deal.

Photo Boy   You're a nice cat.

Vendice   There, I'm afraid, you are very much mistaken. Drink?

Photo Boy   Tonic.

Cool *runs onstage, being chased by a gang of* **Teds**. **Cool** *is cornered; the* **Teds** *circle.*

Ed the Ted   Oi, oi, where you running to, black boy?

Ted 1   We only want a word.

Ted 2   Black boy!

Ed the Ted   We're just asking if you have any cigarettes.

Ted 2   Black boy.

Cool   No.

Ted 2   No?

Ted 1   Wotcha mean, no?

Ed the Ted   Black boy?

Cool   I mean, no.

Ted 2   No, you have no cigarettes?

Ted 1   Or no, you ain't giving us any?

Ed the Ted   Black boy?

Cool   Pick one.

Ed the Ted   That ain't very nice.

Ted 1   Black boy.

Ted 2   Might have to teach you some manners.

Ed the Ted   Black boy!

Cool   Try it.

Ted 2   Which side you want your hair parted?

Ted 1   Black boy?

Cool   What you want?

Ted 2   You –

Ted 1   And your kind –

Ed the Ted   Out of Napoli.

Ted 2   Black boy.

Cool   Never going to happen.

Ted 1   We hate you.

Cool   You don't say?

Ted 2   Get back to your own country.

Cool   This is my country.

Ted 1   Black boy!

Ed the Ted   You're nothing but a monkey.

Cool   Yeah, and when your mother wants a good fuck, she comes to me, instead of yer dad.

Ted 2 *surges forward, but* **Cool** *snaps his fingers. Two of his black mates appear, armed with bats. The* **Teds** *withdraw.*

Ed the Ted   Yes, run and hide, Mr Cool.

Ted 2   We'll dance again!

Ted 1   Black boy!

Suzette *is sitting at the dining table with* **Henley** *at his home in Cookham.*

Henley   Alright, my dear, let's try this again.

Suzette   Yes, Henley, let's. (*Giggles.*)

Henley   No giggling, please.

Suzette   No giggling. I can't believe how big this house is, though. My flat can fit in your bathroom, did you know that?

Henley   No.

Suzette   Sorry, really sorry, I'll pay attention now.

Henley   If you wouldn't mind.

Suzette   This is the life.

Henley   Please?

Suzette   Sorry.

Henley   Now, dinner napkin.

Suzette   You gently lay it on the lap.

Henley   Lay gently *in* the lap.

Suzette   Right, sorry.

Henley   Please remove your elbows. Now, once again. (*Holds up forks.*) This is for your starter, this is for your salad, this one is for your main course, understand?

Suzette   Don't I have a fork for dessert?

Henley   This is where the spoon comes in.

Suzette *is giggling.*

Henley   What is it now?

Suzette   All this. It's unreal. Back home on Fridays, we would eat with our fingers. Dad always bought fish and chips on his way back from work. It was the only day of the week Mum never cooked.

Henley   How interesting.

Suzette   If they could see me now, eh?

Henley   How interesting. Shall we try?

Suzette *lifts up the wrong fork.*

Henley   No, no, from the outside in.

Suzette   Outside in, I keep forgetting, sorry.

Henley   Do not be sorry.

Suzette   I'm just a bit nervous.

Henley   One more time.

Suzette   You've got such a lovely house, Henley.

Henley   Thank you.

Suzette   I can't believe it.

Henley   Suzette, my dear?

Suzette   You ever seen that film where Charlie Chaplin does that things with the forks?

Henley *whacks* **Suzette** *on the fingers with a spoon.* **Suzette** *yelps.*

Suzette (*in pain*)   Bastard!

Henley   There you see, you little silly girl, you have got me all upset. Why don't I leave you alone for a few minutes, try to remember, and then we'll start again, yes? Good girl. Please do not slouch, darling.

Henley *leaves.*

Suzette (*in tears*)   Fucking bastard!

Photo Boy, *now dressed in a smart suit and tie, is clicking away at his camera like a madman.*

Photo Boy   Right, let's be having yer, look lively! That's it. Hop on the bike for me mate, lovely. Hop, tilt yer head for me, super. Jill!

Big Jill   Big boy!

Photo Boy   Lean over for me, beautiful. Hop, to the side, man, let me see yer handsome, lovely! Come on, Hop, crack a smile, yer gorgeous! Jill, light yer fag, beautiful, put it back, slowly, gently, oh smashing, this is great, this is good! Hands on hips, Jill, super, lovely! This is good!

Hoplite   What are you on, dear?

Photo Boy *sees* **Cool**.

Photo Boy   Cool, you want in, mate? Come on, show us some moves!

Cool *ignores him as he walks by*.

Photo Boy   Ah well. Jill, look at me, gorgeous.

Big Jill   Scrumptious.

Photo Boy   Gaze at him, right at him, like you want him! That's it. Don't move, beautiful. Hop, tilt yer hat, great, yer fabulous! Now look away, not at me, just look away, keep yer hands on the handlebars. Oh man, what a profile! Look into the lens for me.

Hoplite   You just told me to look away.

Photo Boy   Now I'm saying, look into the lens. Don't come the acid drop, please! Hold it, right there, smashing! You're going to sell so well, my sweet, just a couple more rolls.

Hoplite   A couple more rolls? I'll be up for hours.

Photo Boy   An hour tops.

Hoplite   Not me, my love, my bed is calling!

Photo Boy   Hop! Come on, Jill, he's a lightweight, pout those lips for me, gorgeous. Jill?

Big Jill   Gotta run. Can't keep my girlies waiting, big boy.

Photo Boy   This is important to me. Jesus! You're supposed to be my mates. Vendice is waiting on this snaps, I gotta make a good impression.

Big Jill   Easy, breezy.

Ed the Ted, *followed by other* **Teds**, *crosses the stage.*

Big Jill   You wanna talk about important, aim yer camera at those sopheads.

Photo Boy   Be a waste of film.

Big Jill   It's all kicking off in Nottingham, you know.

Photo Boy   What do you expect kids to do living in a dump like that? The masses don't want to know.

Big Jill   They should.

Photo Boy   You don't think it's gonna happen here? (*Scoffs.*) Do yer?

Big Jill   Catch you later, doll.

She exits.

Photo Boy *jokingly takes a picture of himself.*

Photo Boy (*to himself*)   A professional teenager.

Ed the Ted *enters. He creeps up behind* **Photo Boy** *and snatches his camera.*

Ed the Ted   Well, look who it isn't.

Photo Boy   Hand it over, Ed.

Ed the Ted   Ain't you gonna take my picture?

Photo Boy   And what would be the point in that?

Ed the Ted   Yeah, cos we're nothing but a bunch of inbreds.

Photo Boy   Correct.

Ed the Ted   Stupid white trash.

Photo Boy   You're catching on, Ed.

Ed the Ted   Bin looking for you.

Photo Boy   Help yer?

Ed the Ted   Wid a couple of things.

Photo Boy   Speak.

Ed the Ted   Fuss of all, about these platters.

Photo Boy   What platters?

Ed the Ted   These here. I wanna flog them.

Photo Boy   Let's have a look. (*Examines the records.*) Exceedingly hip, Ed, I didn't know you had such taste. Knocked off, I suppose?

Ed the Ted   Naturally.

Photo Boy   What you asking?

Ed the Ted   Ten.

Photo Boy   I'll give you two.

Ed the Ted   Two? Ten I said.

Photo Boy   No chance.

Ed the Ted   Don't come it, I know you can afford ten.

Photo Boy   Says who?

Ed the Ted   I've bin hearing. You bin taking pictures for that rich cat, Vendick.

Photo Boy   Vendice.

Ed the Ted   You're all suited and booted now, you're loaded.

Photo Boy   Not yet I am, but that is the plan. And I sure as hell won't be if I'm buying knock-offs from the likes of you. Go find yourself another mug. Now, what's the second thing?

Ed the Ted   Flikker sent me.

Photo Boy *looks concerned.*

Ed the Ted   Yeah, I thought that'd make you shiver.

Photo Boy   What's he want?

Ed the Ted   To see you.

Photo Boy   Tell him to call round.

Ed the Ted   You don't tell Flikker.

Photo Boy   I ain't being summoned by anyone, except the magistrate.

Ed the Ted   I'll tell him you said that.

Photo Boy   Please.

Ed the Ted   There's this Sambo he wants out of here.

Photo Boy   Who?

Ed the Ted   Cool.

Photo Boy   Why?

Ed the Ted   He don't have to say why, he just wants him out. You gotta tell him.

Photo Boy   Ed, you can go piss up your leg!

Ed the Ted (*holds up records*)   I'll take five!

Photo Boy   No deal.

Ed the Ted   How about yer camera? Bet that's worth a few bob.

Photo Boy   In your dreams. You can go now.

Ed the Ted *suddenly attacks him.*

Ed the Ted   Now listen here, Sambo lover! I'm trying to be nice. You tell Cool, or whatever his name is, that Flikker says the clock is ticking.

Cool *sees what is happening from his window and runs down.*
Photo Boy *and* **Ed the Ted** *collapse onto the ground, fighting.*
Photo boy *rises to his feet first and kicks* **Ed the Ted** *in the stomach.*

Photo Boy   You wasted mess of a treacherous bastard!

Cool *comes bursting out.*

Cool   I saw you were in turmoil from the winder. You done?

He inspects an unconscious **Ed the Ted**.

Photo Boy   Ain't dead, is he?

Cool   Don't sweat, he'll die another day.

He lifts up **Ed the Ted**, *and dumps him by the bins.*

Photo Boy   Cool, you got trouble. Teds want you out, that's why they sent him. This geezer calling himself Flikker. He heads his mob.

Cool   I heard of him. Tough number. Can beckon about two hundred teenagers, they say.

Photo Boy   Make that four.

Cool   Summin's happening.

Photo Boy   Yeah, but what? What? I don't feel anything.

Cool   You wouldn't, not with your pale face. You bin hiding yer face behind that camera too long. They're running us down with cars, motorbikes.

Photo Boy   This has happened to you?

Cool   Too many times! Summin's cooking.

Photo Boy   Oh, come on.

Cool   You think I'm lying?

Photo Boy   Easy, Cool, I'm on yer side. But this is London, man, the capital, where every kind of race has lived since the Romans! They'd never allow it.

Cool   Who is they?

Photo Boy   Adults, citizens! The law!

Cool   They're the ones standing by, letting it all boil.

Photo Boy   Come on, Cool, you were born here, you're one of us, you're not exactly a spade, are yer?

Cool (*glaring*)   When it comes to trouble, that's exactly what I am.

The three **Teds** *enter and begin chanting at* **Cool** *who goes back inside.*

Teds   'You put yer right leg in, yer left leg out, in out, in out, you kick the niggers out!'

Photo Boy   Oi!

He starts taking snaps.

Teds   'Yer shite, we're white, yer shite, we're white! Nigger out, nigger out, nigger nigger nigger out!'

Photo Boy (*shocked*)   Jesus!

Photo Boy *is taking* **Wiz**'s *pictures at Chez Nobody.*

Photo Boy   Telling yer, Wiz, it's all going mad down Napoli.

Wiz   What do you want me to do?

Photo Boy   Dunno, come and have a look.

Wiz   What are you worrying for? You're not a colour problem.

Photo Boy   Well, pardon me for thinking all this might disgust you as well.

Wiz   As a matter of fact it does. All these mugs' activities disgust me. Hitting without warning.

Photo Boy   I said I was sorry.

Wiz   Forget the Teds, they're harmless.

Photo Boy   They're bleedin nutters, Wiz.

Wiz   They're bin squeezed out of their own country by the coloureds, can you blame them?

Photo Boy   You should be put to sleep, for even thinking that.

Wiz   Still looking down on me, like I don't know me arse from.

He holds up a wad of notes.

Photo Boy (*trying hard not to drool*)   Where'd you get all that?

Wiz   Me and my girl. Beating punters off with a stick, we are. Keep this up, I'm going to have to find another. You want in?

Photo Boy   How?

Wiz   Bin thinking, kiddo. Phone boxes.

Photo Boy   And?

Wiz   You take the snaps of my lovely girls, we get them printed on cards, number underneath, leave them in phone boxes round Soho, the old pervs can cruise at their leisure. What d'you say?

Photo Boy   You're sick.

Wiz   We'll make a mint. You'll easily make Suze's target, we're talking weeks not months.

Photo Boy   How do you know about that?

Wiz   I know how much Suze will come out for, who doesn't?

Photo Boy   Told yer, I'm doing it my way.

Wiz   You mean Vendice's way. You think he's only interested in making money, but what he's really after is everyone's else's. He'll never let you be as rich as him. (*Waves the money.*) Come on – with me, it's a dead cert.

Photo Boy   No.

Wiz   You want it, you know you want it, it's coming out of yer pores, mate.

Photo Boy   I ain't exploiting chicks.

Wiz   Have a word with yerself, will yer! Nineteen summers old, might as well be fifty! You're a citizen in all but name. Who are you to look down on me?

Photo Boy   See yer then, Wiz. Come and visit, if you ever feel the urge.

Act Three

In August

Photo Boy *is on a boat trip with his* **Dad**.

Photo Boy For our day out, Dad and I took our trip up
the river. The boat was sailing by Cookham, and though I'd
no intention of dropping in on Suze and Henley for tea and
buttered scones, I certainly wanted to have a look at their
place. It was like I needed to. The birthday boy didn't mind,
anything for a quiet life, him. So, what news of Mum and
Verne then?

Dad Mum keeps saying she wants to see yer.

Photo Boy Yeah, well, she knows my address.

Dad Oi, don't be too hard on yer mum, son. I don't like
you taking liberties where she's concerned.

Photo Boy She's the one taking liberties, Dad, for years!
Verne?

Dad He's got himself a job.

Photo Boy No!

Dad Bakery, night work.

Photo Boy I give up eating bread from this day forward.
Tenants?

Dad The Turkish are out. She's got some Greeks in
instead.

Photo Boy Mum is certainly loyal to the
Commonwealth, ain't she? And how is you? You feeling
well, in yourself?

Dad As usual. Never mind me.

Photo Boy I don't mind.

Dad   I do. How's your work? You ain't bin using your darkroom much of late.

Photo Boy   Bin changing my angle, Dad, trying summin new. Some character called Vendice Partners, works in the media, has taken me on, taking pictures for his products, anything to do with the teenage angle, make-up, clothes, shoes, you name it. Tell it as it is. He's given me my own studio, plus an advance, twenty-five.

Dad   Ain't much.

Photo Boy   You don't think so?

Dad   It's not all you could have.

Photo Boy   You saying I should have asked for more?

Dad   Did you sign anything?

Photo Boy   I had to.

Dad   Then you're a bleedin fool.

Photo Boy   Listen, Dad, I've not got your experience, but one thing I ain't, please, is a fool.

Dad *begins coughing violently.*

Photo Boy   How long you bin doing that?

Dad   It's nothing.

Photo Boy   It's like you're coughing for England, Dad.

Dad   It's nothing.

Photo Boy   Fancy a trip?

Dad   We're on a trip.

Photo Boy   I mean another one. Down Harley Street.

Dad   Harley Street! Are you that flush now?

Photo Boy   Vendice knows someone. He's a doctor.

Dad   Well, I wouldn't expect him to be a bleedin plumber, would I?

Photo Boy   He's top-notch!

Dad   All the more reason why I wouldn't want to be wasting his precious time.

Photo Boy   You won't be out of pocket.

Dad   Nor will anyone else.

Photo Boy   He can check you out proper, make sure you're alright.

Dad   I am alright, it's only a bleedin cough!

Photo Boy (*pleads*)   Dad!

Dad   I think someone has been tellin tales. She's bin talking to my doc behind my back, and now she's crying to you. I ain't stupid, son! Since when have you listened to her?

Photo Boy   The evidence is pretty compelling.

Dad   I don't want to talk about it any more.

Photo Boy   Dad?

Dad   End of discussion, boy. Come on, don't ruin this day out for me. Stop worrying about me, worry about yourself.

Photo Boy   Myself? I'm doing alright.

Dad   Flashy suits, money in yer pocket, ain't you, son!

Photo Boy   But being brassic is?

Dad   This Vendice character is ripping you off! He's turning you into a mug.

Photo Boy (*snaps*)   Daddy should know!

Dad   Meaning?

Photo Boy   Meaning, Mum's busy keeping all the lodgers' beds warm, and you happily turn a blind eye, you just sit on yer arse, with yer pipe and yer stupid bleedin book about pre-war Britain, that you'll never finish, that no one cares about, but you'll just keep on writing it.

Dad   Have you finished?

Photo Boy   You just don't dig it, Dad.

Dad   Don't dig what? What they are doing to yer, to all of yer? Exploitation? Assimilation? It's as old as time, boy.

Photo Boy   So what, who cares? Let the money flow.

Dad   You don't mean that.

Photo Boy   So you don't want my help, but don't lecture me. I'm sorry you were born in the wrong decade, Dad.

They arrive back at the bay. **Photo Boy** *catches sight of* **Suzette** *from afar.* **Dad** *gets off the boat.*

Dad   You coming to the pub? Come on, have a wet one with yer old man.

Photo Boy   No, I'm staying on till the next stop.

Dad   Listen, son, every person affects the life of every other person, every single thing you do does matter, to somebody. Yeah?

Photo Boy   Yeah. I'll see yer, Dad.

Photo Boy *and the boat sail off.*

Dad   Yes, see yer, son.

Dad *starts coughing violently again as he exits.*

Photo Boy *jumps off the boat as it arrives in Cookham. He sees* **Suzette** *standing out in the garden of* **Henley**'s *house.*

Photo Boy   Hi, hon.

Suzette   I was just thinking about you.

Photo Boy   And here I am.

Suzette   What are you doing here?

Photo Boy   Went out on a boat trip with Dad. Seeing as I was passing, I thought I'd come out here. Find out what all the fuss is.

Suzette   Have you got something for me? Five hundred?

Photo Boy   Is that all you can say to me, Suze? I come all this way –

Suzette   Answer the question.

Photo Boy   I'm earning, I'm almost there.

Suzette   Almost? Go home, darl.

Photo Boy   Can't you be a little more flexible?

Suzette   I ain't like you. When I make a plan, I stick to it.

Photo Boy   What happened to your hand?

Suzette   It's nothing.

Photo Boy   Let me see.

Suzette (*snaps*)   I want you to go.

Photo Boy   Don't say that.

Suzette   Henley wants to move the wedding forward. We're thinking early autumn.

Photo Boy   This isn't fair, Suze. I'm working on it.

Suzette   Work harder!

Photo Boy   No one is working as hard as I am, Suze. Vendice is spreading me so thin. It's all changing, I'm changing, we're changing, Dean, the Wiz, Cool, it's like the whole world has its eyes on us, like it's expecting, and we don't know what to do with ourselves.

Suzette   I don't care about any of that. Five hundred or I'm marrying him.

Photo Boy   There has got to be summin else.

Suzette   Like what? Passing the supper tray to you every night . . .

Photo Boy   Suze, don't.

Suzette   When I'm not looking for yer sodding pipe and slippers, is that what you want for me?

Photo Boy   Why do you always have to bring it to that?

Suzette   You might as well kill me now.

Photo Boy   You're not yer mum. (*Pleads.*) Suze?

Suzette   You have to go.

Photo Boy   Just listen. You know, I shut my eyes and I can feel you, smell you, see you, and I love it. I'm your boy, Suze, your one and only.

Suzette (*placing her finger on his lips*)   Just come back for me, that's all I want to hear from you.

Photo Boy *leaves.*

Photo Boy   Vendice had decided the *Lorn Lovers* thing wasn't quite the suitable vehicle for Hoplite, but the kid was such a natural that they had to place him somewhere, so he put him in his new show called *Junction*. It's where they throw unexpected pairs together in the studio, to see what happens. When it takes off, Vendice is going to commission a whole series with yours truly as chief talent scout/producer. Never mind five hundred, Suze. When you see me next, I'll be riding you out of Cookham, in a Roller convertible. (*To* **Hoplite**.) You look glorious, Hop, you're going to murder him.

Hoplite   But an admiral? Baby, I shall faint.

Photo Boy   You don't know your own strength. Tilt yer head. (*Takes another picture.*) Lovely! So, is your Yank friend here somewhere?

Hoplite   It's all over between he and me. Over and done with.

Photo Boy   Is it now?

Hoplite   It was, from the moment I saw him in a hat.

Photo Boy   A hat?

Hoplite   Imagine it, baby, he wore a hat! The whole thing faded instantly. I am heartbroken.

Photo Boy   You're on, kid. Just be fabulous for me, yeah? Be brilliant. I'll take you with me, Hop, I'll take you to the big time.

Round of applause.

Vendice   Hello, good evening and welcome to *Junction.* Tonight – teenagers! Where have they all come from? Where are they all going? Are they a wonder, or a hindrance to the British way of life? To discuss this phenomenon, I have with me in this studio, the Fabulous Hoplite.

Hoplite   Mwah!

Vendice   And former Admiral, Sir Amberley Drove. Welcome to the show, gentlemen. Now, the Fabulous Hoplite here poses for pictures, which supposedly capture the life of teenagers, alive.

A photo of **Dean Swift** *appears.*

Vendice (*scornfully*)   Wouldn't like to run into him in a dark alleyway.

Sound of canned laughter.

Hoplite   Charming!

Vendice   Will someone please tell me who or what this teenage creature is supposed to represent?

A photo of **Big Jill** *appears. More canned laughter.*

Hoplite   A little below the belt, darling, don't you think?

A photo of **Crêpe Suzette** *appears.*

Vendice   Ah, far more acceptable, wouldn't you say, Admiral?

Drove (*getting excited*)   Quite.

Vendice   Tell me, Hoplite, are teenagers such as these really as highly sexed as we are led to believe? Actually, what is it that you all believe?

Hoplite   I believe in the flowering of the personality, such as my own.

Vendice   Admiral?

Drove   In my day, we'd make those kind walk the plank.

Hoplite   As you say, in your day, ducks!

Admiral   The root cause of all this nonsense and fighting I see is the unbridled promiscuity that they seem to have inherited by all this coloured influx onto our shores. May I remind you that England is an old and highly civilised nation, but the countries of Africa and the Caribbean are very far from being so indeed. Now it is true that for centuries the West India Islands enjoyed the advantages of British government, but even in these the cultural level was low, to say the least of it. And as for Africa, it should be remembered that, a mere hundred years ago, some parts of that vast continent had never even heard of Christianity.

Hoplite   I wouldn't even call him human.

Vendice (*nervous laughter*)   Now now.

Admiral   In their own setting, black folk are no doubt admirable citizens, according to the standards that prevail there. But transported unexpectedly to a culture of a higher order, serious difficulties and frustrations must inevitably arise.

Hoplite   Must I go on hearing this balls?

Vendice   Too much square from us oldies, huh, Hoplite?

Hoplite   No, just balls.

Admiral   And what is that you think?

Hoplite   Well, for a start, I think how could any personality flower in this boiler room of this old destroyer?!

More canned laughter.

Hoplite   You wanna do something useful, please sort out yer navy uniforms, love. It is so old-style musical. Model yourselves on the French, get yourself some nice pink pompoms.

Vendice   Thank you, Hoplite. Admiral?

Admiral   Typical.

Hoplite   Typical? I will tell you what is typical. People like you! You and your precious navy. For hundreds of years, you spread yourself all over the blooming world, for dear old England. No one invited you, you didn't ask anyone's permission, yet when a few hundred thousand come and settle among our fifty millions, you just can't take it. They have British passports, sweetie, just like us, yet when they show up in the dear old mother country, and show us the damn thing, you throw it back in their faces. Charming! And don't get me started on being a teenager – too late, you already have.

Vendice   Thank you, thank you, the Fabulous Hoplite, everyone.

Hoplite   Shut up, you sad excuse for a cretin, I'm talking. Can you hear me, England, hello? Let me tell you something about this teenage phenomenon. You listening? It was all so good at the beginning, it was wonderful, our world would be our world, the way we wanted it to be, but it's going now, if it's not gone already, satisfied? We're as miserable and as screwed up and as grey as the rest of you. Congratulations. What fun, eh? What glorious fun to be just like you, to be oldies, to be citizens. Make us conform, make us hate, same old crap. I don't want to be like you, we don't want to be like you –

Vendice   Cut!

Blackout.

Photo Boy *enters with* **Vendice**.

Photo Boy   I'm really sorry. He can be a little over-emotional. I'll do better.

Vendice   Of course you will. Don't worry.

Photo Boy   It will be better next week.

Vendice   There won't be a next week.

Photo Boy   Come again?

Vendice   Your friend Hoplite has got me thinking. I don't think *Junction* is quite doing it.

Photo Boy   Yes it is, give it a chance.

Vendice   Sorry, son. It's too angry, too aggressive, too – how I hate this word – political. (*He shudders.*) I'm looking for something else. The public want something light to watch on TV, something they can easily digest when they come home after a hard day's graft, they don't want to think, bless their hearts, you dig?

Photo Boy   Alright, so what do we do instead?

Vendice   Never rush a genius. Look, you just keep taking your snaps, and we'll see what we can come up with in a couple of months.

Photo Boy   I can't wait a couple of months.

Vendice   Spent that advance I gave you already? Why you didn't you say? (*Takes out his wallet.*) What do you need, ten?

Photo Boy   I don't need ten, I need something big, Vendice, and I need it now.

Vendice   Soon.

Photo Boy   Forget soon – now! What about all of your talk, eh? Don't walk away from me. You don't want anyone getting ahead, except you.

Vendice   Are you losing it?

Photo Boy   No.

Vendice   There is nothing more pathetic, son, than –

Photo Boy   I am not losing it.

Vendice   Good. (*Fixes the boy's tie.*) Now keep the faith. Take a break. I'll be in touch.

Photo Boy   Are you sacking me?

Vendice   I think you just sacked yourself.

Vendice *exits.* **Hoplite** *approaches.*

Photo Boy   You mind telling me why you did that?

Hoplite   Who else would? You? Are you not the professional teenager, the voice?

Photo Boy (*snarls*)   You bloody ruined everything!

Hoplite   They were your pictures, and they were laughing at them.

Photo Boy   It was only a joke.

Hoplite   Is that what we are now, a joke? You've sold out, doll.

Photo Boy   Take a look around – adult numbers couldn't give a single cat's lump about what we think. They're laughing at us, you stupid male's whore male maid.

Hoplite   Oh deary, what are you doing?

Photo Boy *is confronting* **Henley** *at his home.*

Photo Boy   Where's Suze?

Henley   I have no idea, young man.

Photo Boy   Don't lie, you're hiding her.

Henley   What on earth do you think this is, a prison? Now, if you don't mind –

Photo Boy   I've got things to say to you.

Henley   Please, by all means.

Photo Boy   Alright, Henley, in the first place, Suze is working class, like me.

Henley   And me.

Photo Boy   You?

Henley   My father was a butler.

Photo Boy   A butler is not working class. No disrespect to your old man, but he's a flunkey.

Henley   Alright, I may not be working class. Anything else?

Photo Boy   These cross-class marriages don't work.

Henley   Nonsense. What next?

Photo Boy   She's young enough to be your great-great-niece!

Henley   Please don't exaggerate, I'm not yet forty-five.

Photo Boy   Forty-five! You're ripe for Chelsea Hospital.

Henley   How old do you think Clark Gable and Cary Grant are?

Photo Boy   They're not marrying my girl.

Henley   You think I'm senile. Anything else?

Photo Boy   I think I'll leave the rest to your imagination.

Henley   Young man –

Photo Boy   Don't call me that.

Henley   You do know that a great many marriages between completely normal people are never consummated.

Photo Boy   So why wed?

Henley   It's what the French call –

Photo Boy   I don't care what they call it, it's disgusting, you're disgusting. Now where is she?

Henley   I think you had better go.

Photo Boy   I ain't leaving without seeing my Suze.

Henley   Then I'm afraid you are stuck here. Which may not perhaps be a bad thing, if I can persuade you to cross the line, perhaps, if you know what I mean?

Photo Boy   Where is she?

Henley   I threw her out. Common little tyke, I should have known better.

Photo Boy   You what?

Henley   I caught her, with one of her nigger friends, in here, rolling around half naked on the floor! The audacity! I told the cheap little bitch, I have standards! She can do whatever she likes, but she will not flaunt it in front of me. Funny, if I didn't know any better, I would say the disgusting little whore wanted to be caught.

Photo Boy   Or maybe she finally opened her eyes, to what you lot are doing to us.

Henley   Think that way if you must.

Photo Boy   Sod you, Henley. Sod Vendice, the lot of yer. If this is what being a adult is all about, I'm staying an Absolute Beginner. You are sick. You just let me stand there and rant on –

Henley   One must amuse oneself. Don't you think?

Photo Boy   I feel sorry for people like you.

Henley (*laughs*)   Whatever for? I suppose you want to fight me.

Photo Boy   I suppose I ought.

Henley   Well, if you really want to, I am quite agreeable. Although I should warn you, I am a dirty fighter.

Photo Boy   You're dirty alright.

Photo Boy *leaves.*

Photo Boy *arrives back in Napoli.*

Photo Boy (*calls*)   Suze? Suze!

He finds he has walked right into the middle of a fascist rally, led by **Ed the Ted** *and his gang.*

Photo Boy (*trying to shout above the noise*)   Suze? Suze!

Big Jill *comes out from her basement.*

Big Jill   Stud, what you doing? Get off the streets, will yer, are you mad?

Photo Boy   Where's Suze?

Big Jill   How the hell should I know?

Photo Boy   She's left him, Jill.

Big Jill   Left who?

Photo Boy   For me. She's here, she has to be. I'm her boy.

Big Jill   Triffic, now will you please get inside?

Photo Boy   What's going on?

Big Jill   Trouble!

Ed the Ted (*spotting* **Photo Boy**)   Nigger lover, nigger lover, hang him, hang him, hang him! Nigger lover, nigger lover, hang him, hang him, hang him! (*Flicks his knife.*) This is what happens to darkie lovers!

Cool *and his gang of blacks show up.* **Ed** *and his gang of Teds forget about* **Photo Boy** *and the two gangs stand on opposite sides of the stage, taunting and jostling as they walk past each other. One of the Teds deliberately brushes past one of the black youths, daring him to take a swing at him. Both sides line up against each other, shouting obscenities as they dare the other to make the first move.* **Photo Boy** *begins taking pictures from the sidelines. After a while he decides he has had enough and joins in, siding with the blacks. The Teds withdraw.*

Carl   See me? I served in the Royal Air Force during the war, I fought for this country, I have a medal to prove it. (*Shows his friend.*) See it deh?

The black youth tosses his medal away.

Good enough to fight, eh? Good enough to nearly get kill, but not good enough to live here?

Marcus   But good enough to get mash up!

Carl   Dis country can go kiss my arse, you hear me? I ain't tekin no more shit from no more Teds, right?

Marcus (*waves his bat*)   Yes, deh gonna find out about summin now!

Carl   Bring dem, bring dem come!

The two youths finally notice **Photo Boy**, *who is taking their pictures. They grab him.*

Marcus   Well, what the rass do we have here?

Carl   Yu mad or what?

Marcus   Him look like juss like ona dem, yu nuh!

Photo Boy   But I'm not.

Carl (*slaps him*)   Is who tell yu to speak?

Marcus   Yu mad?

Photo Boy   I'm sorry.

Marcus   Yu want save yer life, shut yer mout.

Photo Boy   Sorry, sorry, I'll shut up.

Carl   Fool ain't shut up yet. Yu 'fraid?

Photo Boy   Yes.

Carl (*slaps him again*)   Well, you should be.

Marcus   Wa yu have to say for yerself, white bwoi?

Photo Boy   I'm here to help?

Marcus   Yu here to help?

The black youths burst into fits of laughter.

I say yu and yer Teddy bwois have done enough.

Photo Boy   I ain't no Ted!

Carl   What the hell yu have to help us wid?

Photo Boy   My eyes.

Carl   Wat him say?

Marcus   Him eyes?

Carl (*flicks his knife*)   Let me cut out dem blasted eyes fer him.

Photo Boy   I'm a witness.

Black youths jeer.

No, hear me out for a sec. I'm a witness, I'm your witness. And I bet I can get more witnesses for yer. Friends, who can witness this thing, like I'm doing, who can show you all that this two square miles ain't gonna be written off as a ghetto.

Marcus   Him chat shit.

Carl   Yu tink that go mek it alright, mek it sweet?

Photo Boy   Yeah, I do as it goes.

The black youths continue to heckle him.

All you need is a few healthy pale faces out there, to lower the temperature them out there are trying to build up.

Marcus   I need to find some Ted and buss 'im claart!

Photo Boy   If you lot saw a few hundred different kinds of kids who admired yer, and the Teds saw a few hundred of the coloured nurses who'll have to stitch them up in hospital, it's gotta make a difference. This is our chance, our biggest chance, the one we've bin waiting for to prove our words about the kind of country this is. So let's get out there!

Carl   Damn right we're gonna get out there.

Photo Boy   No, let's get out and show them, let's have those public figures who do nothing but haunt the telly studios advise us what to do, let's have the thinkers of the left and the thinkers of the right tell us how they'd handle this one. And let's have the Queen in all her glory, riding through the streets of Napoli and saying, You are *all* my subjects, every one of you is my own!

Teds 1 *and* **2** *are outside. They start chanting.*

Teds (*in unison*)   Niggers out! Niggers out!

Marcus   See dat, deh chat shit.

Photo Boy   Ain't shit, listen!

Carl   I see yu again, I go cut yer throat!

The black youths give chase.

Photo Boy *looks over at his flat. He is delighted when he sees* **Crêpe Suzette** *coming out of his house.*

Photo Boy (*calling*)   Suze? Suze!

His face changes when he sees **Cool** *following her out.* **Cool** *takes* **Suzette** *in his arms and they kiss affectionately, before she runs off.*

Photo Boy (*heartbroken*)   Suze?

Cool (*approaching*)   Hey, young one! Taking the night air, are you?

Photo Boy   I had an encounter with some of your brothers.

Cool   Shit, sorry.

Photo Boy   I wasn't hurt.

Cool   Mad day. Mad times.

Photo Boy   You still cool, *Cool*?

Cool   For sure, white boy.

Photo Boy   None of this, hasn't turned you sour then?

Cool   We don't turn sour.

Photo Boy   Cos yer cool, Mr Cool.

Cool   I suppose it ain't nice for you to feel that your tribe is in the wrong.

Photo Boy   You must be the only spade in Napoli right now who cares about that.

Cool   You ain't all bad.

Photo Boy   And the women?

Cool   Say again, Cat?

Photo Boy   Our women, Cool, they ain't all bad either, wouldn't you say?

Cool   No, I mean yeah.

Photo Boy   Yeah, what?

Cool   Yer women ain't all bad.

Photo Boy   You would say that.

Cool   I'm losing track here. Where is all of this coming from?

Photo Boy   All of those times when I used to confide in you, telling tales about Suze, wondering if she's slept with her hundredth spade yet, it would appear you took that one rather too literally.

Cool   You always used to go on about her. The wonderful Crêpe Suzette.

Photo Boy   You thought you'd have a taste.

Cool   What are you blubbering for? Like yu say, gal had plenty of black man.

Photo Boy   So that means you had to be the next in line, eh, Cool?

Cool   Why not me, what is wrong with me, from all de others?

Photo Boy   You're my friend.

Cool   I'm the spade who lives above you. I'm your spade.

Photo Boy   Same thing.

Cool   It will never be the same thing, in yer life, ever. So, if I want to know what yer gal taste like, I will.

Photo Boy   Even among this?

Cool   She come to me, panting. Or rather she was looking for you. Worried sick about yer. She needed calming down.

Photo Boy   Shut up.

Cool   Asked and answered.

Photo Boy   Cool, it's me, you know I love her, how could you?

Cool   Well, it's like this, you see, the more you shouldn't, the more you want. What?

Photo Boy   Bastard!

Cool   That all? Come, boy, let it out, you wanted to say black bastard, innit?

Photo Boy   No.

Cool   Lie yu tell.

Photo Boy   I wanted to say bastard, cos you are a bastard.

Cool   Black bastard.

Photo Boy   I won't say it, don't make me say it.

Cool   That only means you thought about saying it.

Photo Boy   I love her, and yer taking her from me.

Cool   Hey, you can have the bitch back, I'm done with her. All of yu, man, like we should be grateful for you taking us in. As long as we don't touch what don't belong to us, isn't that right?

Photo Boy   No, it's not right.

Cool   I bet you thought, when we all first come here, 'Yeah, I can play the big white man with these natives, run rings round them, no trouble.' But you hate it when we act that we don't need you any more. It's why we get all this.

Photo Boy   Suze is my love, Cool, she's my hon, that's all I'm telling yer. Why are you being like this?

Cool   Have you had your eyes shut? You can see what is happening here. Suze is not your love.

Photo Boy   Shut up, Cool.

Cool   She say you can only manage two minutes. Girl is laughing at you. She's so far ahead, boy, she's creeping up from behind to make another pass.

Photo Boy   She's my girl.

Cool   She is everybody's girl.

Photo Boy *strikes* **Cool** *with a pipe. He continues to hit* **Cool** *as he falls down.*

Photo Boy   Shut up, shut up, shut up!

By now, a group of Teds, led by, of all people, **Wiz**, *circle* **Photo Boy** *as he continues to beat* **Cool** *to a pulp.*

Wiz   Yes, come on, boy!

The boys are cheering **Photo Boy** *with each blow he lands on* **Cool**. *He is so wrapped up in this, he does not notice the gang behind him. Finally he turns round, when the Teds, including* **Wiz**, *hail him by giving him a round of applause.*

Photo Boy   What?

Wiz   Should be proud, son.

Photo Boy   Wiz, what you doing here?

Wiz   Seeing what's occurring, like you said, why fight on the losing side?

Photo Boy   You're sick.

Wiz   I'm sick? Yer with us. You did the right thing.

Photo Boy *punches* **Wiz** *hard in the face, then he runs as fast as he can.*

Wiz (*chants*)   Keep England white, England white! Keep England white!

The rest of the Teds join in the chanting. **Photo Boy** *keeps on running.*

Photo Boy *has to fight his way through gangs of white and black youths who are out for his blood as well as each other's. He manages to escape and he watches from the sidelines as both gangs finally tear into each other. He sighs when he sees* **Vendice** *and his TV crew appear.*

Vendice (*to* **Photo Boy**)   Isn't this great? This is good, this is sexy, this is what we want.

Photo Boy   Fuck off out of it, Vendice, you ain't wanted here.

Vendice   Tell me you're getting this!

Cameraman   I'm getting it.

Photo Boy   You hearing me? Vendice!

Vendice *and his crew immerse themselves into the riots.* **Photo Boy** *tries several times to stop them from entering but is pushed back always by the* **Cameraman**. *He gets between the rioters and tries in vain to break up the fights. He gets hit several times and falls to the ground.*

Photo Boy (*screams*) STOP IT!!

The heavens open. Rain pours down heavily on all of them. They scatter. There is no one left onstage except **Photo Boy**, *who slumps down and cradles himself on the ground, with the rain pouring down on him.*

Photo Boy (*weeping*)   Cool . . . Suze . . .

Verne *enters. He sees his brother on the ground and goes to him.* **Photo Boy** *jumps when* **Verne** *taps him on the shoulder, thinking it's one of the* **Teds** *coming for him. He grabs* **Verne** *by the neck and is about to strangle him when he realises who it is.*

Verne (*gasping*)   Are you cracked in the head or what?

Photo Boy   What are you doing here?

Verne   Hands!

Photo Boy *releases him.*

Verne (*scanning the area*)   So, they finally done it then? Crazy wogs! They ain't got an ounce of decency in them.

Photo Boy   Shut yer stupid bleedin mouth, Jules, or I will kill yer right now!

Verne   Easy.

Photo Boy   Fuck easy. Cos I've had it, I've fucking had it!

Verne   I didn't come here for a ruck. I need to tell you something.

Photo Boy   This sodding island can sink under the sea for all I care. Gonna take off somewhere, get naturalised, and settle. Fuck it, fuck them all!

Verne   You gotta come home. It's yer dad.

Photo Boy *enters the room of his* **Dad**. *He goes over to the lifeless body lying on the bed, covered by a sheet. He lifts the sheet to see his* **Dad**'*s face.* **Verne** *waits by the door.*

Photo Boy   How long?

Verne   Couldn't say. Ma found him like this about an hour ago. But he's bin up here coughing his lungs out for the past couple of days.

Photo Boy   A couple of days?

Verne   Ma brought the doctor round but he wouldn't see him, made a right show, never seen Ma look so embarrassed.

Photo Boy   You know what you can do with her feelings.

Verne   Bit harsh.

Photo Boy   All those times she's left him on his own, while she's off . . . The slag.

Verne   Oi, she's my ma an all.

Photo Boy   So?

Verne   So leave it out.

Photo Boy   Shut up, Jules, yer boring.

Verne (*snaps*)   Can't you call me Verne just now, just for once? Eh? It is my name, you know. What, is it against the law in that precious teenage world of yours or summin? You tell someone enough times that they are shit, they'll believe it.

Photo Boy   I sincerely hope so. Cos that's the difference between the likes of you and me. I won't let it happen.

Verne   Alright, so don't let that happen.

Photo Boy   Pearls of wisdom?

Verne   Can only keep you on yer knees if you let us. Or ain't you got the fight?

He hands him a box.

Here.

Photo Boy   What?

Verne   For you. Yer dad wanted you to have this, in case, you know, if anything should happen.

Photo Boy *opens the box. Inside, he finds a large notebook, with loads of paper sticking out.*

Photo Boy   No . . . Dad's book . . . He only finished it. (*Reads from the first page.*) ' "History of Pimlico", for my one and only son.' (*Finds a stash of envelopes, opens them to find them stashed with money.*) Jesus!

Verne   Yer dad's fortune, saving it year by year he was.

Photo Boy   Wass he want me to do with it?

Verne   Spend it, you mug.

Photo Boy   You ain't touched this, have yer?

Verne   You little bastard, you don't trust yer own brother! Do you really hate me that much? It's alright, don't answer that. Can't say I have that much love for myself right now, can't say I ever did.

Photo Boy   I can't believe he managed to keep all this from her. One up to Dad!

Verne   You know all that money should go into the estate.

Photo Boy   Is that right?

Verne   It's the law. I'm just saying.

Photo Boy *hands two of the envelopes to* **Verne**.

Verne   I said I was just saying . . . I ain't after yer money . . . Jesus! What have you got me down as, eh? You really think I'm that low?

Photo Boy   Just shut up and take it.

Verne   You must really hate me.

Photo Boy   Verne, I don't hate yer.

Verne *takes the envelopes and stuffs them into his pockets.*

Verne   You won't tell Ma?

Photo Boy   Not if you don't, brother.

Verne   What's made you so nice all of a sudden?

Photo Boy   People in glass houses.

The two of them shake hands. **Verne** *leaves* **Photo Boy** *alone with his* **Dad**. **Photo Boy** *shares a brief moment alone, until his* **Mum** *enters.*

Mum   Coroner will be coming soon to pick him up. He kept asking for you, you know? All the bleeding time, wouldn't shut up.

Photo Boy   I got nuttin to say.

Mum   Oh yes you have.

Photo Boy   Alright, you're really a selfish cow.

Mum   Go on.

Photo Boy   For as long as I can remember, you've made Dad's life a torture. You brought me up to hate yer, how do you think that makes me feel? That I can't stand the sight of my own mother? You make me sick.

Mum   Your father has been of no use to me at all since the day I married him.

Photo Boy   He produced me.

Mum   He just about managed that.

Photo Boy   Whatever my dad was, you married him. Whatever you felt about him, if you had me, you were supposed to love me. Mothers are supposed to love their sons.

Mum   And sons their mothers.

Photo Boy   If they get a chance.

Mum   You listen hard. I don't give a bugger what you think. In the first place, I had you, from in here (*bangs her belly*), and if you think that's easy, try it yourself sometime. Without me, and what I went through, you'd not be here insulting me like you are. In the next place, although your father meant nothing to me, I stood by him, didn't throw him out, and I could have, a hundred times if I wanted, and made things much easier for me by doing so. You don't love or not love because you choose to, you love if you do, and if you don't, you just don't, and there's no good at all pretending.

Photo Boy   I don't want to hear this!

Mum   I still love you.

Photo Boy   Shut up.

Mum   More than air.

She pours them both a drink.

Here.

Photo Boy   I don't drink, Ma.

Mum   Don't be a cunt.

They drink, in silence. **Mum** *giggles.*

Photo Boy   What? What?

Mum   You! You're a real nasty little bastard, ain't yer?

Photo Boy (*smiles*)   Mother should know.

They both chuckle.

Photo Boy *arrives at Chez Nobody to find there is a party going inside. Everyone is there,* **Dean**, **Big Jill**, **Hoplite**, *white and*

black youths dancing together. In the middle of them all is **Suzette**.
She sees **Photo Boy** *and runs over to embrace him.*

Suzette   You trying to kill me, where you been?

Photo Boy   Around.

Suzette   I was worried sick for yer.

Photo Boy   So you decided to throw a party?

Suzette   Not just me. It started off with a few cats, from
either side, getting pissed off with all the fighting, word got
round, we all ended up here. Cool got done over. Fucking
Wiz and the Teds. Since when did Wiz side with the Teds?
You shoulda seen what the spades did to him, they gave him
a right kicking. They only caught him calling me a nigger's
whore, trying to rub soot into my face.

Photo Boy   Bastard!

Suzette   Screaming at me he was. Darl, it's alright, I told
you, the spades had him.

Photo Boy   How's Cool doing?

Suzette   Hospital as well. Wouldn't it be funny if they
both ended up in the same ward? There's poetic justice for
yer.

Photo Boy   How so?

Suzette   Well, it was Wiz and his mates who done him
over. Are you listening?

Photo Boy   How do you know?

Suzette   Cool said.

Photo Boy   Cool said that?

Suzette   Yeah. You alright? Darl, what's bothering you?

Photo Boy   I'm glad you're alright.

Suzette   And you. If anything'd happened to you, I
woulda killed myself, I ain't lying.

Photo Boy   No Henley then?

Suzette   Henley who?

Photo Boy   What happened?

Suzette   He weren't for me. You're for me.

Photo Boy   Serious?

Suzette   Can't help it, and I'm sick of fighting it.

Photo Boy   So, what now?

Suzette   We stay, until it's all over. Then you and me are gonna cut out of here, for ever. Smile!

Photo Boy   Suze, I need to tell you something.

Suzette   Forget it, whatever it is, it don't matter.

Photo Boy   No, listen.

Suzette   No, you listen. It don't matter. Now, gimme a kiss before I change my mind, will yer?

Photo Boy *kisses her.*

Suzette   More like it. Now, party's waiting.

Photo Boy   Suze, it was me.

Suzette   What was you?

Photo Boy   It was me, Suze, I hurt Cool.

Suzette   No, it was Wiz.

Photo Boy   It was me.

Suzette   Shut up.

Photo Boy   Suze, it was me.

Suzette   But why would you do that?

Photo Boy   Why'd you think? I saw you with him.

Suzette   And that made you . . . are you mad?

Photo Boy   I lost it.

Suzette   You lost it, is that all?

Photo Boy   I'm sorry.

Suzette   You beat his face in, cos you lost it, is that what you're saying?

Photo Boy   Yeah.

Suzette   Oh, God!

Photo Boy   Suze?

Suzette   All yer talk – when it comes down to it, yer no better than the adult numbers, full of hate!

Photo Boy   You promised you wouldn't sleep around.

Suzette   You promised you'd get the money.

Photo Boy   I have though!

He shows her his **Dad***'s fortune.*

Photo Boy   See! I got it, Suze, all for you, there's loads of it, see, loads! Well, look at it. I got it, it's what you wanted. We can cut, Suze. Like you said, yeah? Will you stop looking at me like that? Say something.

Suzette   You take it.

Photo Boy   Did I just hear you proper? Crêpe Suzette's turning her nose up at a shedload of dinero!

Suzette   Doesn't matter no more. It's spoilt, hon, you've spoilt what we used to be, it's gone.

Photo Boy   I love you.

Suzette   I'm not your possession.

Photo Boy   Don't say that to me.

Suzette   To what, a form-filling taxpayer, a stupid inbred, cos that's what you are now. I'm musta bin stupid, to even think!

Photo Boy   But we can go.

Suzette   I didn't sleep with Cool. I went to Napoli to find you, cos I was worried sick about you. Do you see what you've done, do you get it now? Why did you have to tell me, why did you have to spoil it?

Photo Boy   Suze? Tell Cool I'm sorry.

He leaves.

Act Four

In September

Photo Boy *is at the airport.*

Photo Boy   Napoli was big stuff in the papers this morning. The old cats were going on about unrestricted immigration, and how unwise it was, just as if it wasn't they who'd allowed it in the first place. As for me, in this present feeling, and thanks to the small fortune Dad left for me, I'm out of this small island for a bit . . . actually, I think it's safe to say, I won't be coming back any time soon.

Teller   Next.

Photo Boy   One single ticket to Brazil.

Teller   Passport please?

Photo Boy *hands her the passport.*

Teller   You don't have a visa.

Photo Boy   What's a visa?

Teller   Something you cannot fly to Brazil without.

Photo Boy   OK, where can I fly to without a visa?

Teller   Somewhere in Continental Europe, Norway for example.

Photo Boy   What's the capital?

Teller   Oslo.

Photo Boy   Fine. One single ticket to Oslo!

Sound of thunder and lightning from outside. A young **African Student** *dressed in robes comes running on, holding his hand luggage over his head against the rain.*

Photo Boy   Welcome to England, mate.

Student   Thank you. Are you from England?

Photo Boy   Not for long.

Student   They said it was summer.

Photo Boy   It was. Do me a favour, when you leave, take some of this bad weather with you.

Student   I am not leaving. I am staying.

Photo Boy   Trust me, you don't want to do that.

Student   Whyever not?

Photo Boy   You'll find out.

Student   I am studying here, medicine.

Photo Boy   Nice one, give them hell, Doc.

Student (*a little unsure*)   Why, thank you.

Photo Boy   My pleasure. (*Aside.*) Has no idea.

Student   I beg your pardon?

Photo Boy   Of what's in store.

Student   I am sure I will find out in the goodness of time.

Photo Boy   Oh, you will.

Student   Right, well, goodbye.

Photo Boy *moves off but stops himself halfway. The sound of Napoli still partying into the early hours is ringing in his ears, as well as* **Suzette**. *He turns back to face the* **Student**.

Student   Yes, can I help you?

Photo Boy   My apologies.

Student   Your apology?

Photo Boy   For not making you feel more welcome.

Student   It does not matter, forget it.

Photo Boy   Sorry, no can do. Because it does matter. Everything we do matters. Now, please allow me the pleasure of welcoming you to London, to England in fact.

Student   Thank you very much.

Photo Boy   Meet your very first teenager.

Student (*shakes his hand*)   How do you do, teenager? Are you not going to miss your plane?

Photo Boy   They'll be another one. Besides (*sighs*), I ain't ready.

He flings his arms around the **Student**.

Photo Boy   Right, first order of business, I am taking you to a ball, sir, a party.

Student   A party. Where?

Photo Boy   Napoli. Trust me, you're going to love it!

They both exit.

Blackout.